Jianyang Zhou

The NCL Natural Constraint Language

Jianyang Zhou

The NCL Natural Constraint Language

With 54 figures

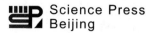
Science Press
Beijing

Springer

Author

Jianyang Zhou
ENGINEST
1, Allée de L'Alzette
54500 Vandoeuvre-Lès-Nancy, France
Email: zhou@enginest.com

ISBN 978-7-03-031784-1
Science Press Beijing

ISBN 978-3-642-23844-4   e-ISBN 978-3-642-23845-1
Springer Heidelberg Dordrecht London New York

Library of Congress Control Number: 2011936024

Printed on acid-free paper

Springer is part of Springer Science + Business Media (www.springer.com)

Preface

Most advices on solving the Sudoku game come from the theorem of an English mathematician of the last century: Philip Hall, "On representatives of subsets". By applying this theorem Jianyang Zhou has studied the constraint "to be all different" over integers, which happens to be the basic constraint of a Sudoku. This was in 1996. Since then Jianyang Zhou has pursued his work which has led to a complete programming language: NCL for Natural Constraint Language. What is it?

I open a parenthesis. As early as in 1977, Donald Knuth studied TeX, his language for editing, which is extensively used for publishing scientific books and journals throughout the world. TeX accumulates and clarifies all the mathematical notations used for generations. When I write in TeX, I am in the mathematical mood! I close this parenthesis.

Thus, by using TeX as basic formalism, NCL immerses me directly in the universe of mathematics and logics. I can see pretty formulas! In fact NCL roughly incorporates first-order logic and set operations. For example, I can build a constraint over integers but also build a constraint over sets of integers.

I forgot to say that Jianyang Zhou is the founder of ENGINEST. It is in this context that with NCL he studies and solves difficult Operational Research problems: Set Partitioning, Heat Exchanger, Pick-up and Delivery, Production Scheduling, Personnel Planning, etc. We will hear from NCL.

Alain Colmerauer
in Marseille
25 September 2011

Contents

1 Introduction

This introduction is a brief presentation of NCL (Natural Constraint Language) and its software platform POEM® (Programming in Operational and Expressive Models). After reading this chapter, readers will have a clear idea about the main features of NCL.

Section 1.1 gives a quick overview of some systems for modeling and solving. At the solver level, a new algorithmic framework called "Mixed Set Programming" is proposed. At the parser level, "Semantic Parser" based on context analysis and implicit typing is presented.

Section 1.2 presents the NCL language and its main features in terms of "Natural Modeling", "Mixed Set Programming" and "Search Rules". The basic differences between NCL and some other systems are discussed.

Section 1.3 presents the software platform POEM, which integrates NCL and visualization facilities for developing industrial solutions.

1.1 Modeling and Solving

Constraint Satisfaction Problems (CSP) are ubiquitous in the real world. Being usually NP-hard, they are in general very difficult to solve. Computational complexity theory suggests that if a problem is NP-complete (or NP-hard), then there does not exist any algorithm to solve it in polynomial time unless P equals NP (Garey and Johnson 1979).

In an informal manner, this section studies critical subjects on dealing with constraint satisfaction problems: "programming framework and algorithm" and "formal grammar and parser", respectively for problem solving and mathematical modeling.

1.1.1 Programming Framework and Algorithm

In this section, some programming frameworks for problem solving will be studied to show the nature of the NCL solver.

Linear Programming

Operations Research (OR) is a scientific discipline which studies management and decision problems in various fields.

In OR, a particularly successful technique is Linear Programming which tackles the optimization of a linear objective function subject to linear equality and/or inequality constraints (Kantorovich 1939). In 1947, George Dantzig invented the simplex method (Dantzig 1990) for solving linear programming problems. Based on Linear Programming and linear relaxation, the OR community has created step by step a mathematical programming paradigm: Linear Programming, Integer

Programming, 0-1 Programming, Mixed Integer Programming, etc. There exists a modeling language AMPL for mathematical programming (Fourer et al. 1993).

Although originally it is not related to computer programming, compared to other programming frameworks, linear programming is viewed in this book as computer programming in linear models.

Logic Programming

Generally speaking, logic programming is the use of mathematical logic for computer programming. As one of the first logic programming languages, Prolog was invented by Alain Colmerauer and his team in Marseille in the early 1970s (Colmerauer et al. 1973). Prolog allows programmers to write programs in a declarative style. For a programmer, with Prolog in mind, declarative programming becomes clearly distinguished from imperative programming of procedural languages such as the C programming language (Kernighan and Ritchie 1988).

Regarding logic programming, this book concentrates on the study of first-order logic (Barwise 1977). First-order logic is mainly distinguished from propositional logic by its use of quantifiers; compared to second-order logic, first-order logic uses only variables that range over the domains of discourse.

Constraint Programming

Constraint Programming (CP) is a programming paradigm where relations between variables are expressed in the form of constraints. Compared to Logic Programming, CP concentrates more on problem-solving algorithms by reasoning over variable domains.

Research work on Constraint Programming was started in the 1980s (Jaffar and Lassez 1987; Dincbas et al. 1988; Colmerauer 1990; Smolka 1995). Principally, its idea is to incorporate "solvers" into declarative programming frameworks such as logic programming and functional programming for solving constraint satisfaction problems. In this sense, Prolog II (Colmerauer 1982) is the first CP system if disequations as well as equations are constraints. Different from linear programming methods, CP breaks through the limitation of linear modeling; it studies problem-solving algorithms in a more general way.

Mixed Set Programming

Linear solvers are efficient in solving problems of linear models. However, algorithms of a linear solver may have the following limitation: Linear programming handles a system of linear constraints with a linear objective function. This means that it necessitates transforming non-linear constraints into linear form, which may be difficult and may pose the problem of readability and clarity to models.

Constraint Programming is a flexible programming paradigm. However, with a short development history, its performance seems not yet satisfactory enough compared to mathematical programming, for example, in solving problems such as Set Partitioning (Hoffman and Padberg 1993) and Vehicle Routing (Solomon 1987).

Based on the above observation, this book proposes an algorithmic framework called Mixed Set Programming (MSP) (Zhou 2008) which deals with constraint satisfaction problems over the mixed domain of real numbers, integers, Booleans, dates/times, references, and in particular sets of integers. Reasoning over sets of integers in the sense of naive set theory (Halmos 1960) is the strongest feature of MSP.

Mixed Set Programming incorporates and combines a simplified form of first-order logic, numeric constraints over integers (Dincbas et al. 1988) and over real numbers (Colmerauer 1990; Benhamou 1994; Colmerauer 1995), set reasoning (Zhou 1998) and date/time management (Zhou 2009). Here, set theoretical formulation is fundamental in problem modeling and set theoretical reasoning is crucial in problem solving. Mixed Set Programming leads to an enhanced expressive and algorithmic power for modeling and solving constraint satisfaction problems.

Search Rules

NP-hard problems pose computational challenges to algorithms. Unless P equals NP, no algorithm can guarantee a solution to an NP-hard problem in satisfactory time; no matter how powerful a solver is, it is always "fragile" facing "NP-hard".

Due to this consideration, to introduce search rules into a problem-solving system becomes a natural idea. Search rules allow a programmer to exploit the specific structure of a problem to well solve it. On one hand, search rules based on the problem logic of a specific field can help to construct a feasible solution rapidly. On the other hand, search rules can help to contain combinatorial explosion by "regulating" the search in the solution space. The combination of search rules and a solver makes a problem-solving system more robust.

1.1.2 Formal Grammar and Parser

A formal language is a set of strings defined over an alphabet. A formal grammar is a set of rules for rewriting strings in a formal language. To the rules a finite set of terminal symbols and a finite set of non-terminal symbols are associated. Among the symbols, a special non-terminal is chosen to be the start symbol (Chomsky 1956).

The rules describe how to produce strings according to the language's syntax. A string in the language is generated by applying the rules in some order, initially on the start symbol, until all non-terminal symbols are removed. The formal language of the grammar amounts to the set of all distinct strings generated in such a way. In this sense, the rules are called production rules.

For the application of production rules, there is a strategy called "leftmost derivation" which means "always rewrite the leftmost non-terminal first". Analogously, "rightmost derivation" means "always rewrite the rightmost non-terminal first".

In this book, context-free and context-sensitive grammars are used to study the NCL language.

Context-Free Grammar

A context-free grammar is a grammar in which every production rule is of the form "$A \rightarrow w$" where A is a single non-terminal symbol and w is a (possibly empty) string of terminals and/or non-terminals.

Backus-Naur Form (BNF) is a meta-syntax used to express context-free grammars (Knuth 1964). Programming languages tend to be specified in terms of a context-free grammar because efficient parsers can be written for them. Almost all modern languages are context free and can be described in BNF (Wikipedia 2010).

For example, the language $\{[^n \,]^n : n \geq 0\}$, where $[^n$ denotes a string of n consecutive ['s, can be produced by the following grammar:

- Non-terminals: S
- Start symbol: S
- Terminals: ⊔, [,]
- Production rules:

$$S \quad \rightarrow \quad ⊔ \tag{1}$$

$$S \quad \rightarrow \quad [S] \tag{2}$$

Here ⊔ is the empty string.

For example, the generation chain for [[]] is: $S \rightarrow_2 [S] \rightarrow_2 [[S]] \rightarrow_1 [[]]$

Note that in NCL, the square brackets [] are used to denote objects such as included file, text file, buffer and database, etc.

To simplify the presentation, the two rules can be written as below with a vertical bar (|) separating them:

$$
\begin{array}{lll}
S & \rightarrow \quad ⊔ & \tag{1}\\
 & | \quad [S] & \tag{2}
\end{array}
$$

Context-Sensitive Grammar

A formal grammar is context-sensitive if all production rules are of the form "$\alpha A \beta \rightarrow \alpha w \beta$" where A is a single non-terminal symbol, α and β are (possibly empty) strings of non-terminals and terminals and w is a non-empty string of non-terminals and terminals.

The term "context-sensitive" comes from the introduction of α and β as a "context" for A, which determines whether A can be replaced by w or not.

The canonical non-context-free grammar for the language $\{a^n b^n c^n : n > 0\}$ is:

- Non-terminals: A, B
- Start symbol: A
- Terminals: a, b, c
- Production rules:

$$
\begin{array}{lll}
A & \rightarrow \quad aBAc \\
 & | \quad abc
\end{array}
$$

$$Ba \quad \rightarrow \quad aB$$

Bb → bb

The form of the rules requires that in "α A β → α w β" w is non-empty. But in practice, rules of the form "A → ⊔" (with ⊔ being the empty string) may be very useful.

For more details, readers are referred to (Chomsky 1956).

Parser, LL Parser and LR Parser

With respect to a given formal grammar, parsing is to determine if and how an input string can be derived from the start symbol of the grammar. A parser is a program for parsing, which checks for correct syntax, builds a data structure, and recognizes semantic information implicit in the input (Aho et al. 1986; Grune and Jacobs 1990).

For a context-free grammar, leftmost derivation or rightmost derivation leads to different types of parsing:

- Top-down parsing: It attempts to find leftmost derivations of the input by using a top-down expansion of the production rules. LL parsers (Left to right, Leftmost derivation) are examples of top-down parsers;
- Bottom-up parsing: It attempts to rewrite the input to the start symbol by applying the production rules reversely. That is, instead of derivation it works by creating a "leftmost reduction" of the input; the end result, after reversed, will be a rightmost derivation. LR parsers (Left to right, Rightmost derivation) are examples of bottom-up parsers. An efficient type of LR parser is look-ahead LR parser (LALR).

Ambiguity of a Context-Free Grammar

A context-free grammar is said to be ambiguous if there exists a string which can be generated by the grammar in more than one way by leftmost derivation. For example, the context-free grammar

$$A \quad \rightarrow \quad A + A \qquad\qquad\qquad (1)$$
$$| \quad A - A \qquad\qquad\qquad (2)$$
$$| \quad a \qquad\qquad\qquad\qquad (3)$$

is ambiguous since there are two leftmost derivations for the string a+a−a (Figure 1.1):

- A →₁ A+A →₃ a+A →₂ a+A−A →₃ a+a−A →₃ a+a−a
- A →₂ A−A →₁ A+A−A →₃ a+A−A →₃ a+a−A →₃ a+a−a

These two derivations represent the following structures:

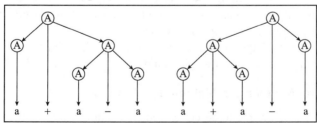

Figure 1.1 Two Structures Interpreted for the String a+a−a

However, for the above example there exist parser generators such as YACC (Johnson 1979) that can disambiguate this kind of ambiguity by using the precedence and associativity constraints.

Vagueness in Reduction

Besides ambiguity in derivation, for a LR parser there may be the problem of vagueness in terms of leftmost reduction. In a bottom-up reduction, when more than one rule have the same right-hand side, reduction conflicts may need to be settled. One way to accommodate such conflicts is by introducing context-sensitive rules; see Section 3.2.

Semantic Parser

The parsing for a description language like NCL is complex. It necessitates an intelligent parsing system, referred to as "Semantic Parser" (Zhou 2000), to understand natural problem formulation in mathematical logic and submits abstract models to embedded algorithms for efficiently solving problems.

Semantic parser of NCL is different from that of an imperative programming language such as C, logic programming languages such as Prolog and modeling languages such as AMPL. Differences will be discussed in the next section.

1.2 The NCL Language

NCL is a description language in mathematical logic. It offers user a language, which is fast to learn and easy to use, for modeling and solving constraint satisfaction problems in a natural and concise way.

Designing the NCL language became its author's idea around 1995 during his PhD study. The idea is quite simple: Using TeX (Knuth 1984) as basic formalism to express combinatorial problems and solving them by a constraint solver. A paper on the first NCL prototype was submitted in December 1997 to The Third International Conference on Systems Science and Systems Engineering (Zhou 1998). A formal paper (Zhou 2000) was submitted in March 1998 to The Journal of Logic Programming, official journal of the Association for Logic Programming at that time. The NCL language has greatly evolved in the past 10 years. Its main features can be outlined as below:

- Natural Modeling: Building models that are problem descriptions in conventional mathematical logic;
- Mixed Set Programming: Solving problems over a mixed domain of real numbers, integers (generalized to dates/times, strings, references, etc.), Booleans, and sets in a cooperative manner;
- Search Rules: Supporting concise search specifications. This makes the programming of search strategies simple and straightforward.

1.2.1 Natural Modeling in Mathematical Logic

NCL allows a programmer to describe problems naturally, within the conventions of mathematical logic. Its semantic parser supports context-based analysis and reasoning for typing, model recognition, model diagnosis, and model optimization; see Section 6.2. In this sense, natural modeling supports precise, concise and clear problem description. A programmer can concentrate on modeling at the problem logic level and can be liberated from low-level algorithmic details.

Technically speaking, NCL supports implicit typing in the global context, modeling abstraction and context-based analysis. These concepts will be developed in Chapter 3 and Chapter 6.

1.2.2 Cooperative Solving

NCL adopts a cooperative problem-solving scheme. By cooperative solving, the author does not mean cooperation between different solvers (e.g., constraint programming and linear programming solvers) but within a single system over different domains and with multiple techniques. Briefly, the idea is to integrate parser, solver and search rules in a description language:

- Combining "parser" and "solver" allows a problem-solving system to naturally and clearly define problems using concise mathematical logic models;
- Combining "search rules" and "solver" allows a problem-solving system to regulate the search for solutions in accordance with the problem logic.

Mixed Set Programming and Search Rules

Set theory being a ubiquitous part of mathematics, set operations should be introduced to support set programming for solving problems. By Set Programming, this book does not mean the simple use of set notations, set variables or set constraints in a problem-solving system, but rather rigorous and complete set theoretical formulation and reasoning in a systematic way to solve problems. "Set Programming" should not be only a term, but must be effective in practice. Through this book, especially in the part of industrial applications, the modeling and solving of most problems are centered on set programming.

By Mixed Set Programming, this book means: Reasoning and solving with a simplified form of first-order logic, numeric constraints, set operations and date/time management in a cooperative way. In a practical sense, MSP aims to create a more generic algorithmic system for efficiently modeling and solving constraint satisfaction problems such as Set Partitioning, Production Scheduling and Vehicle Routing.

NCL's simplified form of first-order logic includes at least the following features:

- Universal and existential quantifiers are introduced;
- Besides predefined functions such as cosine, the definition of user functions and predicates is allowed. This can help to encapsulate modeling in a more structured and modular way;
- Logical connectives such as conjunction, disjunction, implication, biconditional and negation can be trivially replaced by Boolean operations with the "$\wedge, \vee, \rightarrow, \equiv, \neg$" operators.

What merits more attention is that, for a quantifier, its domain of discourse can be a set variable. This is referred to as "dynamic quantification" in NCL (Zhou 2000). The technique of dynamic quantification is particularly useful for aggregate functions such as $\sum_{i \in A} x_i$ and $\cup_{i \in A} C_i$ where A is a set variable, x_i's are integer variables and C_i's are set variables. In some sense, dynamic quantification enables "fuzzy reasoning" and greatly enhances expressive and algorithmic power.

To better support the modeling of planning and scheduling problems, date/time management in a natural manner is also incorporated into MSP. Thus, a high-level management of the date/time resource is available in NCL.

Furthermore, NCL supports search rules to specify solution strategies in a highly concise and straightforward manner. Search rules allow user to rapidly develop and maintain industrial solutions, which is important because the change in user's requirements may be frequent. On one hand, in every business field there exist heuristic rules that can be used as search rules to regulate the tree search for solutions. On the other hand, research work on Operations Research has accumulated many heuristic strategies such as least-slack, least-regret and greedy-search which can be used in search rules to contain combinatorial explosion.

In the following, NCL's problem-solving scheme will be illustrated.

Solving by Cutting and Branching

The constraint solving scheme of NCL is simple. Briefly, it is based on the following algorithm: It uses constraints to cut the solution space of a problem to contain combinatorial explosion. Each time such *cutting* process terminates, if a solution is not concluded (for example, all integer variable domains are not singletons), a *branching* scheme will be used to search for solutions. The method is, for example, to split the domain of some variable into two parts and deal with their corresponding sub-problems respectively. As such *cutting* and *branching* go on, the system will either reach some solution at a search node or will prove "no solution" to that node, provided that initially all variable domains are finitely splittable. In both cases, the system backtracks to search other branches for solutions.

For an optimization problem, the system always attempts to search for a better solution after one is found. At the end of a complete exploration of the solution space, the system reaches a proof of optimality and it concludes: The last solution is optimal.

Problem-Solving Phases

After the model of a problem is submitted, the solving of the problem is carried out in 3 phases:

- Parsing: NCL's Semantic Parser adopts modeling abstraction in syntactic and semantic analysis on the model. This parsing phase ensures syntactic correctness and preliminarily verifies consistency of the model.
- Pre-Search: After the parsing, this phase globally reasons with all the constraints to cut the solution space (i.e., variable domains) to the maximum extent before the search starts. Model diagnosis and consistency checking are also enforced.

- Search: If the pre-search phase cannot identify a solution to the problem, NCL will start to construct a search tree to separate solutions or prove "no solution" to the problem. The complexity of this phase is the highest; cutting and branching alternate recursively.

A Tutorial of Solving

Readers are invited to study the following constraint system to understand the problem-solving scheme.

```
x ∈ [2,5],
y ∈ [1,4],

x < y,

x = ?,
y = ?,

min  y.
```

After parsing and pre-search, the solution space is cut to the maximum extent: $x = <2..3>$, $y = <3..4>$. Readers can verify that, for the constraint $x < y$, NCL cuts the inconsistent values 4..5 off x's domain (<2..5>) and cuts the inconsistent values 1..2 off y's domain (<1..4>). However, the domains of x and y are not yet singletons. So the queries "x = ?" and "y = ?" will trigger the tree search to identify solutions. The search process is as follows:

```
to enumerate x: <2..3> -> 2
to enumerate y: <3..4> -> 3
C2: ' y ' decreased to 3
to backtrack at y: <3..4> -> 4
optimization objective ' y ': bounding fails
to backtrack at x: <2..3> -> 3
optimization objective ' y ': bounding fails
C5: optimal solution proved
```

The first solution found by NCL is:

```
x = 2, y = 3.
```

There is no better solution found by backtracking. The first solution is proved optimal after the whole search tree is explored.

A second example is about NCL's pre-search ability for set reasoning. The NCL program is:

```
#A = 2,                      % cardinality of A is 2
∀ i ∈ [1,6]
    xᵢ = 0,                  % input to xᵢ

A ⊂ [1,6],
Σᵢ∈A xᵢ = 6,

A = ?.
```

In this example, the NCL syntax is trivial for even beginners. What is a bit special is that O signifies "input". Suppose for example, the input to the integer array x_i with i from 1 to 6 is:

```
1    -2    3    8    4    7
```

NCL will find the following solution without launching a search:

```
A = {2, 4}
x₂ = -2
x₄ = 8
```

Readers can verify that there is only one possibility: $x_2 + x_4 = 6$.

1.2.3 Comparison with Some Other Systems

NCL stems from CP. However, its basic differences from CP systems and scripting modeling languages are two-fold:

- At the parser level, NCL's "Semantic Parser" understands natural problem formulation in mathematical logic and submits abstract models to its solver;
- At the solver level, NCL adopts the algorithmic framework of Mixed Set Programming and search rules.

An additional explanation to MSP is: NCL encapsulates sophisticated problem-solving algorithms under a simple logical interface. Traditional CP systems strengthen the capability of problem modeling and solving by introducing Global Constraints (Aggoun and Beldiceanu 1993; Régin 1994). For comparison, in NCL no special predicate such as "sort", "alldifferent", "alldisjoint", "cumulative", "cycle"/"path", "sequencing", "global cardinality", "among" or "distribute" is introduced, though NCL includes algorithms for solving these related problems and many others. Global constraints do not fit in NCL due to two reasons:

- Besides hundreds of elementary algorithms, several tens of specialized algorithms such as "sort" (Zhou 1997; Bleuzen-Guernalec and Colmerauer 2000) exist in NCL. Even "sort" alone has four variants for each of the domains of real numbers, integers and sets (Zhou 2008). More complicated, it may be linked to peripheral concepts such as "UnaryResource", "AscendingSorting" and "RegretBasedSearch". This suggests that global (or specialized) constraints cannot be explicitly defined in NCL. Otherwise too many specific names and peripheral concepts will be introduced;
- From a global point of view, context-based reasoning and context-based constraint solving are crucial. Sophisticated reasoning links between algorithms are often the key to solving complex problems. This suggests that there should be some mechanism beyond "global constraints" to support context-based analysis and to coordinate embedded algorithms. In NCL, it is "Semantic Parser" that recognizes mathematical logic formulation, identifies algorithms and coordinates algorithmic links for solving a problem.

Lexically, NCL exclusively adopts conventional mathematical logic notations which can be cleanly expressed in the mathematical mode of TeX. Syntactically and semantically, NCL supports semantic parsing, set programming, logical function, fuzzy reasoning and date/time management. Regarding constraint handling capability, controls such as dynamic quantification, referencing, extraction, switch, if-then-else, query and optimization objective are introduced in a natural way. Moreover, embedded SQL query, included file, sub-model and OS command make NCL become a practical language for modeling, data processing and system integration.

1.3 The POEM Platform

To effectively implement a project, development platform that supports software engineering is indispensable. POEM is such a software platform. It aims to provide user with a general-purpose programming environment for efficiently modeling and solving problems.

In the sense of "programming language", the POEM platform is an efficient implementation of the NCL language. In the sense of "practical system", POEM integrates NCL and practical peripheral facilities. The platform is composed of a development toolkit, a computation server and two software components.

After 10 years of industrialization, the POEM package becomes a software system developed with more than 800,000 lines of C++ code. The integration of peripheral facilities makes it become a software engineering platform for rapidly developing, debugging, testing, deploying and maintaining industrial projects.

The graphical user interface and visualization components are implemented by Jiande Zhou.

1.3.1 Development Toolkit

The POEM development toolkit includes the following facilities:
- Workspace and Model Folder;
- Information tables: Constants, Variables, Constraints, Running Models;
- Visualization facilities: Quick Watch, Browser, Solution Viewer;
- Debuggers: Constraint Debugger, Visual Debugger;
- Trace Window.

The design of these modules conforms to software conventions. User can easily learn to use POEM if, for example, he is already a Visual C++ or Visual Basic programmer.

1.3.2 Component and Server

The POEM platform provides user with peripheral modules to support a client/server architecture. For POEM applications two software components and a computation server are available:
- ComPoem: a computation component;
- ComView: a visualization component;
- PoemServer: computation server.

This book concentrates on the NCL language and will not present peripheral modules in detail. However, the POEM development toolkit will be presented in Chapter 5; a detailed description of ComPoem is given in Appendix 2.

References

Aho, A.V., Sethi, R., Ullman, J.D.: Compilers: Principles, Techniques, and Tools. Addison-Wesley Longman Publishing Co., Inc. Boston, MA, USA (1986)

Aggoun, A., Beldiceanu, N.: Extending CHIP in order to solve complex scheduling and placement problems. Mathl. Comput. Modelling, 17 (7): 57–73 (1993)

Barwise, J.: An introduction to first-order logic. In: Barwise J. ed. (1982), Handbook of Mathematical Logic (Studies in Logic and the Foundations of Mathematics). North-Holland (1977)

Benhamou, F.: Interval constraint logic programming. Constraint Programming 1994: 1–21 (1994)

Bleuzen-Guernalec, N., Colmerauer, A.: Optimal narrowing of a block of sortings in optimal time. Constraints, 5(1/2): 85–118 (2000)

Chomsky, N.: Three models for the description of language. IRE Transactions on Information Theory, 2(3): 113–124 (1956)

Colmerauer, A., Kanoui, H., Pasero, R., Roussel, P.: Un système de communication homme-machine en français. Technical Report, Groupe Intelligence Artificielle, Université d'Aix-Marseille II (1973)

Colmerauer, A.: PROLOG II reference manual and theoretical model. Technical report, Groupe Intelligence Articielle, Université Aix-Marseille II (1982)

Colmerauer, A.: An introduction to Prolog III. Communications of the ACM, 33(7): 69–90 (1990)

Colmerauer, A.: Prolog IV Specifications. Reference Manual WP7/R25, Esprit project 5246, TRD Prince (1995)

Dantzig, G.B.: Origins of the simplex method. In: Nash SG (ed.), A History of Scientific Computing. Boston: Addison-Wesley, 141–151 (1990)

Dincbas, M., Van Hentenryck, P., Simonis, H., Aggoun, A., Graf, T., Berthier, F.: The constraint logic language CHIP. Proc. of the 3rd Annual ACM Symposium on Theory of Computing, 151–158 (1988)

Fourer, R., Gay, D.M., Kernighan, B.M.: AMPL: A Modeling Language for Mathematical Programming. The Scientific Press, San Francisco, CA (1993)

Garey, M.R., Johnson, D.S.: Computers and Intractability: A Guide to the Theory of NP-Completeness. W.H. Freeman (1979)

Grune, D., Jacobs, C.J.H.: Parsing Techniques – A Practical Guide. VU University Amsterdam, Amsterdam, The Netherlands. Originally published by Ellis Horwood, Chichester, England (1990)

Halmos, P.: Naive Set Theory. Princeton, NJ: D. Van Nostrand Company (1960)

Hoffman, K.L., Padberg, M.: Solving airline crew scheduling problems by branch-and-cut. Management Science, 39(6): 657–682 (1993)

Jaffar, J., Lassez, J.L.: Constraint Logic Programming. Proc. of the 14th ACM POPL Conference, Munich, 111–119 (1987)

Johnson, S.C.: YACC: Yet Another Compiler-Compiler. Unix Programmer's Manual. Vol 2b (1979)

Kantorovich, L.V.: Mathematical Methods of Organizing and Planning Production. Management Science, 6(4): 366–422 (1960)

Kernighan, B.W., Ritchie, D.M.: The C Programming Language (2nd ed.). Englewood Cliffs, NJ: Prentice Hall (1988)

Knuth, D.E.: Backus Normal Form vs. Backus Naur Form. Communications of the ACM 7, (12): 735–736 (1964)

Knuth, D.E.: The TeX Book (Computers and Typesetting, Volume A). Reading, Massachusetts: Addison-Wesley (1984)

Régin, J.C.: A filtering algorithm for constraints of difference in CSPs. Proc. of AAAI, 1: 362–367 (1994)

Smolka, G.: The Oz programming model. Computer Science Today, 324–343 (1995)

Solomon, M.M.: The vehicle routing and scheduling problems with time window constraints. Operations Research, 35: 254–265 (1987)

Wikipedia: Comparison of parser generators (2010)

Zhou, J.: A permutation-based approach for solving the Job-shop problem. Constraints, 2(2): 185–213 (1997)

Zhou, J.: A unified framework for solving Boolean, integer and set constraints. Proc. of ICSSSE, Beijing, 205–210 (1998)

Zhou, J.: Introduction to the constraint language NCL. JLP, 45(1-3): 71–103 (2000)

Zhou, J.: A note on mixed set programming. Proc. of the 7th International Symposium on Operations Research and Its Applications, 131–140 (2008)

Zhou, J.: The NCL Natural Constraint Language (in Chinese). Science Press, Beijing (2009)

2 Data Types and Lexical Conventions

This chapter presents NCL's data types and lexical conventions. Data types are presented with an emphasis on sets, dates/times and floating-point numbers. Lexical conventions of NCL respect those of the C language (Kernighan and Ritchie 1988) and TeX (Knuth 1984).

2.1 Data Types

Before the presentation of the grammar in Chapter 3, an overview of basic data types shows some differences between NCL and other computer languages.

2.1.1 Generality

NCL supports four basic data types: Boolean, float, integral and set of integrals. The *integral* type includes data types of *integer*, *date/time*, *string* and *reference* which all reduce internally to the *integer* type. A reference is a logical pointer to a Boolean, a float, an integral or a set expression. Therefore, a set can be a set of integers, a set of dates/times, a set of strings, or a set of references.

This book studies the NCL grammar by using *bool*, *float*, *integral* and *set* to represent respectively Boolean, float, integral and set expressions. NCL's basic data types are outlined in Table 2.1.

2.1.2 Set

Sets are one of the most fundamental concepts in mathematics (Halmos 1960). So it is important to introduce set concepts (e.g., set types and set operations) and set reasoning into a problem-solving system. On this aspect, some researches on logical sets can be found in (Gervet 1997; Zhou 1998).

In NCL, the elements of a set can be any data of the integral type: integer, date/time, string, reference, etc.

Thanks to sets, quantifiers are introduced in NCL; aggregate functions are powerful in NCL; user-defined functions are flexible in NCL.

Set being a compact data type, set programming makes problem modeling simple and concise. With set programming as one of the main features, Mixed Set Programming (Zhou 2008) forms NCL's algorithmic framework.

2.1.3 Date/Time

Most of the industrial problems in this book are related to "date" and "time" which are considered the most important resource in people's life.

In order to model real-world problems in a natural way, NCL supports date/time management by introducing date/time types: date (e.g., '02/02/2008'), time (e.g., '10:30:00'), date-time (e.g., '02/02/2008 10:00'). Times are available in

Table 2.1 Data Types

Type	Sub-Type	Explanation	Example
bool	bool	Boolean	T
float	float	float	1.0
integral	int	integer	1
	date	date	31/01/2008
	time	time	08:00
	date-time	date-time	31/01/2008 08:00
	str	string	"student"
	bool-ref	Boolean reference	`T`
	float-ref	float reference	`1.0`
	int-ref	integer reference	`1`
	set-ref	set reference	`{1, 3, 5}`
set	int set	set of integers	{1, 3, 5}
	date set	set of dates	{31/01/2008}
	time set	set of times	{08:00}
	date-time set	set of date-times	{31/01/2008 08:00}
	str set	set of strings	{"boy", "girl"}
	bool-ref set	set of Boolean references	{`T`, `F`}
	float-ref set	set of float references	{`1.0`, `3.0`, `5.0`}
	integral-ref set	set of integral references	{`1`, `3`, `5`}
	set-ref set	set of set references	{`{1, 3}`, `[1, 5]`}

minutes as well as in seconds. The date/time types significantly improve the readability of an NCL program, especially in scheduling applications.

Internally dates/times are encoded to integers. The date-time at 0 is fixed to '01/01/2000 00:00' with precision in minutes and is fixed to '01/01/2000 00:00:00' with precision in seconds.

For the practical use of the date/time types, readers are referred to industrial applications in Chapter 7.

2.1.4 Numeric

The representation of any data type is logical in NCL. Due to limited bits (16, 32, or 64 bits, etc.), neither irrational numbers (e.g., e and π) nor rational numbers such as 1/3 can be precisely encoded by a computer. To support logical reasoning with limited computer bits, NCL adopts interval approximation (Cleary 1987; Benhamou 1994; Colmerauer 1995; Zhou 1994) to logically represent data, either rational or irrational numbers.

Interval Arithmetic for Real Numbers

For a real number, a floating-point interval is used to approximate it at the precision of one bit. For example:

- $1/3 = <0.3333333134651..0.3333333432674>$

- e = <2.7182817459106..2.7182819843292>

So for a float variable, its domain is splittable if and only if its domain width is more than 2 floating point units (each of which is representable by 1 bit). For the problem solving scheme described in Section 1.2.2, a branching is possible over a float variable only when its domain is splittable.

Infinities for Integers

The symbol ∞ is introduced to represent the infinities: $-\infty$ for negative infinity and $+\infty$ for positive infinity. In this way, the universe of integers can be represented by $[-\infty, +\infty]$. In particular, $[-\infty$, minimum computer integer] and [maximum computer integer, $+\infty]$ are used to represent the smallest integer and the greatest integer.

2.2 Lexical Tokens

In an informal way, this section presents the notation for tokens such as characters, identifiers, constants, non-instantiated values, and comments.

2.2.1 Characters

Letters

a b c d e f g h i j k l m n o p q r s t u v w x y z
A B C D E F G H I J K L M N O P Q R S T U V W X Y Z

Digits

0 1 2 3 4 5 6 7 8 9

Special Symbols

| & = < > + - * / . , ( ) [ ] @ ' " ` ? ; : #

Backslash Escapes

Some special characters (e.g., double quote, horizontal tab) can be included in a string by escaping each of them with a backslash (\). Examples:
- \\ (literal backslash)
- \" (double quote)
- \' (single quote)
- \t (horizontal tab)
- \n (line feed)

Invisible Characters in TeX

Some characters are invisible in TeX (thus in NCL), for example:
    _ ^ { } % ~ $
Some others are also considered invisible in NCL, for example:
    é è ç à ¨ £ $ ¤ ù µ § ²

In particular, the symbol ⊔ is used to represent the space character or "empty".

2.2.2 Identifiers

An identifier is a token composed of letters or digits or underline symbols (_) starting with a letter or the underline symbol such as:

abc12   VAR   A101   var_1

Note that the underline symbol alone can be an identifier. It signifies either "anonymous" or "default":

- In an NCL program, it represents an anonymous variable;
- In a data file, it represents a default value.

2.2.3 Predefined Identifiers

A predefined identifier is a token quoted by two single quotes (') such as:

- '@'
- 'Search Depth'
- 'dd/mm/yyyy hh:mm:ss'

2.2.4 Constants

Boolean

Boolean constants are defined in an NCL configuration file. Usually they are:

T   F

Float

A float is a token composed of digits, including a decimal point (.) or an 'e' or an 'E' and possibly preceded by a sign, such as:

1.0   +0.1   −1.1   0.001   1.0e12   0.2E−10   −2.5e−7

Integer

An integer is a token composed of digits, possibly preceded by a sign, such as:

1000   0   9   123   −7   +1

or it is the positive or negative infinity denoted in TeX as below:

\infty   +\infty   −\infty

Date/Time

Denoting a date/time in a program is different from that in input/output.

Date/Time in Input/Output

- Date: A token composed of digits and two slashes (/) or two hyphens (-), e.g.:
  29/01/2008
  2008-01-29
- Time: A token composed of digits and one or two colons (:), e.g.:
  10:30
  10:30:00
- Date-Time: A token composed of a date and a time separated by a space, e.g.:

01/01/2008 10:00
29/01/2008 08:30:00

Date/Time in a Program

In a program, a date/time must be quoted by two single quotes (') so as to be recognized correctly, for example, '2008-02-02'. Otherwise for the parser it is not clear whether to consider 2008-02-02 a date or two consecutive subtractions of three integers. Examples:

- Date: '29/01/2008'
- Time: '10:00'
- Date-Time: '29/01/2008 08:30:00'

String

A string is a token quoted by double quotes (") such as:

"This is an NCL string"

Reference

A reference is a token quoted by two back quotes (`) such as:

`var` `x`

Set

Denoting a set in a program is different from that in input/output.

Sets in Input/Output

A set is a token composed of data of a same type, grouped by curly brackets ({}) or by square brackets ([]), separated by commas (,) or by double point (..), such as:

- {1..4, 8, 10..20}
- {"student", "12", "+ −"}
- [1, 3]

In particular, the empty set is denoted as { }.

Sets in a Program

In a program, set delimiters are denoted in TeX as \{ and \} because otherwise they cannot be distinguished from the curly brackets { and } used in an aggregate function. For example for the set {1, 3, 5} in input/output, its coding is \{1, 3, 5\} in a program.

Default Values

In input/output, the underline symbol (_) represents a default value of any type.

2.2.5 Non-Instantiated Values

Data, quoted by angle brackets (<>) and separated by double point (..) and/or comma (,), signify a non-instantiated value. But the representation for the value of a non-instantiated Boolean variable is an exception.

Boolean

The non-instantiated Boolean value is initialized in an NCL configuration file. Usually it is:

U

Float

<0.0..0.9>

Integer

<-\infty..+\infty>   <1..5>   <1..3, 5, 10..20>

Date

<01/01/2008..31/12/2008>

Time

<10:00..12:30>
<10:00:30..12:30:00>

Date-Time

<01/12/2008 08:00..31/12/2008 23:59>
<01/12/2008 08:00:00..31/12/2008 23:59:59>

String

<"", "abc">

Reference

<`x`, `var`>

Integer Set

{<1, 3, 5>}   {<1..3, 5>, 10..20}

Date/Time Set

{<01/12/2008 08:00..31/12/2008 23:59>}

String Set

{<"">, <"abc">}

Reference Set

{<`x`>, `var`}

2.2.6 Comments

TeX-Style Inline Comments

As in TeX, an inline comment is all texts following % in one line, such as:
    % This is an NCL remark

C-Style Block Comments

As in C, a block comment is all texts grouped between /* and */, such as:
    /* This is also an NCL remark */

2.3 Mathematical Notations

NCL adopts TeX as the basic formalism for denoting mathematical symbols. Beginners are required to learn them by heart.

2.3.1 Mathematical Symbols

The coding of NCL's mathematical symbols is given in Table 2.2. TeX symbols commonly start with a backslash (\) and are grouped with curly brackets ({}). For some symbols, simplified coding is also used. For example, empty set (∅) can be denoted as \emptyset in TeX or {} in plain text; "logic and" (∧) can be denoted as \wedge in TeX or && in plain text; "logic or" (∨) can be denoted as \vee in TeX or || in plain text.

Table 2.2   Mathematical Symbols

Symbol	Coding	
	TeX	Plain Text
∀	\forall	
∃	\exists	
∅	\emptyset	{}
∞	\infty	
O	\bigcirc	()
::		::
:=		:=
=		=
≠	\neq	<>
≡	\equiv	==
≢	\not\equiv	!=
⇒	\Rightarrow	=>
⇐	\Leftarrow	<=
→	\rightarrow	->
←	\leftarrow	<-
∧	\wedge	&&
∨	\vee	||
⊕	\oplus	
¬	\neg	!
>		>
<		<
≥	\geq	>=
≤	\leq	=<
+		+

Continued

Symbol	Coding	
	TeX	Plain Text
-		-
×	\times	*
÷	\div	
/		/
$\frac{f}{g}$	\frac{f}{g}	
∪	\cup	
∩	\cap	
\	\setminus	
>>		>>
<<		<<
⊂	\subset	
⊄	\not\subset	
⊃	\supset	
⊅	\not\supset	
≺	\prec	
⊀	\not\prec	
≻	\succ	
⊁	\not\succ	
∈	\in	
∉	\not\in	
∧	\bigwedge	
∨	\bigvee	
∪	\bigcup	
∩	\bigcap	
⊗	\bigoplus	
∑	\sum	
max	\max	
min	\min	
sin	\sin	
arcsin	\arcsin	
cos	\cos	
arccos	\arccos	
tan	\tan	
arctan	\arctan	

Continued

Symbol	Coding	
	TeX	Plain Text
log	\log	
exp	\exp	
inf	\inf	
sup	\sup	
$\sqrt{\ }$	\sqrt	
{	\{	
}	\}	
⌈	\lceil	
⌉	\rceil	
⌊	\lfloor	
⌋	\rfloor	
|		|
#		#
‾	\overline	
_	\underline	
Δ	\Delta	

2.3.2 Predefined Functions

NCL adopts TeX in mathematical mode as basic formalism for denoting prede-fined functions (Table 2.3). Beginners are required to learn them by heart.

Table 2.3   Predefined Functions

Unary Boolean Functions		
Function	Coding	Explanation
$\neg a$	\neg a	logical negation

Binary Boolean Functions		
Function	Coding	Explanation
$a \wedge b$	a \wedge b	logical and
$a \vee b$	a \vee b	logical or
$a \oplus b$	a \oplus b	exclusive-or
$a \rightarrow b$	a \rightarrow b	implication
$a \equiv b$	a \equiv b	equivalence
$a \not\equiv b$	a \not\equiv b	non-equivalence

Unary Numeric Functions		
Function	Coding	Explanation
$-f$	-f	negative

Continued

Unary Numeric Functions

Function	Coding	Explanation
$|f|$	|f|	absolute
$\arccos f$	\arccos{f}	arccosine
$\arcsin f$	\arcsin{f}	arcsine
$\arctan f$	\arctan{f}	arctangent
$\cos f$	\cos{f}	cosine
$\sin f$	\sin{f}	sine
$\tan f$	\tan{f}	tangent
$\exp f$	\exp{f}	exponential, i.e., e^f
$\log f$	\log{f}	natural logarithm, i.e., $\log_e f$
$\sqrt{f}$	\sqrt{f}	square root

Binary Numeric Functions

Function	Coding	Explanation
f^g	{f}^{g}	exponentiation
$f + g$	f + g	addition
$f - g$	f - g	subtraction
$f \times g$	f \times g	multiplication
f / g	f / g	division
$\dfrac{f}{g}$	\frac{f}{g}	division
$\min(f, g)$	\min(f, g)	binary min
$\max(f, g)$	\max(f, g)	binary max

Numeric Transformation Function

Function	Coding	Explanation
$\lceil f \rceil$	\lceil f \rceil	ceiling
$\lfloor f \rfloor$	\lfloor f \rfloor	floor

Binary Integer Functions

Function	Coding	Explanation
$x \div y$	x \div y	integer division
$x \bmod y$	x \mod y	modulo

Conditional Evaluation Functions

Function	Coding	Explanation
$(a\,?\,b : c)$	(a ? b : c)	conditional Boolean evaluation

Continued

Conditional Evaluation Functions

Function	Coding	Explanation
$(a ? f : g)$	(a ? f : g)	conditional float evaluation
$(a ? x : y)$	(a ? x : y)	conditional integer evaluation
$(a ? A : B)$	(a ? A : B)	conditional set evaluation

Functions

Function	Coding	Explanation
$\#f$	#{f}	domain width of a float
$\#(x, str)$	#(x, str)	record count of a data pool
$\#str$	#{str}	string length
$\#A$	#{A}	cardinality

Set Functions

Function	Coding	Explanation
$\{x\}$	\{x\}	singleton
$[x, y]$	[x, y]	interval
$A \cup B$	A \cup B	set union
$A \cap B$	A \cap B	intersection
$A \setminus B$	A \setminus B	set difference (complement)
$A \setminus x$	A \setminus x	exclusion of an element from a set
$A \ll x$	A << x	leftward set shift
$A \gg x$	A >> x	rightward set shift

Set Transformation Functions

Function	Coding	Explanation
ΣA	\sum{A}	sum of the elements of a set
$\inf A$	\inf{A}	infimum of a set
$\sup A$	\sup{A}	supremum of a set

Substring, Element and Subset Functions

Function	Coding	Explanation
$str[x]$	str[x]	character of a string
$str[x..y]$	str[x..y]	substring
$A[x]$	A[x]	element of a set
$A[x..y]$	A[x..y]	subset of a set

Boolean Aggregate Functions

Function	Coding	Explanation
$\bigwedge_{i \in A} a_i$	\bigwedge_{i \in A}{a_{i}}	global and
$\bigvee_{i \in A} a_i$	\bigvee_{i \in A}{a_{i}}	global or
$\bigotimes_{i \in A} a_i$	\bigoplus_{i \in A}{a_{i}}	global exclusive-or

Continued

Numeric Aggregate Functions		
Function	Coding	Explanation
$\min_{i \in A} f_i$	\min_{i \in A}{f_{i}}	minimum
$\max_{i \in A} f_i$	\max_{i \in A}{f_{i}}	maximum
$\sum_{i \in A} f_i$	\sum_{i \in A}{f_{i}}	sum

Set Aggregate Functions		
Function	Coding	Explanation
$\bigcup_{i \in A} C_i$	\bigcup_{i \in A}{C_{i}}	global union
$\bigcap_{i \in A} C_i$	\bigcap_{i \in A}{C_{i}}	global intersection

Lower Bound Extraction Functions		
Function	Coding	Explanation
$\underline{a}$	\underline{a}	Boolean lower bound
$\underline{f}$	\underline{f}	float lower bound
$\underline{x}$	\underline{x}	integer lower bound

Upper Bound Extraction Functions		
Function	Coding	Explanation
$\overline{a}$	\overline{a}	Boolean upper bound
$\overline{f}$	\overline{f}	float upper bound
$\overline{x}$	\overline{x}	integer upper bound

Domain Extraction Functions		
Function	Coding	Explanation
Δa	\Delta{a}	domain of a Boolean
Δx	\Delta{x}	domain of an integer
ΔA	\Delta{A}	candidate elements of a set variable
$\underline{A}$	\underline{A}	accepted elements of a set
$\overline{A}$	\overline{A}	all possible elements of a set

2.3.3 Delimiters of TeX

The following delimiters of TeX for grouping tokens are useful in coding but are invisible when it is visualized:

{ }   _{ }   ^{ }

Normally:

- Between { and } is a grouped expression;
- Following _ is a subscripted expression grouped by { and };
- Following ^ is a superscripted expression grouped by { and }.

Note that in an NCL program the coding is in TeX mathematical mode while in NCL's input/output the coding is in plain text. This mainly concerns set delimiters: Set delimiters in an NCL program are always denoted in TeX as \{ and \}, while in NCL's input/output they are plainly { and }.

References

Benhamou, F.: Interval constraint logic programming. Constraint Programming 1994: 1–21 (1994)

Cleary, J.G.: Logical arithmetic. Future Computing Systems, 2(2): 125–149 (1987)

Colmerauer, A.: Prolog IV Specifications. Reference Manual WP7/R25, Esprit project 5246, TRD Prince (1995)

Gervet, C.: Interval propagation to reason about sets: definition and implementation of a practical language, Constraints, 1(3): 191–244 (1997)

Halmos, P.: Naive Set Theory. Princeton, NJ: D. Van Nostrand Company (1960)

Kernighan, B.W., Ritchie, D.M.: The C Programming Language (2nd ed.). Englewood Cliffs, NJ: Prentice Hall (1988)

Knuth, D.E.: The TeX Book (Computers and Typesetting, Volume A). Reading, Massachusetts: Addison-Wesley (1984)

Zhou, J.: Approximate solving of y = cos(x) and other real constraints by Cartesian products of intervals. Technical Report, LIM, Université d'Aix-Marseille II (1994)

Zhou, J.: A unified framework for solving Boolean, integer and set constraints. Proc. of ICSSSE, Beijing, 205–210 (1998)

Zhou, J.: A note on mixed set programming. Proc. of the 7th International Symposium on Operations Research and Its Applications, 131–140 (2008)

3 Grammar and Semantics

This chapter presents NCL's grammar and its semantics. Different from imperative languages such as C (Kernighan and Ritchie 1988) and declarative languages such as Prolog (Colmerauer et al. 1973), NCL uses mathematical logic to model a problem and uses mixed set programming algorithms to solve it.

To facilitate the presentation, the NCL grammar is separated into context-free and context-sensitive parts. Section 3.1 presents the context-free rules. Section 3.2 studies the context-sensitivity of some NCL elements.

Along the definition of the grammar, semantics of its statements are presented. To illustrate the grammar, tutorial programs are given in Chapter 4. For a more structured presentation of the grammar, readers are referred to Appendix 1.

3.1 Context-Free Rules

This section will progressively present NCL's context-free rules and related semantics in seven steps: Overall Structure, Expression, Constraint, Declaration, Declarative Control, Temporal Control, Search and Optimization.

3.1.1 Overall Structure

program	→	statements .
statements	→	statement
	|	statement , statements
statement	→	declaration
	|	elementary
	|	control
declaration	→	explicittyping
	|	functiondef
	|	labeled
elementary	→	⊔
	|	constraint
	|	assignment
	|	query
	|	objective
	|	print
	|	expectation
control	→	compound

	selection
	quantified
	jump
	dataconnection

compound   →   grouped
	included
	soft
	(message : statements)

As the start symbol, *program* defines the overall structure of an NCL program. A *program* is a sequence of statements separated by commas (,) and ended by a point (.). A *statement* is a *declaration* statement, or an *elementary* statement, or a *control* structure:

- A *declaration* can be an *explicittyping*, a function definition (*functiondef*) or the label of a *labeled* statement;
- An *elementary* statement can be an empty statement (⊔), a *constraint*, an *assignment*, a search *query*, an optimization *objective*, a *print* or an expected constraint (*expectation*);
- A *control* structure can be a *compound* statement, a *selection* statement (*switch* or *if-then-else*), a *quantified* statement, a *jump*, or a data connection (*dataconnection*) .

For a declaration statement, in the *explicittyping* part, explicit typing for variables can be given; in *functiondef*, a user-defined function can be described; finally a label can always be added to a statement to define a "jump" point for a *jump* statement.

For an elementary statement, in the *constraint* part, NCL can handle constraints over all kinds of expressions; in *assignment*, user can assign an expression to a variable; in *query*, critical variables will be instantiated; in *objective*, user can specify multiple-criteria optimization objectives; in *print*, expressions of any types can be output; in *expectation*, programmed debugging facilities can be used to supervise the semantic evolution of a constraint.

Similar to control structures (compound statement, selection, iteration) in a procedural language, NCL provides logical and temporal controls. In particular for a compound statement, an *included* file can be included verbatim into the program; a custom *message* (a string expression) can be associated to a sequence of statements so that a personalized message can be given when a constraint in the statements fails. Similarly, a Boolean expression *bool* can be associated to a sequence of statements so that constraints involved in the statements become "soft". In other words, such constraints will not fail if the Boolean expression *bool* is not false. In *dataconnection*, connection/disconnection to data pools such as files, memory buffers and databases can be specified.

Some other facilities and controls such as referencing, logical function, submodel, SQL query and OS command are available in NCL but do not appear yet at the definition of the *statement* rule. They will be presented in the *expression* part.

3.1.2 Expression

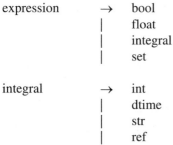

expression   →   bool
                          | float
                          | integral
                          | set

integral   →   int
                          | dtime
                          | str
                          | ref

Immediately after the overall structure, expressions are presented so that readers can see what kinds of data types, constants, variables, functions, etc. are available in NCL.

In NCL, the definition of an expression is closed over all kinds of data types. First, it conforms to mathematical and logical conventions in notation, evaluation order and associativity of operations. Second, an expression can occur where a constant of the same type can be, anywhere either at a subscript of a variable or at an argument of a function.

Internally, a date/time (*dtime*), a string (*str*) or a reference (*ref*) is in fact an integer. So from a general point of view, these types together with integer (*int*) are labeled as *integral*.

To simplify the presentation, referencing is only expanded to references of integral expressions (*integral*), no more detailed to references of integers (*int*), dates/times (*dtime*), strings (*str*), sets (*set*) or references (*ref*). For the same reason, sets of references are simply denoted as *refset*; they are not classified further into sets of Boolean references, float references, integer references or date/time references.

Boolean

bool   →   constraint

All form of constraint (to be defined in Section 3.1.3) can be used as a Boolean expression. This makes it flexible for NCL to manipulate constraints.

In the form of tautology, a Boolean expression becomes a constraint.

Numeric

num   →   float
                          | int

In terms of numerical reasoning, a floating-point expression (*float*) or an integer expression (*int*) is called a numeric expression (*num*).

Integer

int   →   + int
                          | - int
                          | bool + bool
                          | bool + int

	int + bool
|	int + int
|	int - int
|	bool × bool
|	bool × int
|	int × bool
|	int × int
|	int ÷ int
|	int mod int
|	intgroup
|	(int)

intgroup	→	intcst
	|	intvar
	|	intfunc
	|	intextract
	|	pool

|	$\lfloor num \rfloor$
|	$\lceil num \rceil$
|	$\mid int \mid$
	int^{int}
|	(bool ? int : int)
|	min (int , int)
|	max (int , int)
|	#str
|	#set
|	inf intset
|	sup intset
|	Σ intset
|	$\Sigma_{subidx} int$
|	$\Sigma_{subidx} bool$
	$min_{subidx} int$
	$max_{subidx} int$
|	intsetgroup [int]

Integer expressions involve unary operators +, − and binary operators +, −, ×, ÷ (integer division) and mod.

The handle of a data *pool* can also be used as an integer. Readers are referred to Data Management and Data Pool in Section 3.1.6.

$\lfloor num \rfloor$ and $\lceil num \rceil$ signify respectively floor and ceiling of *num*. $\mid int \mid$ represents the absolute value of *int*. int^{int} represents the exponentiation, the first *int* being the base and the second *int* being the exponent. The expression (*bool* ? *int* : *int*) signifies the conditional evaluation which gives the first *int* if *bool* is true and evaluates to the second *int* if *bool* is false. *min*(*int* , *int*) and *max*(*int* , *int*) are respectively functions of binary minimum and binary maximum.

#*str* represents the length of string *str*. #*set* represents the cardinality of set expression *set*. The functions inf *intset*, sup *intset* and Σ*intset* evaluate respectively infimum, supremum and weight of the integer set *intset*. The aggregate functions Σ_{subidx}*int*, Σ_{subidx}*bool*, min_{subidx}*int*, max_{subidx}*int* represent respectively integer sum of *int*, Boolean sum of *bool*, global minimum of *int*, and global maximum of *int*.

The element function *intset*[*int*] needs a bit more explanation. In general, for *set* (an integer set or a date/time set), whose elements can be sorted, *set*[*n*] signifies the *n*-th element of *set*. Currently in NCL, references and strings are not sortable.

Float

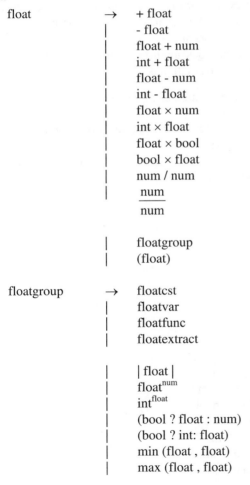

floatgroup $\rightarrow$ floatcst
| floatvar
| floatfunc
| floatextract

| | float |
| float^{num}
| int^{float}
| (bool ? float : num)
| (bool ? int: float)
| min (float , float)
| max (float , float)

$$
\begin{array}{l}
| \quad \min_{\text{subidx}} \text{float} \\
| \quad \max_{\text{subidx}} \text{float} \\
| \quad \sum_{\text{subidx}} \text{float}
\end{array}
$$

$$
\begin{array}{l}
| \quad \arccos \text{ num} \\
| \quad \arcsin \text{ num} \\
| \quad \arctan \text{ num} \\
| \quad \cos \text{ num} \\
| \quad \sin \text{ num} \\
| \quad \tan \text{ num} \\
| \quad \exp \text{ num} \\
| \quad \log \text{ num} \\
| \quad \sqrt{\text{num}}
\end{array}
$$

Almost all operations available on integers (except integer operators such as $\div$ and mod) can apply to real numbers. For example: (*bool* ? *float* : *float*) shares the same signification as (*bool* ? *int* : *int*) except for their types. *float*^{num} is the exponentiation with *float* as the base and *num* as the exponent; *int*^{float} is the exponentiation with *int* as the base and *float* as the exponent.

Note that in NCL the division operations are different for *int* and *float*:

- For integer division of x and y, the notation is: $x \div y$;

- For float division of f and g, the notation is: f / g or $\dfrac{f}{g}$.

Most of the numeric operations can be mixed on *int* and *float*. But the results in the above rules are always of float type.

There is a rich set of operations for a float expression, including the following conventional functions which evaluate always to *float*:

- arccos (arccosine)
- arcsin (arcsine)
- arctan (arctangent)
- cos (cosine)
- sin (sine)
- tan (tangent)
- exp (exponential)
- log (logarithm)
- $\sqrt{\ }$ (square root)

Date/Time

$$
\begin{array}{lcl}
\text{dtime} & \rightarrow & \text{dtime} + \text{int} \\
& | & \text{dtime} - \text{dtime} \\
& | & \text{dtime} + \text{bool} \\
& | & \text{dtime} \times \text{int} \\
& | & \text{int} \times \text{dtime} \\
& | & \text{dtime} \div \text{dtime} \\
& | & \text{dtime mod dtime}
\end{array}
$$

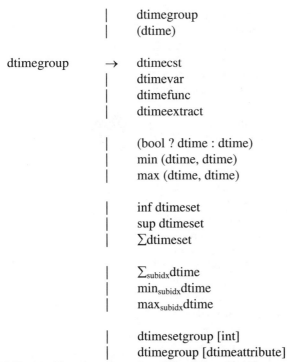

	dtimegroup
	(dtime)
dtimegroup →	dtimecst
	dtimevar
	dtimefunc
	dtimeextract
	(bool ? dtime : dtime)
	min (dtime, dtime)
	max (dtime, dtime)
	inf dtimeset
	sup dtimeset
	Σdtimeset
	Σ_{subidx}dtime
	$\min_{\text{subidx}}$dtime
	$\max_{\text{subidx}}$dtime
	dtimesetgroup [int]
	dtimegroup [dtimeattribute]

An NCL date/time is a natural coding of date and/or time. Its representation is defined in the "Data Format" part.

To be meaningful, operations defined on dates/times are a limited version of those for integer expressions. They include binary operators +, −, ×, ÷, mod, conditional evaluation (*bool* ? *dtime* : *dtime*), binary min, binary max and aggregate functions over dates/times as those for integers.

For date/time types, element function *dtimeset*[*int*] and date/time attribute function *dtime*[*dtimeattribute*] are defined. Element function for dates/times is the same as that for integers. Date/time attribute function *dtime*[*dtimeattribute*] signifies a date/time transformation for the date/time expression *dtime*; for the detail, readers are referred to the "Data Format" part in this section.

String

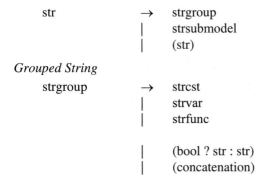

str →	strgroup
	strsubmodel
	(str)

Grouped String

strgroup →	strcst
	strvar
	strfunc
	(bool ? str : str)
	(concatenation)

		strgroup [int]
		strgroup [int..int]

Concatenation

concatenation	→	group group
		group concatenation

group	→	boolgroup
		floatgroup
		intgroup
		dtimegroup
		strgroup
		boolrefgroup
		floatrefgroup
		integralrefgroup
		setrefgroup
		intsetgroup
		dtimesetgroup
		strsetgroup
		refsetgroup

A string is a sequence of characters. Conditional evaluation (*bool* ? *str*: *str*) and substring functions are available for strings. There are two kinds of substring functions:

- *str*[*n*] signifies the *n*-th character of string *str*;
- *str*[*n1*..*n2*] is the substring (characters from *n1*-th to *n2*-th) of *str*.

A flexible function for strings is concatenation (*group group*) which generates new strings by concatenating the two expressions *group* and *group* of all types.

Finally, a sub-model (*strsubmodel*) can also be used as a string expression. The detail on this functionality is to be presented in "Temporal Control" since there is a procedural semantics for sub-model.

Reference

ref	→	boolref
		floatref
		integralref
		setref

Boolean Reference

boolref	→	boolrefgroup
		(boolref)

boolrefgroup	→	`bool`
		boolrefvar
		boolreffunc

		(bool ? boolref : boolref)

Float Reference

floatref	→	floatrefgroup
	|	(floatref)

floatrefgroup	→	`float`
	|	floatrefvar
	|	floatreffunc
	|	(bool ? floatref : floatref)

Integral Reference

integralref	→	integralrefgroup
	|	(integralref)

integralrefgroup	→	`integral`
	|	integralrefvar
	|	integralreffunc
	|	(bool ? integralref : integralref)

Set Reference

setref	→	setrefgroup
	|	(setref)

setrefgroup	→	`set`
	|	setrefvar
	|	setreffunc
	|	(bool ? setref : setref)

A reference is a notation of an expression (of any type except string) quoted by two back quotes. It is a logical pointer to an expression. It can also be considered the name of an expression; when a reference is printed, the name of the referenced expression is written to output. References are often used together with quantification, set constraints and aggregate functions for the consideration of flexibility and efficiency. In this sense, referencing is also viewed as a control.

To simplify the presentation, referencing is only expanded to references of integral expressions (*integral*), not detailed to references of integers (*int*), dates/times (*dtime*), strings (*str*) or references (*ref*).

Set

set	→	intset
	|	strset
	|	dtimeset
	|	refset

Integer Set

intset	→	intset \ int
	|	intset \ intset

		intset $\cap$ intset
	|	intset $\cup$ intset
	|	intset $\gg$ int
	|	intset $\ll$ int
	|	intsetgroup
	|	(intset)
intsetgroup	$\rightarrow$	intsetcst
	|	intsetvar
	|	intsetfunc
	|	intsetextract
	|	[int , int]
	|	{ intcollection }
	|	(bool ? intset : intset)
	|	$\cap_{\text{subidx}}$intset
	|	$\cup_{\text{subidx}}$intset
	|	intsetgroup [int..int]
intcollection	$\rightarrow$	intlist
	|	$\forall$ index int
	|	$\forall$ doubleidx int
intlist	$\rightarrow$	int
	|	int..int
	|	int , intlist
	|	int..int , intlist

Date/Time Set

dtimeset	$\rightarrow$	dtimeset \ dtime
	|	dtimeset \ dtimeset
	|	dtimeset $\cap$ dtimeset
	|	dtimeset $\cup$ dtimeset
	|	dtimeset $\gg$ int
	|	dtimeset $\ll$ int
	|	dtimesetgroup
	|	(dtimeset)
dtimesetgroup	$\rightarrow$	dtimesetcst
	|	dtimesetvar
	|	dtimesetfunc
	|	dtimesetextract

		[dtime , dtime]
		{ dtimecollection }
		(bool ? dtimeset : dtimeset)
		$\cap_{\text{subidx}}$dtimeset
		$\cup_{\text{subidx}}$dtimeset
		dtimesetgroup [dtimeattribute]
		dtimesetgroup [int..int]
dtimecollection	→	dtimelist
		∀ index dtime
		∀ doubleidx dtime
dtimelist	→	dtime
		dtime..dtime
		dtime , dtimelist
		dtime..dtime , dtimelist

String Set

strset	→	strset \ str
		strset \ strset
		strset ∩ strset
		strset ∪ strset
		strsetgroup
		(strset)
strsetgroup	→	strsetcst
		strsetvar
		strsetfunc
		strsetextract
		{ strcollection }
		(bool ? strset : strset)
		$\cap_{\text{subidx}}$strset
		$\cup_{\text{subidx}}$strset
strcollection	→	strtlist
		∀ index str
		∀ doubleidx str
strtlist	→	str
		str , strtlist

Reference Set

| refset | → | refset \ ref |

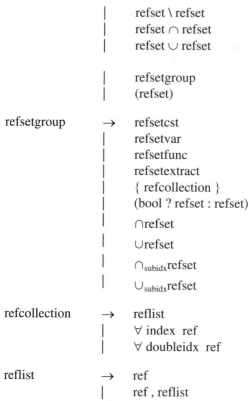

	refset \ refset
	refset ∩ refset
	refset ∪ refset
	refsetgroup
	(refset)

refsetgroup	→	refsetcst
		refsetvar
		refsetfunc
		refsetextract
		{ refcollection }
		(bool ? refset : refset)
		∩refset
		∪refset
		∩_{subidx}refset
		∪_{subidx}refset

refcollection	→	reflist
		∀ index ref
		∀ doubleidx ref

reflist	→	ref
		ref , reflist

A set is a collection of distinct objects. A set expression *set* can be a set of integers, a set of dates/times, a set of strings, or a set of references. To simplify the presentation, sets of references are simply denoted as *refset*; they are not classified further into sets of Boolean references, float references, integer references, or date/time references, etc.

The symbols \, ∩, ∪, ≫, ≪ signify respectively set difference (or set exclusion), set intersection, set union, rightward set shift and leftward set shift operators. The \ operator has a special case (set exclusion between a set and an integer): the operation (*intset* \ *int*) gives as result a set with *int* excluded from *intset*.

Examples about set shift are as below:

$\{1..3, 6..7\} \gg 1 \rightarrow \{2..4, 7..8\}$

$\{1..3, 6..7\} \ll 1 \rightarrow \{0..2, 5..6\}$

The symbols ∩ and ∪ signify operators for global intersection and global union of sets. For ∩*refset* and ∪*refset,* set expression *refset* is restricted to be a set of set references. They compute respectively the global union and global intersection of the set expressions referenced in *refset*.

The collection operations {∀ *index integral*} and {∀ *doubleidx integral*} signify respectively sets of integrals collected by the universal quantification.

The subset function *set*[*n1*..*n2*] is available for integer and date/time sets. It signifies the subset (elements from *n1*-th to *n2*-th) of *set*.

Finally, date/time attribute functions *dtimeset*[*dtimeattribute*] are defined for date/time sets. See the "Date/Time Format" part in this section for a detailed presentation on date/time attribute functions.

Constant

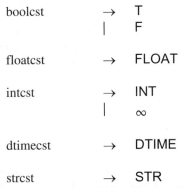

Boolean, float, integer, date/time and string constants are special terminals with meanings as below:

- T and F represent the Boolean values "true" and "false" which can be initialized in NCL's configuration file;
- FLOAT is a floating-point number, e.g., 1.01, 1.7E+134, 1.0E 34;
- INT is an integer number, e.g., 0, 100;
- ∞ is the infinity symbol;
- DTIME is a date/time constant, e.g., '08:00', '2008-02-02', '2008-02-02 08:00';
- STR is a string, e.g., "student", "abc".

There is no terminal symbol for reference constants.

The syntax for set constants is strongly context-sensitive. This will be explained in detail in Section 3.2. Before further defining production rules over set constants, they are symbolized by *intsetcst*, *dtimesetcst*, *strsetcst*, *refsetcst* and are considered "terminals" for the moment.

Variable

Variables are the most "liberal" objects in NCL and provide user with a great programming convenience. As will be explained in Section 3.2, the syntax for variable is strongly context-sensitive.

Before further defining production rules over variables, they are for the moment considered "terminals" and are symbolized by *boolvar*, *floatvar*, *intvar*, *dtimevar*, *strvar*, *boolrefvar*, *floatrefvar*, *integralrefvar*, *setrefvar*, *intsetvar*, *dtimesetvar*, *strsetvar*, *refsetvar*.

Function

The definition of a user-defined function is given in the "Function Definition" part. Logically, in the sense of function there is no essential difference between a user function and a conventional function like cosine. Calling a user function consists in matching the names, matching the arities and passing arguments from the caller to the receiving function. Such a function call also adds derived constraints (argument unification and constraints in the function's body) into the constraint system.

The syntax for user-defined function is strongly context-sensitive. This will be explained in Section 3.2.

Before further defining production rules over functions, they are symbolized by *boolfunc, floatfunc, intfunc, dtimefunc, strfunc, boolreffunc, floatreffunc, integralreffunc, setreffunc, intsetfunc, dtimesetfunc, strsetfunc, refsetfunc* and are considered "terminals".

Data Format

dataformat	$\rightarrow$	alignment
	|	floatformat
	|	dtimeformat

There are mainly three kinds of data formats: *alignment, floatformat* and *dtimeformat*. Date/time attribute and set format should also be taken into consideration. Moreover, data format for input will be presented in Section 3.2.2.

Alignment

alignment	$\rightarrow$	int

Length of any expression and its alignment style can be specified in the format option of an output; see Section 3.1.6 for the output statement. The output is leftward aligned if *alignment* is a positive integer; otherwise it is rightward aligned. If the length of the output is greater than that specified by *alignment*, the printed result will be truncated to the required length |*alignment*|.

Float Format

floatformat	$\rightarrow$	(decimallen , alignment)

decimallen	$\rightarrow$	int

For a float expression *float*, a format option in the form of (*decimallen, alignment*) can be given. Here *decimallen* determines the number of digits after the decimal point, and *alignment* tells the whole length and alignment style of *float*.

Date/Time Format

dtimeformat	$\rightarrow$	"dd/mm/yyyy hh"
	|	"mm/dd/yyyy hh"
	|	"yyyy-mm-dd hh"
	|	"dd/mm/yyyy hh:mm"
	|	"mm/dd/yyyy hh:mm"
	|	"yyyy-mm-dd hh:mm"
	|	"dd/mm/yyyy hh:mm:ss"
	|	"mm/dd/yyyy hh:mm:ss"
	|	"yyyy-mm-dd hh:mm:ss"
	|	"dd/mm/yyyy"

```
|     "mm/dd/yyyy"
|     "yyyy-mm-dd"
|     "yyyymmdd"

|     "hh"
|     "hh:mm"
|     "hh:mm:ss"

|     ""
```

An input or an output can be of date/time format. NCL supports explicit setting for date/time format in an input or an output statement. In particular, user is required to pay attention to the 3 different output formats of a date: American, European and Chinese.

For a date/time expression, the following data formats are supported:

- "dd/mm/yyyy": European date format;
- "mm/dd/yyyy": American date format;
- "yyyy-mm-dd": Chinese date format;
- "yyyymmdd": compact date format of (year month day);

- "hh": time format in hours;
- "hh:mm": time format in minutes;
- "hh:mm:ss": time format in seconds;

- "dd/mm/yyyy hh": European date-time format (precision in hours);
- "mm/dd/yyyy hh": American date-time format (precision in hours);
- "yyyy-mm-dd hh": Chinese date-time format (precision in hours);
- "dd/mm/yyyy hh:mm": European date-time format (precision in minutes);
- "mm/dd/yyyy hh:mm": American date-time format (precision in minutes);
- "yyyy-mm-dd hh:mm": Chinese date-time format (precision in minutes);
- "dd/mm/yyyy hh:mm:ss": European date-time format (precision in seconds);
- "mm/dd/yyyy hh:mm:ss": American date-time format (precision in seconds);
- "yyyy-mm-dd hh:mm:ss": Chinese date-time format (precision in seconds);

- "": An empty string signifies that internal integer representation for a date/time is required for an input or an output.

NCL's parser can intelligently coordinate the date/time format according to the context.

Date/Time Attribute

```
dtimeattribute    →    "dd/mm/yyyy"
                  |    "mm/dd/yyyy"
                  |    "yyyy-mm-dd"

                  |    "hh"
                  |    "hh:mm"
```

| "hh:mm:ss"

| "yyyy"
| "mm"
| "dd"

For a date/time expression, attribute functions are defined as below:

- Transforming from a date-time to a date by attribute format "dd/mm/yyyy", "mm/dd/yyyy" or "yyyy-mm-dd";
- Transforming from a date-time to a time by attribute format "hh", "hh:mm" or "hh:mm:ss";
- Transforming a date to an integer (year, month or day) by attribute format "yyyy", "mm" or "dd".

NCL does not define attribute transformation functions such as hour, minute or second for a time expression. But user can define such functions easily with integer division ($\div$) and modulo (mod).

Set Format

Note that there are two data formats for sets in input/output:

- In all cases, curly brackets ({ }) can be used to group elements or intervals. For example, { 1, 3..5, 7..9 };
- In the case of an interval, [*n1*, *n2*] can be used to represent the set of elements from *n1* to *n2*. In the general case, [*n1*, *n2*] can be of course also written as {*n1*..*n2*}.

Set format can be initialized in NCL's configuration file; see Section 5.2.2.

3.1.3 Constraint

constraint	$\rightarrow$	boolctr
	|	numctr
	|	dtimectr
	|	strctr
	|	refctr
	|	setctr

In NCL, the definition of constraints is closed over all kinds of NCL expressions. It conforms to mathematical and logical conventions in notation, evaluation order and associativity of operations.

In general the symbols =, $\neq$ represent respectively the (binary) equality and disequality relations over all types of expressions (*bool, float, integral, set*).

Boolean Constraint

boolctr	$\rightarrow$	bool = bool
	|	bool $\neq$ bool
	|	$\neg$ bool
	|	bool $\wedge$ bool
	|	bool $\vee$ bool
	|	bool $\oplus$ bool

| bool → bool
| bool ≡ bool
| bool ≢ bool

| boolsubmodel
| sqlquery
| oscommand

| boolgroup
| (boolctr)

The symbols ¬, ∧, ∨, ⊕, →, ≡, ≢ signify respectively logical negation, and, or, exclusive-or, equivalence, non-equivalence.

A sub-model (*boolsubmodel*), an SQL query (*sqlquery*) or an OS command (*oscommand*) can also be used as a Boolean expression. The detail on these functionalities is to be presented in the "Temporal Control" part since they each have a procedural semantics.

boolgroup   →   boolcst
| boolvar
| boolfunc
| boolextract

| ∧refset
| ∨refset
| ⊕refset

| ∧$_{subidx}$ bool
| ∨$_{subidx}$ bool
| ⊕$_{subidx}$ bool

The operators ∧, ∨, and ⊕ are respectively global conjunction, global disjunction and global exclusive-or. In the case of global exclusive-or, it evaluates to true if and only if one and only one argument is true.

Note that for ∧*refset*, ∨*refset* and ⊕*refset,* the expression *refset* is restricted to be a set of Boolean references. These functions represent respectively global conjunction, global disjunction and global exclusive-or of the Boolean expressions referenced by the references in *refset*.

Numeric Constraint

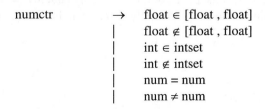

numctr   →   float ∈ [float , float]
| float ∉ [float , float]
| int ∈ intset
| int ∉ intset
| num = num
| num ≠ num

	num < num
	num ≤ num
	num > num
	num ≥ num
	(numctr)

Equality, disequality and inequality relations =, ≠, <, ≤, >, ≥ apply to integer and float expressions in accordance with mathematical conventions. The symbols ∈ and ∉ signify the membership relations.

Note that numeric constraints over mixed expressions of *float* and *int* are naturally supported.

Date/Time Constraint

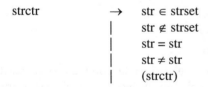

dtimectr	→	dtime ∈ dtimeset
		dtime ∉ dtimeset
		dtime = dtime
		dtime ≠ dtime
		dtime < dtime
		dtime ≤ dtime
		dtime > dtime
		dtime ≥ dtime
		(dtimectr)

In NCL, dates/times can be sorted. So in addition to equality (=), disequality (≠) and membership relations (∈, ∉), order relations (<, ≤, >, ≥) also apply to date/time expressions.

String Constraint

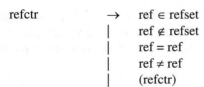

strctr	→	str ∈ strset
		str ∉ strset
		str = str
		str ≠ str
		(strctr)

Reference Constraint

refctr	→	ref ∈ refset
		ref ∉ refset
		ref = ref
		ref ≠ ref
		(refctr)

Currently in NCL, references and strings are not sortable. So only equality (=) and disequality (≠) and membership relations (∈, ∉) apply to string and reference expressions.

Set Constraint

setctr	→	set = set
		set ≠ set

	set $\prec$ set
	set $\stackrel{\prec}{\scriptstyle\sim}$ set
	set $\succ$ set
	set $\stackrel{\succ}{\scriptstyle\sim}$ set
	set $\subset$ set
	set $\not\subset$ set
	set $\supset$ set
	set $\not\supset$ set
	(setctr)

To simplify the presentation, for set constraints, sets are not classified further into integer, date/time, string or reference sets.

The $\prec$ symbol is the set precedence notation with its reverse being $\stackrel{\prec}{\scriptstyle\sim}$. Inversely, they are $\succ$ and $\stackrel{\succ}{\scriptstyle\sim}$. Analogously, the symbols $\subset$, $\supset$, $\not\subset$, $\not\supset$ signify the set inclusion relations (subset/superset) and their reverse relations.

3.1.4 Declaration

Typing

Implicit Typing

NCL supports implicit typing which depends globally on the context (Zhou 2000). The implicit typing follows the principles below:

- In a mathematical model, the type of a variable is implicit in the global context in accordance with naive mathematical logic conventions;
- The implicit typing is not always static in a program. The typing may be dynamic as the parser analyzes the program and its input;
- By default, integer type or integer set type is imposed to a variable whose type is unclear in the global context.

Implicit typing is one of the main functionalities that makes the NCL grammar strongly context-sensitive; see Section 3.2.

Explicit Typing

explicittyping	$\rightarrow$	bool :: bool
		float :: float
		int :: int
		dtime :: dtime
		str :: str
		boolref :: boolref
		floatref :: floatref
		integralref :: integralref
		setref :: setref

| intset :: intset
| dtimeset :: dtimeset
| strset :: strset
| refset :: refset

NCL also supports explicit typing (Zhou 2009). The symbol :: is a typing operator that unifies the types of the expressions on its two sides. It can be used intuitively to type or declare expressions (variables). For example,

```
Datetime :: { '31/01/2008 08:00' },
```

Here *Datetime* is explicitly declared to be a date-time set.

Function Definition

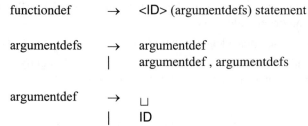

functiondef   →   \<ID\> (argumentdefs) statement

argumentdefs   →   argumentdef
               | argumentdef , argumentdefs

argumentdef   →   ⊔
               | ID

Similar to the C language, NCL supports logical functions of all types and a function can be used in any expression of its type. The list of identifiers *argumentdefs*, which may be empty, is the list of arguments for the function \<ID\>.

All constraints derived from calling a function become a part of the constraint system. If only constraints occur in a function, then the function is similar to a conventional function like cosine. See the Cotangent example in Section 4.10.

Function Identifier

Different from procedural languages, a function in NCL is logical. The function identifier ID itself is a variable and can be constrained internally to determine the type and value of the function. Externally it should be consistent with the whole constraint system.

Argument

Arguments are passed to a function by setting up unification relations over arguments between the caller and the receiving function.

Global Variable

Variables defined outside of a function are considered global to the function.

Local Variable

Variables introduced in a function, which are not global variables, are local to the function and are invisible from outside of the function.

Encapsulation

The definition of an NCL function is flexible. In *statement* (body of the function), most kinds of statements including constraints, search queries and optimization objectives can be encapsulated.

Recursion

Calling functions is allowed in a function. This implies that function can be recursive in NCL.

Recursive reasoning goes on along the recursive calls. The termination of a recursion is determined in two cases:

- There is no more recursive call. The recursion ends normally;
- Termination state variable ('.') becomes true in the function. The recursion is interrupted.

See the factorial example in Section 4.10.

Limitation

Not all kinds of statements are allowed in a function. To reduce the complexity, some special statements are forbidden in the body of a function:

- function definition
- sub-model

Predicate

Usually the type of a function depends on the context. By default the function takes the Boolean type and it plays a role similar to that of a predicate. See the Predicate example in Section 4.10.

Labeled Statement

labeled   →   <ID> statement
                  | (labeled)

In NCL, a label of the form <ID> can be added to a statement. Here ID is an NCL identifier. A label defines a jump point for NCL's jump statement which will be presented in the "Temporal Control" part.

3.1.5 Declarative Control

Compound Statement

A compound statement can be a grouped statement, an *included* file, a statement with a custom *message*, or a *soft* statement.

Grouped Statement

grouped   →   (statement , statements)

A compound statement can be a sequence of statements grouped by parentheses.

Included File

included   →   [path]
                  | (included)

path   →   str
                  | concatenation

In an NCL program, an *included* file can be added similar to that of a procedural language like C. The file will be included verbatim into the program.

In a model, NCL parser expands an included file only once and will neglect repeated occurrences of the same included file.

Soft Statement

    soft $\rightarrow$ (bool : statements)

Sometimes a *soft* statement in the form of *(bool : statements)* may occur. In preference, user does not hope that *statements* fail; but a failure of such statements can be tolerated if the Boolean expression *bool* is not false. This is a flexible mechanism to program soft constraints since *bool* can be any Boolean expression.

Custom Message

    message $\rightarrow$ str
                             | concatenation

In an NCL program a custom message can be used for the failure of a statement (constraint, quantified statements, if-then-else and switches, etc.).

A custom message is a string. It is associated to a group of statements separated by a colon: *(message : statements)*. The *message* will replace standard NCL messages in case of a constraint failure.

Selection

    selection $\rightarrow$ switch
                             | ifthenelse

There are two kinds of selection statements: switch and if-then-else.

Switch

    switch $\rightarrow$? float (floatswitch)
                             | ? integral (integralswitch)
                             | ? set (setswitch)
                             | (switch)

    floatswitch $\rightarrow$ floatbranch
                             | floatbranch ; floatswitch

    floatbranch $\rightarrow$ $\sqcup$: statements
                             | floatcase : statements

    floatcase $\rightarrow$ float
                             | float , floatcase

    integralswitch $\rightarrow$ integralbranch
                             | integralbranch ; integralswitch

    integralbranch $\rightarrow$ $\sqcup$: statements
                             | integralcase : statements

    integralcase $\rightarrow$ integral

		integral , integralcase

| setswitch | → | setbranch |
| | \| | setbranch ; setswitch |

| setbranch | → | ⊔ : statements |
| | \| | setcase : statements |

| setcase | → | set |
| | \| | set , setcase |

The functionality of logical switch is similar to that of "switch" in C. In NCL, there are switches for float, integral and set types. A switch contains an option, which is an expression after a question mark (?), and some branches, each of which corresponds to a case and a sequence of statements separated by a colon (:). The option and its cases should be of the same type (*float*, *integral* or *set*). In particular, a branch can be a default one with its case being empty.

The statements in a branch can be executed only once when no earlier case is matched with the option. That is, NCL executes (only) the first branch whose case is matched. If no case at all is matched with the option, it is the default branch that is executed.

If-Then-Else

ifthenelse	→	bool ⇒ boolswitch
	|	(ifthenelse)

| boolswitch | → | statement |
| | \| | (statements ; statements) |

An if-then-else can be considered a Boolean switch and has at most two branches, with the second one being the default branch. If its option is true the first branch will be executed; otherwise NCL executes its second branch if it exists.

If-then-else plays an important role when it is used together with NCL's system variables (see Section 3.1.6). For example, an external call (e.g., SQL query or OS command) or an internal call (sub-model) must be executed at an input or an output state.

Quantification

quantified	→	existential
	|	universal
	|	(quantified)

NCL supports quantification over integral variables (*int*, *date/time*, *str*, *ref*). In particular, a quantified variable can be a reference (referenced Boolean/integral/set/float variable). Quantification includes universal quantification and existential quantification.

Existential Quantification

existential	→	∃ index statement

| ∃ indices statement

Universal Quantification

universal   →   ∀ index body
                   | ∀ indices body

body   →   statement
                   | → (criteria) statement

For a universally quantified statement, query criteria, grouped by parentheses and following a right arrow (→), can be added before the statement. It signifies that the ordering of quantifier indices should respect the criteria.

An existential quantifier will trigger an existential query. For query under quantification, readers are referred to the "Query and Search" part in Section 3.1.7.

Indexing

index   →   varidx ∈ set
                   | varidx ∈ set : varidx ≠ integral
                   | varidx ∈ set : varidx ≤ integral
                   | varidx ∈ set : varidx ≥ integral
                   | varidx ∈ set : varidx < integral
                   | varidx ∈ set : varidx > integral

indices   →   varidxlist ∈ set

varidxlist   →   varidx , varidx
                   | varidx , varidxlist

doubleidx   →   index , index
                   | doublevaridx ∈ set

doublevaridx   →   varidx ≤ varidx
                   | varidx < varidx
                   | varidx ≥ varidx
                   | varidx > varidx
                   | varidx ≠ varidx
                   | varidx , varidx

varidx   →   ID
                   | `ID`

Indexing in NCL is a powerful and flexible functionality that to some extent distinguishes NCL from other modeling systems. Indexing techniques are widely used in quantification, subscripts and superscripts.

Subscript and Superscript

subidx	$\rightarrow$	`integral` `varidx=integral`
		index
		doubleidx

Indices can be used in subscripts (or superscripts) to a variable or to an aggregate function.

Index Leak

An NCL model is protected against any subscript/superscript/reference leak. The measures are as below:

- A variable becomes invalid if one of its subscripts leaks (out of its range defined at its initial occurrence);
- An expression involving an invalid variable is considered invalid. Especially, a reference over an invalid expression is referred to as an empty reference or an empty pointer;
- NCL will neglect invalid expressions. Especially, 1) constraints over invalid expressions are neglected; 2) An empty reference is regarded as a pointer to a default value.

See the tutorial program "Subscript Leak" in Section 4.6 for an example. See also the modeling of the Knight problem in Chapter 6 for another example.

3.1.6 Temporal Control

In a procedural language like C, a programmer can write an increment statement like $x = x + 1$.

However, a constraint system involving a logic statement in such a form will crash since logically "$x = x + 1$" can never be true. But for a programming language, procedural functionality is practical in applications. It is important to introduce "temporal control" in NCL:

- Temporal reasoning such as extraction, assignment, system variables and expectation;
- Procedural operations such as sub-model, jump, data connection, input, output, SQL query and OS command.

To ensure the soundness and efficiency of logic reasoning, all temporal reasoning and procedural operations must be arranged to be executed only once at an input or output state. Especially, sub-model, SQL query, OS command, jump, etc. must be placed in the body of an if-then-else statement at input or output state ('O' $\Rightarrow (\ldots)$ or '@' $\Rightarrow (\ldots)$).

Data Management

NCL manages data through *pool*.

Data Pool

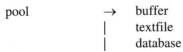

pool	$\rightarrow$	buffer
		textfile
		database

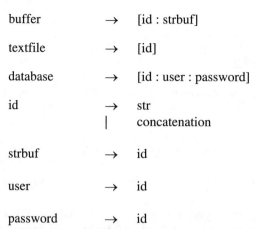

buffer	→	[id : strbuf]
textfile	→	[id]
database	→	[id : user : password]
id	→	str
	|	concatenation
strbuf	→	id
user	→	id
password	→	id

Grouped by square brackets, a *pool* can be a *buffer*, a *textfile* or a *database*:

- A buffer pool accesses data in memory. It is specified by its identifier *id* and a string buffer *strbuf*: [*id: strbuf*];
- A text file pool is specified by its file path *id*: [*id*];
- A database pool is specified by its identifier *id*, a user name *user* and a *password*: [*id : user : password*].

For example,

- ["*prog*" : "@ \"Hello\""]: a program buffer with "*prog*" as its identifier and a string buffer "@ \"Hello\"" as the content of the program;
- ["*output*" : *x*]: an output buffer with "*output*" as its identifier and *x* as its output buffer which is a variable;
- ["\\models*knight.n*"]: a program file with "\\models*knight.n*" as its file path;
- ["*DB*" : "*user*" : "*password*"]: a database with "*DB*", "*user*", "*password*" as its identifier, user name and password.

The type of a pool is integer (*int*). That is, the handle of a data *pool* can be used as an integer. Readers are referred to integer expression in Section 3.1.2.

Note that a text file pool should be distinguished from an included file. The latter always occurs alone as a statement while the former can be part of an integer expression (a pool handle) or part of a control such as *dataconnection*.

Data Connection

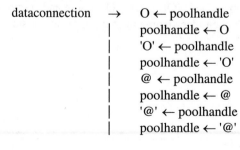

dataconnection	→	O ← poolhandle
	|	poolhandle ← O
	|	'O' ← poolhandle
	|	poolhandle ← 'O'
	|	@ ← poolhandle
	|	poolhandle ← @
	|	'@' ← poolhandle
	|	poolhandle ← '@'
poolhandle	→	int

Here, *dataconnection* is used to specify and control input and output pools. *pool-handle* represents the handle of a data pool. To connect/disconnect to an input pool, the operations are as below:

- 'O' ← ["*knight.dat*"]: connection to input pool ["*knight.dat*"]
- ["*knight.dat*"] ← 'O': disconnection to input pool ["*knight.dat*"]

To connect/disconnect to an output pool, the operations are as below:

- ["*knight.sol*"] ← '@': connection to output pool ["*knight.sol*"]
- '@' ← ["*knight.sol*"]: disconnection to output pool ["*knight.sol*"]

For *dataconnection,* in the place of the symbol 'O' user can also simply write O and instead of '@' user can simply write @.

Input

Input is treated as a special kind of variable. See Section 3.2.2.

Output

print	→	@ expression
	|	@ expression : dataformat
	|	(print)

In NCL, user can print any expression. All data in NCL can be treated as a string. A format option can be attached to an output; its definition is more complex than that for an input; see the "Data Format" part in Section 3.1.2.

Extraction

One strong feature of NCL is its extraction functions. As a low-level function, extraction allows access, control and temporal reasoning over partial information (e.g., bounds and domain) of an expression; it evolves temporally and does not conform to the logic of "declarative programming". User should be careful with this function and pay attention to their presence in all kinds of expressions.

Boolean Extraction

boolextract	→	$\overline{bool}$
	|	$\underline{bool}$

$\underline{bool}$ and $\overline{bool}$ are respectively the lower and upper bounds of *bool*.

Float Extraction

floatextract	→	$\overline{float}$
	|	$\underline{float}$
	|	#float

$\underline{float}$ and $\overline{float}$ are respectively the lower and upper bounds of *float*. #*float* is the domain width of *float*. A real number is not always representable by a floating-point number. Sometimes such a representation is by a floating-point interval. This is why for *float*, the extraction function of domain width is specially introduced.

Integer Extraction

$$\text{intextract} \quad \rightarrow \quad \overline{\text{int}}$$
$$| \quad \underline{\text{int}}$$
$$| \quad \#(\text{poolhandle , delimiter})$$

$$\text{delimiter} \quad \rightarrow \quad \text{STR}$$

$\underline{int}$ and $\overline{int}$ are respectively the lower and upper bounds of *int*. #(*poolhandle, delimiter*) represents the record count of a data pool, where *poolhandle* is the handle of the pool and *delimiter* is the delimiter character. For a database, it is the record number; for a text file or a buffer, it is the number of lines if the delimiter is "\n".

In general the # operator signifies "size" and it has different meanings for different types:

- #(*poolhandle, delimiter*) signifies the record count of pool *poolhandle*;
- #*float* signifies the domain width of *float*;
- #*set* signifies the cardinality of *set*;
- #*str* signifies the string length of *str*.

Date/Time Extraction

$$\text{dtimeextract} \quad \rightarrow \quad \overline{\text{dtime}}$$
$$| \quad \underline{\text{dtime}}$$

$\underline{dtime}$ and $\overline{dtime}$ are respectively the lower and upper bounds of *dtime*.

Integer Set Extraction

$$\text{intsetextract} \quad \rightarrow \quad \Delta \, \text{bool}$$
$$| \quad \Delta \, \text{int}$$
$$| \quad \overline{\text{intset}}$$
$$| \quad \underline{\text{intset}}$$
$$| \quad \Delta \, \text{intset}$$

For a Boolean expression *bool*, Δ *bool* represents the integer set for its domain. Here Boolean values "false" and "true" are respectively transformed to 0 and 1.

Δ *int* represents the domain of integer *int*.

$\underline{intset}$ is the set of certainly accepted elements of the integer set *intset*. $\overline{intset}$ is the total set of all possible elements of *intset*. Δ *intset* is the set of candidate elements of *intset*. For an integer set, the following relations hold:

- $\overline{\text{intset}} = \Delta \, \text{intset} \cup \underline{\text{intset}}$;
- $\Delta \, \text{intset} \cap \underline{\text{intset}} = \varnothing$.

Date/Time Set Extraction

$$\text{dtimesetextract} \quad \rightarrow \quad \Delta \, \text{dtime}$$

| dtimeset

| $\overline{dtimeset}$

| Δ dtimeset

Δ *dtime* represents the domain of date/time expression *dtime*.

dtimeset is the set of certainly accepted elements of the date/time set *dtimeset*.

$\overline{dtimeset}$ is the total set of all possible elements of *dtimeset*. Δ *dtimeset* is the set of candidate elements of *dtimeset*.

String Set Extraction

strsetextract →   Δ str

| strset

| $\overline{strset}$

| Δ strset

Δ *str* represents the domain of string *str*.

strset is the set of certainly accepted elements of the string set *strset*. $\overline{strset}$ is the total set of all possible elements of *strset*. Δ *strset* is the set of candidate elements of *strset*.

Reference Set Extraction

refsetextract →   Δ ref

| refset

| $\overline{refset}$

| Δ refset

Δ *ref* represents the domain of reference *ref*.

refset is the set of certainly accepted elements of the reference set *refset*.

$\overline{refset}$ is the total set of all possible elements of *refset*. Δ *refset* is the set of candidate elements of *refset*.

Examples

Table 3.1 gives some examples.

Table 3.1   Examples of Extraction

variable in a context	value	variable	$\overline{\text{variable}}$	Δ variable
A ⊂ [1, 9], A ⊃ [2, 5]	A = {<1>, 2..5, <6..9>}	$\underline{A}$ = [2, 5]	$\overline{A}$ = [1, 9]	Δ A = {1, 6..9}
B = {2..5, 8}	B = {2..5, 8}	$\underline{B}$ = {2..5, 8}	$\overline{B}$ = {2..5, 8}	Δ B = {}
a ∈ [1, 3] ∪ [5, 8]	a = <1..3, 5..8>	$\underline{a}$ = 1	$\overline{a}$ = 8	Δ a = {1..3, 5..8}
b = 4	b = 4	$\underline{b}$ = 4	$\overline{b}$ = 4	Δ b = {4}
c :: T	c = U	$\underline{c}$ = F	$\overline{c}$ = T	Δ c = [0, 1]
d = T	d = T	$\underline{d}$ = T	$\overline{d}$ = T	Δ d = {1}

System Variable

systemvar	$\rightarrow$	systembool
	|	systemfloat
	|	systemint
	|	systemtime
	|	systemstr

System variables play a coordination role in an NCL program.

Up to today, NCL provides user with five types of system variables for system-level control: Boolean, float, integer, date/time and string.

Boolean

systembool	$\rightarrow$	'O'
	|	'@'
	|	'.'
	|	''

Boolean system variables are important in NCL. They allow programmers to flexibly control the NCL engine. Four variables are available:

- 'O' represents the input state. It becomes true in NCL's program-parsing phase; it is unknown in all other running states;
- '@' represents the output state. It becomes true when a solution is found; it is unknown in all other running states;
- '.' represents the termination state. It becomes true when NCL terminates; it is unknown in all other running states;
- '' (with nothing between the two quotes) signifies a programmed break. An NCL program will break at '' and waits for user to send a "resume" message. The variable takes the true value when NCL breaks; it is unknown in all other running states.

These variables can be programmed to control the NCL states of input, output, termination or break.

- If 'O' becomes true again, it tells the system to return to input state and re-start the search tree with an improved objective bound;
- If '@' becomes true, it tells the system that a "solution" is reached;
- If '.' becomes true, it tells the system to "terminate";
- If '' becomes true, it tells the system to "break".

Float

systemfloat	$\rightarrow$	'Global Time'
	|	'Local Time'

There are two float system variables:

- 'Global Time' represents global running time in seconds;
- 'Local Time' represents local time in seconds (local to each function or model).

These variables help to manage the running time of NCL.

Integer

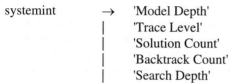

There are five integer system variables:

- 'Model Depth' represents model depth in a sub-model calling process;
- 'Trace Level' represents the trace level of NCL;
- 'Solution Count' represents the number of solutions found;
- 'Backtrack Count' represents the number of backtracks;
- 'Search Depth' represents the search depth.

These variables help to manage a model and the search for solutions.

Date/Time

systemtime	→	'dd/mm/yyyy hh'
	|	'mm/dd/yyyy hh'
	|	'yyyy-mm-dd hh'
	|	'dd/mm/yyyy hh:mm'
	|	'mm/dd/yyyy hh:mm'
	|	'yyyy-mm-dd hh:mm'
	|	'dd/mm/yyyy hh:mm:ss'
	|	'mm/dd/yyyy hh:mm:ss'
	|	'yyyy-mm-dd hh:mm:ss'
	|	'dd/mm/yyyy'
	|	'mm/dd/yyyy'
	|	'yyyy-mm-dd'
	|	'yyyymmdd'
	|	'hh'
	|	'hh:mm'
	|	'hh:mm:ss'

The following date/time variables tell user the current real-world dates/times in different formats:

- 'dd/mm/yyyy': current date (European format)
- 'mm/dd/yyyy': current date (American format)
- 'yyyy-mm-dd': current date (Chinese format)
- 'yyyymmdd': current date (compact format)

- 'hh': current time in hours
- 'hh:mm': current time in minutes
- 'hh:mm:ss': current time in seconds

- 'dd/mm/yyyy hh': current date-time in hours (European format)

- 'mm/dd/yyyy hh': current date-time in hours (American format)
- 'yyyy-mm-dd hh': current date-time in hours (Chinese format)
- 'dd/mm/yyyy hh:mm': current date-time in minutes (European format)
- 'mm/dd/yyyy hh:mm': current date-time in minutes (American format)
- 'yyyy-mm-dd hh:mm': current date-time in minutes (Chinese format)
- 'dd/mm/yyyy hh:mm:ss': current date-time in seconds (European format)
- 'mm/dd/yyyy hh:mm:ss': current date-time in seconds (American format)
- 'yyyy-mm-dd hh:mm:ss': current date-time in seconds (Chinese format)

String

> systemstr   →   'Work Directory'

There is only one string system variable:

- 'Work Directory' represents the work directory of an NCL project.

This variable helps to manage the path of a project, a file, or a database, etc.

Programmed Control

System variables enable programmed control through logical combination. For example, a programmer can control input, output, termination or break of NCL.

Programmed Restarting

Sometimes, when a solution to an optimization problem is found, instead of normal backtracking programmer may want to restart the search with an improved objective bound. This can be done by forcing the input state variable to become true when a solution is reached:

```
'@' → 'O',
```

Programmed Output

User can enable approximate solving of a problem by a logical combination of system variables 'Local Time', 'Backtrack Count', 'Search Depth', and '@', etc. For example, the following temporal control requires accepting an approximate solution when search depth reaches 100, computation time reaches 1 hour and the number of backtracks reaches 1000.

```
'Search Depth' ≥ 100 ∧
'Local Time' ≥ 3600.00 ∧
'Backtrack Count' ≥ 1000 → '@',
```

Programmed Termination

An important NCL state is the termination state. Usually for solving hard industrial problems, it's not necessary or even not possible to wait till an NCL project terminates after it explores all the solution space. In real life people often only need feasible solutions. To force the termination of an NCL model after it finds a satisfactory solution and after it runs for at least 300 seconds, the statement below can be used:

```
'Solution Count' ≥ 1 ∧ 'Local Time' ≥ 300.00 → '.',
```

More simply, the statement below forces the termination of an NCL model immediately after it finds a solution:

'@' → '.',

Note that 'Global Time' is the global running time and 'Local Time' is the running time local to its hosting function or model. 'Global Time' is always the same as 'Local Time' for the main (outmost) model but are different in functions or sub-models.

Programmed Break

User can add a programmed break ' ' (a notation with nothing between two single quotes) in his program for debugging purposes. The NCL engine will break at ' ' and waits for a resumption message to continue. For example, if user hopes to have a break whenever an NCL model finds a solution, he may program simply as follows:

'@' → ' ',

Assignment

assignment	→	boolvar := bool
	|	floatvar := float
	|	intvar := int
	|	dtimevar := dtime
	|	strvar := str
	|	boolrefvar := boolref
	|	floatrefvar := floatref
	|	integralrefvar := integralref
	|	setrefvar := setref
	|	intsetvar := intset
	|	dtimesetvar := dtimeset
	|	strsetvar := strset
	|	refsetvar := refset

Assignment is a special extraction function. Similar to that of a procedural language, an *assignment* assigns the value of an expression to a variable. The assignment symbol (:=) is different from "logical equal" = or "Boolean equivalent" ≡. It is simply a unidirectional data transmission and never fails. For example, an increment operation can be programmed as follows:

x := x + 1,

But it cannot be expressed with logical equal as below:

x = x + 1,

In fact, the value of an assignment function varies from time to time as NCL reasons. Usually in an NCL program, assignment is used to represent a complex expression (involving extraction functions) by a simple variable; such a variable can then be used frequently in the program (e.g., in query criteria).

Jump

jump	→	≫ ID

| (jump)

The definition of a Jump control ">> ID" is similar to that of C. During the running of an NCL program, >> ID leads the execution of NCL to the statement labeled by <ID>.

All labeled statements and Jump controls must be executed at the output ('@') state.

Sub-Model

submodel	$\rightarrow$	[prog , config , level]
prog	$\rightarrow$	int
config	$\rightarrow$	int
level	$\rightarrow$	int

In an NCL program, sub-models can be called. For a sub-model, its program pool *prog* and configuration pool *config* are integer expressions which represent the handles of the pools. The integer expression *level* represents the trace level for the sub-model.

The above production rules are for defining an "abstract" sub-model which do not take type into consideration. A typed sub-model is either *boolsubmodel* (see the rule for Boolean constraint *boolctr* in Section 3.1.3) or *strsubmodel* (see the rule for string *str* in Section 3.1.2). The non-terminal *submodel* is introduced here to facilitate the presentation. To complete the production rules, in Section 3.2 context-sensitive rules will be added to reduce *submodel* to *boolsubmodel* or *strsubmodel*.

Following the context, a Boolean value (true or false) for *boolsubmodel* or a message (string) for *strsubmodel* will be returned. In the *strsubmodel* case, user may receive one of the following messages from a sub-model:

- "no solution exists";
- "all solutions found";
- "optimal solution proved" ;
- "approximate solution found" ;
- "stopped with solution" ;
- "stopped without solution" .

The above standard messages can be configured in an NCL configuration file.

Since a sub-model should be executed only once, it must be called at the input ('O') or output ('@') state. For example,

'@' $\Rightarrow$ [[*"knight.n"*] , [*"ncl.cfg"*] , 1], where

- ["knight.n"] is the program file;
- ["ncl.cfg"] is the configuration file;
- The trace level is 1.

It is ideal if sub-models of an NCL model are well separated and each accomplishes a reasoning task. The structures of sub-model, included file and user-defined function help to support modular programming.

SQL Query

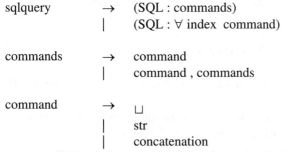

User must use SQL queries to get/update information from/to a database. An SQL query returns Boolean true if it succeeds or it returns false if it fails.

Database Connection

Connecting to a database is similar to opening a text file. User must specify the database, a user name and a password. Once connected, user can communicate with the database using SQL queries.

To connect to a database, it can be stated as below:

'O' ← [*database* : *user* : *password*], or [*database* : *user* : *password*] ← '@',

To close a connection, it can be stated as below:

[*database* : *user* : *password*] ← 'O', or '@' ← [*database* : *user* : *password*],

Executing an SQL Query

In the same manner as a sub-model, SQL queries always appear at input ('O') or output ('@') state, that is:

state ⇒ (SQL : query),

where *state* is one of the NCL states ('O' and '@') and where *query* is an SQL query.

SQL queries can be a sequence of queries separated by commas. They can also be introduced using a universal quantifier. SQL queries are represented in the string format.

Input from a Database

Reading data with a "SELECT" query works in the same manner as reading data from text files. The procedural semantics are:

- The number of selected records will be returned first in reply to the first input symbol O;
- Each of the selected fields will be returned upon an input O in a successive manner.

OS Command

oscommand   →   (OS : commands)
          | (OS : ∀ index command)

Operating system commands can be executed in an NCL program. In the same manner as an SQL query, they always appear at the input ('O') or output ('@') state, that is:

```
state ⇒ (OS : command),
```

where *state* is one of the NCL states ('O' and '@') and *command* is an OS command.

An OS command will return Boolean true if it succeeds, otherwise it will return false.

OS commands can be a sequence of commands separated by commas. They can also be introduced using a universal quantification.

Expectation and Debugging

expectation   →   ?? bool

| (expectation)

A programmer may need to carry out advanced debugging for his NCL model. For this purpose, an expectation constraint in the form of "?? *bool*" (a Boolean expression preceded by a double question mark) can be used to supervise the evolution of the domain of a variable in *bool*. By its name, an expectation constraint "expects" the Boolean expression *bool* to be true, that is to say, constraints involved in *bool* are expected to be satisfied. Otherwise, system will send warning messages.

The usefulness of an expectation constraint lies in the supervision of variable domains. Some examples are:

- "?? ¬ *boolvar*" expects that *boolvar* is false;

- "?? Δ *intvar* ⊂ *intset*" expects that the domain of *intvar* is a subset of *intset*;

- "?? *intvar* ∉ *intset*" expects that *intvar* is not an element of *intset*;

- "?? *intset* ⊂ *intsetvar*" expects that *intset* is a subset of *intsetvar*;

- "?? *intsetvar* ∩ *intset* = ∅" expects that no element of *intset* can be in *intsetvar*.

For example, the following program can supervise the integer variable x on unexpected integer 1 and on expected values 5, 7, 9:

```
x ∈ [1, 10],
?? Δx ⊂ {5, 7, 9},
?? x ∉ {1},
```

Once the variable x is instantiated to 1 (domain of x = {1}) or any of the 3 values of {5, 7, 9} is removed from x's domain, an NCL warning message will be sent and a break will be given if Debug mode is set to be active (see Section 5.6).

Note that an expectation constraint should be stated immediately after the first occurrence of the variable to be supervised. This is to avoid the possible loss of trace in the domain evolution of the variable.

3.1.7 Search and Optimization

Search and optimization are special types of control in NCL. After compact data and constraint models are created for a problem, it is important to design a search strategy to efficiently explore the solution space of the problem.

In an NCL program, the search for a solution is controlled by search rules which specify query criteria and enumeration modes.

A global view of NCL's search logic is presented below.

Query and Search

query	$\rightarrow$	standardquery
	|	fastquery
	|	(query)

In order to find a solution to a problem, it is necessary to instantiate all variables that are critical to the problem. To do this, NCL needs to select query variables (critical and not instantiated) and enumerate their domains to identify solutions.

In NCL there are three kinds of queries: 1) standard query which tends to explore the solution space completely; 2) existential query which instantiates quantified variable of an existential quantification; 3) fast query which straightforwardly constructs a solution with heuristic search criteria.

Query Statement

Standard Query

standardquery	$\rightarrow$	expression = ? enummode
	|	bool $\equiv$? enummode
	|	bool ?

In *query*, the question mark (?) signifies that an expression (either known or unknown) should be instantiated through an enumerative search.

Note that "*bool* $\equiv$?" inquires whether *bool* is true or false. In particular, "*bool* ?" is a natural way of conducting a query to a Boolean expression. For example: "$x \neq y$?" inquires if x is not equal to y.

Existential Query

In addition to explicit queries, an existentially quantified variable will also be instantiated through a search. The behavior of such a query is the same as that for a standard query. The only difference is that the enumeration mode is the default one.

Note that if the quantified is a reference of the form `ID`, then the existential query is on the reference, not on the referenced variable.

Fast Query

fastquery	$\rightarrow$	expression = ?? enummode
	|	bool $\equiv$?? enummode
	|	bool ??

Sometimes fast and direct construction of a solution is sufficient: There is no need to traverse all the solution space. The programmer knows that there will be no backtrack before reaching a solution and the system will immediately terminate once the solution is obtained. In such a case, fast query symbolized by a double question mark (??) can be used to quickly search for a solution.

A fast query makes sense only when the following conditions hold:
- No standard query exists in the program;
- No existential query exists in the program;
- No optimization objective exists in the program.

If any of the above conditions is violated, the fast query will become a standard one.

Enumeration Mode

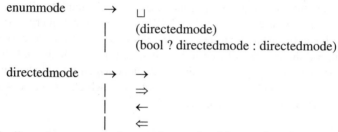

NCL allows two enumeration modes, each with two directions:
- Binary Domain Splitting ($\Rightarrow$ and $\Leftarrow$): The domain of a variable is split into two parts. The solver first branches to the lower part if the mode is $\Rightarrow$ or it first branches to the upper part if the mode is $\Leftarrow$. Next, the remaining part of the domain will be searched in a recursive way;
- Bound Enumeration ($\rightarrow$ and $\leftarrow$): The solver first tries the lower bound of the variable domain if the mode is $\rightarrow$ or it first tries the upper bound if the mode is $\leftarrow$. Next, the remaining part of the domain will be searched in a recursive way.

To be flexible, conditional enumeration can be specified. For example, $(x < 0 ?\ \Rightarrow :\ \Leftarrow)$ signifies that if $x < 0$ is true, NCL will first branch to the lower part; otherwise NCL will first branch to the upper part.

Default Enumeration Mode

The default enumeration modes are different for different types:
- For Boolean and integral types, it is bound enumeration and the enumeration direction is Lower-Bound-First ($\rightarrow$);
- For the float type, it is Binary-Domain-Splitting and the enumeration direction is Lower-Part-First ($\Rightarrow$). See Section 4.14;
- For the set type, it is always bound enumeration (there is no sense for "Binary Domain Splitting") and by default the enumeration direction is Lower-Bound-First ($\rightarrow$).

Query Criterion

criteria	$\rightarrow$	criterion

| criterion , criteria
| (criteria)

criterion → ⊔
| min bool
| max bool
| min float
| max float
| min int
| max int
| min dtime
| max dtime

Query criteria are defined within a universal quantification which contains a query statement: In a quantified statement such as "∀ *index* → (*criteria*) *statement*", *criteria*, grouped by parentheses, are added between a right arrow (→) and the statement. A critical index value is determined by *criteria*.

In an NCL program, the selection of a query variable is by query criteria: A quantifier index that minimizes or maximizes the criteria identifies a most critical query variable. An expression of Boolean, float, integer or date/time type can be used as a criterion in such a min/max query logic.

For a Boolean criterion, NCL supposes that Boolean "false" is less than Boolean "true". Internally Boolean false corresponds to integer 0 and Boolean true corresponds to integer 1.

In addition, programmers should try to ensure that query criteria take fixed values. If the value of a certain criterion is uncertain, NCL will calculate the mean value of its domain and will use it as the final criterion in the choice of query variables.

Optimization Objective

objective → min float
| max float
| min float : step
| max float: step
| min int
| max int
| min int: step
| max int: step
| min dtime
| max dtime
| min dtime: step
| max dtime: step
| (objective)

step → num
| dtime

In NCL, a programmer can specify multiple optimization *objectives* with float, integer and date/time expressions. The precedence relation follows their order in the program.

What is flexible is that user can also specify an optimization *step* which can be a numeric or date/time expression corresponding to the type of the objective to control the scale or precision of the optimization.

3.2 Context-Sensitivity of NCL

This section analyzes context-sensitivity of NCL. Most symbols on the left-hand side of the production rules in this section were not expanded in previous sections. However, once expanded, they become "conflict" rules: It is difficult for an LR parser to parse a grammar with such rules because the bottom-up reduction (to the start symbol *program*) is unclear and inefficient. In particular, implicit typing in the global context may require an unlimited number of looking ahead for an LR parser. For example, a variable can be introduced at the beginning of a program, but its type becomes clear only toward the end of the program; or worse, its type is not identified statically but can only be recognized dynamically as the parser analyzes the program and its input.

NCL is mathematically natural. This means its context-sensitivity is in accordance with conventions of mathematical logic. This section shows how to use such conventions as "contexts" in the rules to accommodate conflicts in the bottom-up reduction.

3.2.1 Constant

$$intsetcst \quad \rightarrow \quad \varnothing$$

$$dtimesetcst \quad \rightarrow \quad \varnothing$$

$$strsetcst \quad \rightarrow \quad \varnothing$$

$$refsetcst \quad \rightarrow \quad \varnothing$$

Though there are an infinite number of set constants, there is only one terminal symbol for set constants: the empty set symbol ($\varnothing$). It can be an empty integer set, an empty date/time set, an empty string set or an empty reference set.

It is vague on how to reduce $\varnothing$ to one of the non-terminals *intsetcst*, *dtimesetcst*, *strsetcst* and *refsetcst*. Even with the look-ahead technique, an LR parser still encounters the problems of dynamic typing in a global context. To settle this problem, it is helpful to transform the conflict rules into context-sensitive ones. Intuitively, for example, if the symbol $\varnothing$ is in an integer set operation context, it will be restricted to be an empty integer set.

In NCL, the implicit typing of an empty set symbol is supported by naive mathematical conventions. Syntactically, all possible contexts for $\varnothing$ should be taken into consideration. Among all, some such context-sensitive rules are:

- $intsetcst \cap intset \quad \rightarrow \quad \varnothing \cap intset$

This rule tells the parser to reduce $\varnothing$ to *intsetcst* in the context of intersection of integer sets.

- strsetcst ∪ strset   → $\varnothing$ ∪ strset

This rule tells the parser to reduce $\varnothing$ to *strsetcst* in the context of union of string sets.

- refsetcst \ refset   → $\varnothing$ \ refset

This rule tells the parser to reduce $\varnothing$ to *refsetcst* in the context of difference of reference sets.

3.2.2 Variable

boolvar	→	var
	|	systembool
floatvar	→	var
	|	systemfloat
intvar	→	var
	|	systemint
dtimevar	→	var
	|	systemtime
strvar	→	var
	|	systemstr
boolrefvar	→	var
floatrefvar	→	var
integralrefvar	→	var
setrefvar	→	var
intsetvar	→	var
dtimesetvar	→	var
strsetvar	→	var
refsetvar	→	var
var	→	ID
	|	ID$_{subscripts}$
	|	input
	|	–

Variables are the most "liberal" objects in NCL. NCL's syntax is designed to provide user with a great programming convenience.

Declaration

There is no need to explicitly declare variables in NCL though user can do this using the typing operator (::) . However, a variable's allocation happens at its first occurrence in a program. At its first occurrence, either its type is explicit in the context, or NCL will force it to be an integer variable.

Array and Subscript

subscripts $\rightarrow$ integral
                    | integral , subscripts

NCL supports array (subscripted variable) and multi-dimensional array. One limitation is that, at the first occurrence of a subscripted variable, there should be enough information on the ranges of its subscripts so that the system can allocate a finite array. Otherwise, an error message will be sent.

A subscript can be an expression of any integral type (integer, date/time, string or reference).

System Variable

A special class of variables which plays a significant role in an NCL program is called system variables. For example, through these variables user can have access to system information such as system states (input, output, termination and break), running time (global or local) and search information (search depth, number of backtracks, number of solutions). See "System Variable" in Section 3.1.6.

Input and Format

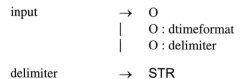

input $\rightarrow$ O
                | O : dtimeformat
                | O : delimiter

delimiter $\rightarrow$ STR

In NCL, user can get his input through an input variable O. The type of an input depends on the context and on the data from the input pool. In particular, for an input of date/time or date/time set or string, a format option exists after the symbol O, separated by a colon.

For an input of date/time or date/time set, a date/time format *dtimeformat* can be added. See "Date/Time Format" in Section 3.1.2.

In the case of string input, a string format *delimiter* can be added. It tells the terminating character (e.g., "\n", "\t", " ", etc.) for the string to be read. See the "String Input" example in Section 4.5.

Anonymous Variable

Sometimes anonymous variables are useful. The underline symbol (_) is introduced to represent an anonymous variable.

Implicit Typing

In NCL, the implicit typing of a variable is supported by naive mathematical conventions. For example, the two programs below are both legal in NCL:

$$\#s = 3, \quad 1 \in s. \tag{1}$$

$$\#s = 3, \quad s \in A. \tag{2}$$

But the statements "$\#s = 3$" have different semantics. In (1) s is a set variable and $\#s$ signifies the cardinality of s; in (2) s is a string variable and $\#s$ signifies the string length of s. Implicit typing in the global context takes effects in the second statements "$1 \in s$" and "$s \in A$". Things become even more complex if domain width function $\#f$ for float expression f and record count function $\#(poolhandle, delimiter)$ are taken into consideration.

Syntactically, all possible contexts for ID or O or _ should be considered in their context-sensitive rules. For example, among all, some such rules are:

- boolvar $\vee$ bool $\qquad \rightarrow \qquad$ ID $\vee$ bool
  This rule tells the parser to reduce ID to *boolvar* in the context of logical or.
- intsetvar $\cap$ intset $\qquad \rightarrow \qquad$ _ $\cap$ intset
  This rule tells the parser to reduce the anonymous variable _ to *intsetvar* in the context of intersection of integer sets.
- strsetvar \ strset $\qquad \rightarrow \qquad$ O \ strset
  This rule tells the parser to reduce O (input) to *strsetvar* in the context of string set and set difference.
- floatrefvar = \`float\` $\qquad \rightarrow \qquad$ ID = \`float\`
  This rule tells the parser to reduce ID to *floatrefvar* in the context of unification and float reference.

3.2.3 Function

boolfunc	$\rightarrow$	func
floatfunc	$\rightarrow$	func
intfunc	$\rightarrow$	func
dtimefunc	$\rightarrow$	func
strfunc	$\rightarrow$	func
boolreffunc	$\rightarrow$	func
floatreffunc	$\rightarrow$	func
integralreffunc	$\rightarrow$	func
setreffunc	$\rightarrow$	func

intsetfunc	$\rightarrow$	func
dtimesetfunc	$\rightarrow$	func
strsetfunc	$\rightarrow$	func
refsetfunc	$\rightarrow$	func
func	$\rightarrow$	ID (arguments)
arguments	$\rightarrow$	argument
	$\mid$	argument , arguments
argument	$\rightarrow$	⊔
	$\mid$	expression

The list of expressions *arguments*, which may be empty, is the list of arguments for function *func*.

The introduction of function in NCL makes the grammar more context-sensitive. For function definition, readers are referred to Section 3.1.4.

Encapsulation for Control

Apart from encapsulation for local variables and constraints, an important feature of function is its encapsulation capability for control:

- If a search query occurs in a function, it is local to the function. The query will be focused on the local query variables before moving to query variables outside of the function;
- If an optimization objective occurs in a function, it is local to the function and it means to tell NCL to carry out a local optimization toward the objective;
- System variables play an important role in control. Some of them become local in a function.

A good example illustrating encapsulation of search query and optimization objective is model decomposition for the Pick-up and Delivery problem in Section 8.2.2.

Global System Variable

Not all system variables become local in a function. The following variables are always global:

- 'Work Directory'
- 'Global Time'
- Date/time variables such as 'yyyy-mm-dd hh:mm:ss'

The following system variables can also be regarded as global:

- "
- 'Model Depth'
- 'Trace Level'

- 'Search Depth'

Local System Variable

The evolution of system state variables in a function will only produce local impacts to the function. For example,

- If 'O' becomes true, it tells the function to return to input state and restart the local search tree with an improved local objective bound;
- If '@' becomes true, it tells the function that a "local solution" is reached;
- If '.' becomes true, it tells the function to "terminate".

The following system variables related to search and optimization become local in a function:

- 'Solution Count' tells the number of local solutions found in a function call;
- 'Backtrack Count' tells the number of backtracking caused by a function call;
- 'Local Time' tells the execution time in the local search and/or optimization.

Implicit Typing

Implicit typing plays an important role in defining and calling functions. Either externally or internally in the function definition, the types of function identifiers and arguments should be consistent in the whole context.

Similar to that for a variable, all possible implicit-typing contexts for ID should be considered. For example, some context-sensitive rules are:

- $\neg$ boolfunc $\rightarrow$ $\neg$ ID (arguments)
  This rule tells the parser to reduce ID to *boolfunc* in the context of Boolean negation.
- intsetfunc $\cup$ intset $\rightarrow$ ID (arguments) $\cup$ intset
  This rule tells the parser to reduce ID to *intsetfunc* in the context of union of integer sets.
- strfunc $\in$ strset $\rightarrow$ ID (arguments) $\in$ strset
  This rule tells the parser to reduce ID to *strfunc* in the context of string membership relation.

3.2.4 Sub-Model

  boolsubmodel $\rightarrow$ submodel

  strsubmodel $\rightarrow$ submodel

The typing for a sub-model (Boolean or string) is the same as that for a variable and is left to be settled by mathematical logic conventions. For example, some context-sensitive rules for sub-model are:

- , boolsubmodel , $\rightarrow$, [int , int , int] ,
  This rule tells the parser to reduce *[int, int, int]* to *boolsubmodel* in the context of tautology.
- (bool ? strsubmodel : str) $\rightarrow$ (bool ? [int , int , int] : str)
  This rule tells the parser to reduce *[int, int, int]* to *strsubmodel* in the context of conditional string evaluation.

References

Colmerauer, A., Kanoui, H., Pasero, R., Roussel, P.: Un système de communication homme-machine en français. Technical Report, Groupe Intelligence Artificielle, Université d'Aix-Marseille II (1973)

Kernighan, B.W., Ritchie, D.M.: The C Programming Language (2nd ed.). Englewood Cliffs, NJ: Prentice Hall (1988)

Zhou, J.: Introduction to the constraint language NCL. JLP, 45(1-3): 71–103 (2000)

Zhou, J.: The NCL Natural Constraint Language (in Chinese). Science Press, Beijing (2009)

4 Tutorial Programs

NCL is a description language in mathematical logic for modeling and solving problems. This chapter uses examples to illustrate NCL's syntax and semantics. After reading them, user will feel closer to NCL.

4.1 Getting Started

4.1.1 Input and Output

With the data file as follows:

```
5
1      23
3      6     5     4
2      6     7
5      1     3     5     7     9
2      1     2
```

and given the program:

```
n = 0,

∀ i ∈ [1,n] (
      xᵢ ∈ [1, 10],
      xᵢ = 0,

      ∀ j ∈ [1, xᵢ] (
            yᵢ,ⱼ :: 0,
            yᵢ,ⱼ = 0,
      )
),

∀ i ∈ [1,n] (
      @ (xᵢ  "\t"),
      ∀ j ∈ [1, xᵢ] @(yᵢ,ⱼ "\t"),
      @ "\n",
).
```

the answer is:

```
1      23
3      6     5     4
2      6     7
5      1     3     5     7     9
2      1     2
```

Note that it is necessary to define a finite domain for variable x_i (in the above example it is [1,10]) so that NCL can determine subscript range and allocate memory for variable $y_{i,j}$.

4.1.2 Default Value

Given default values in the input file:

_ _ _ _ _ _ _ _ _ _ _ _ _ _

and given the program:

```
true,

boolDefault                        :: true,
intDefault                         :: 1,
floatDefault                       :: 1.0,
SetDefault                         :: [1, 5],

dateDefault                        :: '31/01/2008',
timeMMDefault                      :: '08:00',
timeSSDefault                      :: '08:00:00',
dateTimeMMDefault                  :: '31/01/2008 08:00',
dateTimeSSDefault                  :: '31/01/2008 08:00:00',

strDefault                         :: "abc",
boolRefDefault                     :: `true`,
intRefDefault                      :: `1`,
floatRefDefault                    :: `1.0`,
setRefDefault                      :: `[1, 5]`,

boolDefault                        = O,
intDefault                         = O,
floatDefault                       = O,
SetDefault                         = O,
strDefault                         = O,

dateDefault                        = O,
timeMMDefault                      = O,
timeSSDefault                      = O,
dateTimeMMDefault                  = O,
dateTimeSSDefault                  = O,

boolRefDefault                     = O,
intRefDefault                      = O,
floatRefDefault                    = O,
setRefDefault                      = O,

@ ("boolDefault = "  boolDefault          "\n"),
```

```
@ ("intDefault = "   intDefault            "\n"),
@ ("floatDefault = "   floatDefault        "\n"),
@ ("SetDefault = "   SetDefault            "\n\n"),

@ ("dateDefault = "   dateDefault          "\n"),
@ ("timeMMDefault = "   timeMMDefault      "\n"),
@ ("timeSSDefault = "   timeSSDefault      "\n"),
@ ("dateTimeMMDefault = "   dateTimeMMDefault   "\n"),
@ ("dateTimeSSDefault = "   dateTimeSSDefault   "\n\n"),

@ ("strDefault = \""   strDefault          "\"\n"),
@ ("boolRefDefault = "   boolRefDefault     "\n"),
@ ("intRefDefault = "   intRefDefault       "\n"),
@ ("floatRefDefault = "   floatRefDefault   "\n"),
@ ("setRefDefault = "   setRefDefault       "\n").
```

the answer is:

```
boolDefault              = F
intDefault               = 0
floatDefault             = 0.000000000000
SetDefault               = {}

dateDefault              = 01/01/2000
timeMMDefault            = 00:00
timeSSDefault            = 00:00:00
dateTimeMMDefault        = 01/01/2000 00:00
dateTimeSSDefault        = 01/01/2000 00:00:00

strDefault               = ""
boolRefDefault           = F
intRefDefault            = 0
floatRefDefault          = 0.0
setRefDefault            = {}
```

Note that default values are initialized in NCL's .cfg file. The above result displays the initialized default values for Boolean, float, integer, date, time (in minutes), time (in seconds), date-time (in minutes), date-time (in seconds), string, Boolean reference, integer reference, float reference, set reference and set.

The default value symbol (_) should be distinguished from the anonymous variable (_). They use the same notation but have different representations; see Section 4.8 for the example of anonymous variables.

4.1.3 Data Buffer

The following example illustrates how to use a string buffer as a data pool (input or output).

Given the program:

```
input_buf = "1  2  3  4  5  6  7  8",
output_buf :: "",
```

```
'O' ← ["input" : input_buf],

∀ i ∈ [1,8] (
    x_i = O,
),
["input" : input_buf] ← 'O',

["output" : output_buf] ← '@',

∀ i ∈ [1,8] (
    @ (x_i "\t"),
),
@ "\n",

'@' ← ["output" : output_buf],

@ output_buf.
```

the answer is:

```
1   2   3   4   5   6   7   8
```

4.2 Boolean Logic

Given the program:

```
true,
¬ false,
a ≡ (b → c),
b ≡ (true ⊕ a),
c ∨ false,
c ∧ true,

a = ?,
b = ?,
c = ?,

@ ("a = "   a   "\tb = "   b   "\tc = "   c   "\n").
```

the answer is:

```
a = T    b = F    c = T
```

Boolean constants such as T for truth and F for false, which are initialized in the NCL configuration file, are necessary for input and output. But it is not necessary to use Boolean constants in a model. To introduce the Boolean values of truth and false in a model, user can simply define the tautology "true" and the tautology "¬ false" so as to introduce the truth value to the variable true and the false value to the variable false.

4.3 Numerical Reasoning

Due to computer's bits limitation (32 bits, 64 bits, etc), NCL adopts interval approximation to logically represent numbers:

- It approximates a real number by a floating-point interval at the precision of one bit, for example, <1.5707962512970..1.5707963705063>;
- It represents the universe of real numbers or the universe of integers by interval $[-\infty, +\infty]$.

4.3.1 Integer Equation

Given the program:

```
c ∈ [-2000,2000],
c⁴ + 4×c³ - 7×c² - 22×c + 24 = 0,
c = ?,

@ (`c⁴ + 4×c³ - 7×c² - 22×c + 24 = 0` ":\tc = " c "\n").
```

the answer is:

```
c⁴ + 4×c³ - 7×c² - 22×c + 24 = 0:   c = -4
c⁴ + 4×c³ - 7×c² - 22×c + 24 = 0:   c = -3
c⁴ + 4×c³ - 7×c² - 22×c + 24 = 0:   c =  1
c⁴ + 4×c³ - 7×c² - 22×c + 24 = 0:   c =  2
```

Note that NCL's computational capability is limited over integers. User should avoid precision problems caused by a computer's bits limitation.

4.3.2 Infinity

NCL uses the symbol ∞ to represent infinity. Reasoning over infinities is illustrated in the following program.

```
x ∈ [0, 100],

y = ∞ ÷ 3,

z = ∞ mod 3,

w = ∞ - ∞,

f = exp(∞),
g = log(1e-105),

h = ∞ / x,
@ ("y = " y "\n"),
@ ("z = " z "\n"),
@ ("w = " w "\n"),
@ ("f = " f "\n"),
@ ("g = " g "\n"),
@ ("h = " h "\n").
```

The answer is:

```
y = +∞
z = <0..2>
w = <-∞..+∞>
f = +∞
g = <-∞..-103.2789230346680>
h = +∞
```

4.4 Date/Time

NCL supports date/time types (date, time and date-time). This makes it easier and more straightforward to model and solve planning and scheduling problems.

Given the program:

```
∀ i ∈ [1, 7] (
    dayofweekᵢ :: "",
    dayofweekᵢ = O,
),

@ 0 : "mm/dd/yyyy",
@ " is internally ",
@ 0 : "",
@ "\n\n",

∀ d ∈ [-2, 2] (
    @ d : "dd/mm/yyyy",
    @ " is ",
    @ dayofweek(d + 5) mod 7 + 1,
    @ "\n"
),
@ "\n",
@ "Current date information:\n",
@ ('dd/mm/yyyy'  "\n"),
@ ('mm/dd/yyyy'  "\n"),
@ ('yyyy-mm-dd'  "\n"),
@ ('yyyymmdd'  "\n\n"),

@ "Current time information:\n",
@ ('hh'  "\n"),
@ ('hh:mm'  "\n"),
@ ('hh:mm:ss'  "\n\n"),

@ "Current date time information:\n",
@ ('dd/mm/yyyy hh'  "\n"),
@ ('mm/dd/yyyy hh'  "\n"),
```

```
@ ('yyyy-mm-dd hh'   "\n\n"),

@ ('dd/mm/yyyy hh:mm'   "\n"),
@ ('mm/dd/yyyy hh:mm'   "\n"),
@ ('yyyy-mm-dd hh:mm'   "\n\n"),

@ ('dd/mm/yyyy hh:mm:ss'   "\n"),
@ ('mm/dd/yyyy hh:mm:ss'   "\n"),
@ ('yyyy-mm-dd hh:mm:ss'   "\n\n").
```

and given the input:

```
"Monday" "Tuesday" "Wednesday" "Thursday" "Friday"
"Saturday" "Sunday"
```

the answer is:

```
01/01/2000 is internally 0

30/12/1999 is Thursday
31/12/1999 is Friday
01/01/2000 is Saturday
02/01/2000 is Sunday
03/01/2000 is Monday

Current date information:
08/11/2010
11/08/2010
2010-11-08
20101108

Current time information:
00
00:01
00:01:22

Current date time information:
08/11/2010 00
11/08/2010 00
2010-11-08 00

08/11/2010 00:01
11/08/2010 00:01
2010-11-08 00:01

08/11/2010 00:01:22
11/08/2010 00:01:22
```

2010-11-08 00:01:22

4.5 String

4.5.1 String Input

In NCL, to facilitate string input, a special string delimiter can be used to specify the terminating character when reading a string.

With the data file `["StringInput.dat"]` as follows:

```
123   456   789
abc   def   ghi
!@#   $%&   *?|
```

Given the program:

```
file = ["StringInput.dat"],
n = #(file, "\n"),

∀ i ∈ [1, n]
    xᵢ = O : "\n",

∀ i ∈ [1, n]
    @ ("\""    xᵢ    "\""    "\n").
```

the answer is:

```
"123   456   789"
"abc   def   ghi"
"!@#   $%&   *?|"
```

In this example, "\n" is the delimiter. It tells NCL to read strings in three lines.

4.5.2 Concatenation

Concatenation in NCL is a flexible functionality for string. It plays an important role in data processing. It allows concatenation of all kinds of expressions and data transformation between string and all types.

Given the program:

```
x :: 0,
y :: 0,
p :: "",
q :: "",
a :: "",
b :: "",
#a = 8,
#b = 6,
(a   " "   b) = "20000101 113006",

@ (`(a   " "   b)`   " = "   (a   " "   b)   "\n"),
```

```
@ (`a`   " = "   a   "\n"),
@ (`b`   " = "   b   "\n\n"),


#p = 8,
#q = 6,
(p   " "   y) =   "20000101 113006",
(x   " "   q) =   "20000101 113006",


@ (`(x   " "   y)`   " = "   (x   " "   y)   "\n"),
@ (`x`   " = "   x   "\n"),
@ (`y`   " = "   y   "\n\n"),


f :: 0.0,
g :: 0.0,
(a   " "   f) = "20000101 0.0123449992388",
(f   " "   a) = "0.0123449992388 20000101",
(a   " "   g) = "20000101 0.0000000000000",


@ (`(a   " "   f)`   " = "   (a   " "   f)   "\n"),
@ (`a`   " = "   a   "\n"),
@ (`f`   " = "   f   "\n\n"),
@ (`(a   " "   g)`   " = "   (a   " "   g)   "\n"),
@ (`a`   " = "   a   "\n"),
@ (`g`   " = "   g   "\n\n"),


c1 :: T,
c2 :: T,
(f   " "   c1) = "0.0123449992388 T",
(f   " "   c2) = "0.0123449992388 F",


@ (`(f   " "   c1)`   " = "   (f   " "   c1)   "\n"),
@ (`(f   " "   c2)`   " = "   (f   " "   c2)   "\n"),
@ (`f`   " = "   f   "\n"),
@ (`c1`   " = "   c1   "\n"),
@ (`c2`   " = "   c2   "\n\n"),


A :: Ø,
B :: Ø,
C :: Ø,
D :: Ø,
(a   " "   A) = "20000101 {}",
(B   " "   a) = "[12, 34] 20000101",
(C   " "   b) = "{1..3, 12..34, 55} 113006",
(b   " "   D) = "113006 {12345}",


@ (`A`   " = "   A   "\n"),
```

```
@ (`B`    " = "   B   "\n"),
@ (`C`    " = "   C   "\n"),
@ (`D`    " = "   D   "\n\n"),

@ ("abc"    (A   a   B   p   q)    (x+y)).
```

the answer is:

```
(a " " b)  = 20000101 113006
a = 20000101
b = 113006

(x " " y)  = 20000101 113006
x = 20000101
y = 113006

(a " " f)  = 20000101 0.0123449992388
a = 20000101
f = 0.0123449992388

(a " " g)  = 20000101 0.0000000000000
a = 20000101
g = 0.0000000000000

(f " " c1)  = 0.0123449992388 T
(f " " c2)  = 0.0123449992388 F
f    = 0.0123449992388
c1 = T
c2 = F

A = {}
B = [12, 34]
C = {1..3, 12..34, 55}
D = {12345}

abc{}20000101[12, 34]2000010111300620113107
```

4.6 Referencing

4.6.1 Reference in a Subscript

Subscripts of a variable can be any general integer. The following example illustrates the use of subscripts of integer, date/time, string, and reference types.

Given the program:

```
x = 1,
y = 3,
```

```
f = 0.1,
g = 0.2,

E = {`x`, `y`},
A = {"a", "d"},
B = {`x`, `y`},
C = {`f`, `g`},
D = {`{x}`, `∅`, `E`},

∀ `j` ∈ B (
   ∀ i ∈ A (
      ∀ `k` ∈ C (
         ∀ `l` ∈ D (
            x_{i,`j`,`k`,`l`} = (i" " j " " k̲ " " l),
         )
      )
   )
),

∀ k ∈ C (
   ∀ j ∈ B (
      ∀ i ∈ A (
         ∀ l ∈ D (
            @ `x_{i,j,k,l}` : 21,
            @ "=",
            @ ("\"""x_{i,j,k,l}"\"") : 40,
            @ "\n",
         ),
         @ "\n",
      ),
      @ "\n",
   ),
   @ "\n",
),

@ "\n\n",

∀ i ∈ A (
   ∀ `j` ∈ B (
      ∀ `k` ∈ C (
         ∀ `l` ∈ D (
            @ `x_{i,`j`,`k`,`l`}` : 21,
            @ "=",
            @ ("\"" x_{i,`j`,`k`,`l`}"\"") : 40,
            @ "\n",
```

```
                ),
                @ "\n",
            ),
            @ "\n",
        ),
        @ "\n",
    ),
    @ "\n\n",
```

the answer is:

```
x_{"a",`x`,`f`,`{x}`} = "a 1 0.100000 {1}"
x_{"a",`x`,`f`,`{}`} = "a 1 0.100000 {}"
x_{"a",`x`,`f`,`E`} = "a 1 0.100000 {`x`, `y`}"
x_{"d",`x`,`f`,`{x}`} = "d 1 0.100000 {1}"
x_{"d",`x`,`f`,`{}`} = "d 1 0.100000 {}"
x_{"d",`x`,`f`,`E`} = "d 1 0.100000 {`x`, `y`}"

x_{"a",`y`,`f`,`{x}`} = "a 3 0.100000 {1}"
x_{"a",`y`,`f`,`{}`} = "a 3 0.100000 {}"
x_{"a",`y`,`f`,`E`} = "a 3 0.100000 {`x`, `y`}"
x_{"d",`y`,`f`,`{x}`} = "d 3 0.100000 {1}"
x_{"d",`y`,`f`,`{}`} = "d 3 0.100000 {}"
x_{"d",`y`,`f`,`E`} = "d 3 0.100000 {`x`, `y`}"

x_{"a",`x`,`g`,`{x}`} = "a 1 0.200000 {1}"
x_{"a",`x`,`g`,`{}`} = "a 1 0.200000 {}"
x_{"a",`x`,`g`,`E`} = "a 1 0.200000 {`x`, `y`}"
x_{"d",`x`,`g`,`{x}`} = "d 1 0.200000 {1}"
x_{"d",`x`,`g`,`{}`} = "d 1 0.200000 {}"
x_{"d",`x`,`g`,`E`} = "d 1 0.200000 {`x`, `y`}"

x_{"a",`y`,`g`,`{x}`} = "a 3 0.200000 {1}"
x_{"a",`y`,`g`,`{}`} = "a 3 0.200000 {}"
x_{"a",`y`,`g`,`E`} = "a 3 0.200000 {`x`, `y`}"
x_{"d",`y`,`g`,`{x}`} = "d 3 0.200000 {1}"
x_{"d",`y`,`g`,`{}`} = "d 3 0.200000 {}"
x_{"d",`y`,`g`,`E`} = "d 3 0.200000 {`x`, `y`}"

x_{"a",`x`,`f`,`{x}`} = "a 1 0.100000 {1}"
x_{"a",`x`,`f`,`{}`} = "a 1 0.100000 {}"
x_{"a",`x`,`f`,`E`} = "a 1 0.100000 {`x`, `y`}"
x_{"a",`x`,`g`,`{x}`} = "a 1 0.200000 {1}"
x_{"a",`x`,`g`,`{}`} = "a 1 0.200000 {}"
x_{"a",`x`,`g`,`E`} = "a 1 0.200000 {`x`, `y`}"

x_{"a",`y`,`f`,`{x}`} = "a 3 0.100000 {1}"
```

```
x_{"a",`y`,`f`,`{}`}  = "a 3 0.100000 {}"
x_{"a",`y`,`f`,`E`} = "a 3 0.100000 {`x`, `y`}"
x_{"a",`y`,`g`,`{x}`} = "a 3 0.200000 {1}"
x_{"a",`y`,`g`,`{}`}  = "a 3 0.200000 {}"
x_{"a",`y`,`g`,`E`} = "a 3 0.200000 {`x`, `y`}"

x_{"d",`x`,`f`,`{x}`} = "d 1 0.100000 {1}"
x_{"d",`x`,`f`,`{}`}  = "d 1 0.100000 {}"
x_{"d",`x`,`f`,`E`} = "d 1 0.100000 {`x`, `y`}"
x_{"d",`x`,`g`,`{x}`} = "d 1 0.200000 {1}"
x_{"d",`x`,`g`,`{}`}  = "d 1 0.200000 {}"
x_{"d",`x`,`g`,`E`} = "d 1 0.200000 {`x`, `y`}"

x_{"d",`y`,`f`,`{x}`} = "d 3 0.100000 {1}"
x_{"d",`y`,`f`,`{}`}  = "d 3 0.100000 {}"
x_{"d",`y`,`f`,`E`} = "d 3 0.100000 {`x`, `y`}"
x_{"d",`y`,`g`,`{x}`} = "d 3 0.200000 {1}"
x_{"d",`y`,`g`,`{}`}  = "d 3 0.200000 {}"
x_{"d",`y`,`g`,`E`} = "d 3 0.200000 {`x`, `y`}"
```

4.6.2 Referenced Operator

With NCL's referencing mechanism, an expression can be referenced as a logical pointer. This lets user be able to manipulate operations at the meta-level.

Given the program:

```
x = 1,
y = 3,
z = 4,
f = 0.1,
g = 0.2,
E = {`x`, `y`},
A = {"abc",  "d"},
B = {`x`, `y`},
C = {`f`, `g`},
D = {`{x, y}`,`∅`,`E`},

∀ `i ∈ A (
   ∀ `j` ∈ B (
      ∀ `k` ∈ C (
         ∀ `l` ∈ D (
            @ `(⌊j + k⌋∈ l)`,
            @ "\n",
         ),
         @ "\n",
      ),
```

```
            @ "\n",
        ),
        @ "\n",
    ),
    @ "\n\n",

    ∀ `j` ∈ B (
        ∀ i ∈ A (
            ∀ `l` ∈ D (
                ∀ `k` ∈ C (
                    @ `(⌊j + k⌋ ∈ l)`,
                    @ "\n",
                ),
                @ "\n",
            ),
            @ "\n",
        ),
        @ "\n",
    ),
    @ "\n\n".
```

the answer is:

⌊x+f⌋ ∈ {x, y}   ⌊x+f⌋ ∈ ∅
⌊x+f⌋ ∈ E
⌊x+g⌋ ∈ {x, y}   ⌊x+g⌋ ∈ ∅
⌊x+g⌋ ∈ E

⌊y+f⌋ ∈ {x, y}   ⌊y+f⌋ ∈ ∅
⌊y+f⌋ ∈ E
⌊y+g⌋ ∈ {x, y}   ⌊y+g⌋ ∈ ∅
⌊y+g⌋ ∈ E

⌊x+f⌋ ∈ {x, y}   ⌊x+f⌋ ∈ ∅
⌊x+f⌋ ∈ E
⌊x+g⌋ ∈ {x, y}   ⌊x+g⌋ ∈ ∅
⌊x+g⌋ ∈ E

⌊y+f⌋ ∈ {x, y}   ⌊y+f⌋ ∈ ∅
⌊y+f⌋ ∈ E
⌊y+g⌋ ∈ {x, y}   ⌊y+g⌋ ∈ ∅
⌊y+g⌋ ∈ E

⌊x+f⌋ ∈ {x, y}   ⌊x+g⌋ ∈ {x, y}
⌊x+f⌋ ∈ ∅   ⌊x+g⌋ ∈ ∅
⌊x+f⌋ ∈ E   ⌊x+g⌋ ∈ E

$\lfloor x+f \rfloor \in \{x,y\}$ $\lfloor x+g \rfloor \in \{x,y\}$
$\lfloor x+f \rfloor \in \emptyset$ $\lfloor x+g \rfloor \in \emptyset$
$\lfloor x+f \rfloor \in E$ $\lfloor x+g \rfloor \in E$

$\lfloor y+f \rfloor \in \{x,y\}$ $\lfloor y+g \rfloor \in \{x,y\}$
$\lfloor y+f \rfloor \in \emptyset$ $\lfloor y+g \rfloor \in \emptyset$
$\lfloor y+f \rfloor \in E$ $\lfloor y+g \rfloor \in E$

$\lfloor y+f \rfloor \in \{x,y\}$ $\lfloor y+g \rfloor \in \{x,y\}$
$\lfloor y+f \rfloor \in \emptyset$ $\lfloor y+g \rfloor \in \emptyset$
$\lfloor y+f \rfloor \in E$ $\lfloor y+g \rfloor \in E$

4.6.3 Subscript Leak

Given the program:

```
∀ `i` ∈ {`1<2`, `1 ∈ [-1,10]`, `a ≡ b`} (
    ∀ `j` ∈ {`a → b`, `b → a`, `a ∨ b`}(
        x·i·,·j· ≡ i ∧ j,
        x·i·,·j· = ?,

        @ `x·i·,·j·` : 40,
        @  x·i·,·j·  : 4,
    ),
    @ "\n",
),
@ "\n",

¬a,
b,
e,

@ ("Subscripts of "   `x·1<2·, `a ∨ b·`   " are OK\n"),
@ (`x·1<2·, `a ∨ b·`   " = "   x·1<2·, `a ∨ b·   "\n\n"),
@ ("Subscript" `e`   " leaks for x·e·, ·a·. No output.\n"),
@ (`x·e·, ·a·`   x·e·, ·a·   "\n\n") .
```

the answer is:

```
x·1<2·,·a→b·    T    x·1<2·,·b→a·    F    x·1<2·,·a∨b·    T
x·1∈[-1,10]·,·a→b·  T   x·1∈[-1,10]·,·b→a·  F   x·1∈[-1,10]·,·a∨b·   T
x·a≡b·,·a→b·    F    x·a≡b·,·b→a·    F    x·a≡b·,·a∨b·    F


Subscripts of x·1<2·,·a ∨ b· are OK
x·1<2·,·a∨b· = T


Subscript e leaks for x·e·, ·a·. No output.
```

In Debug mode, user gets warning messages as below:

Warning C20: subscript ' `e` ' of ' x·`e`, ·`a`· ' out of range: {`1<2`..`a = b`} instead of {`e`} expected
Warning C20: subscript ' `a` ' of ' x·`e`, ·`a`· ' out of range: {` a→b `..`a∨b`} instead of {`a`} expected

An expression (or a constraint) involving any variable with a subscript leak is invalid. The NCL engine will neglect such invalid constraints and expressions.

4.7 Set Reasoning

4.7.1 A General Example

Given the program:

```
A ∪ B = [1, 3] ∪ [5, 8],
A ∩ B = [2, 3] ∪ [6, 7],

inf A ≥ 2,
sup B ≤ 7,
#A = 6,

A = ?, B = ?,

@ ("A = " A   "\n"),
@ ("B = " B   "\n\n").
```

the answer is:

```
A = {2..3, 5..8}
B = {1..3, 6..7}
```

The infimum (inf) and supremum (sup) of the empty set (∅) can take any value. So user must pay special attention to empty set so that the modeling ensures logical soundness and completeness.

4.7.2 Attributes of a Set

This example illustrates the attributes of a set: infimum (inf), supremum (sup) and cardinality (#) of any set; weight of an integer set (Σ); conjunction (∧), disjunction (∨) and exclusive-or (⊕) of a set of Boolean references; intersection (∩) and union (∪) of a set of set references.

Given the program:

```
A = {1, 2+3, 3+4},
B = {`1 = 2`, `2 > 4`, `1 ∈ [1, 4]`},
C = {`{1, 3, 5}`, `[7, 10]`, `{2, 4, 6}`},

@ (`inf A`   " = "   inf A   "\n"),
@ (`sup A`   " = "   sup A   "\n"),
@ (`#A`   " = "   #A   "\n"),
```

```
@(`ΣA`   " = "   ΣA   "\n\n"),

@(`∧B`   " = "   ∧B   "\n"),
@(`∨B`   " = "   ∨B   "\n"),
@(`⊕B`   " = "   ⊕B   "\n\n"),

@(`∩C`   " = "   ∩C   "\n"),
@(`∪C`   " = "   ∪C   "\n\n").
```

the answer is:

```
inf A = 1
sup A = 7
#A = 3
ΣA = 13

∧B = F
∨B = T
⊕B = T

∩C = ∅
∪C = [1, 10]
```

4.7.3 Piecewise Intervals from a Set

The following program illustrates how to obtain piecewise intervals [1, 2], {4}, {6}, [8, 9] from the set {1..2, 4, 6, 8..9} using set shift and set difference operations.

Given the program:

```
A = {1..2,   4,   6, 8..9},
Start = A \ (A >> 1),
End = A \ (A << 1),
n = #Start,
∀ i ∈ [1,n]
    @ ([Start[i],End[i]]   "   ").
```

the answer is:

```
[1,2]     {4}     {6}     [8,9]
```

4.8 Special Variable

4.8.1 Anonymous Variable

In NCL, the underline symbol (_) represents an anonymous variable. For example, user can write an NCL program as follows:

```
true,

    _  = true,
    _  = 1,
    _  = 1.0,
    _  = [1, 5],
    _  = "abc",
    _  = `true`,
    _  = `1`,
    _  = `1.0`,
    _  = `[1, 5]`,
    A  = [_, _],

∀ i ∈ [1,8]
    _ = i.
```

The anonymous variable (_) has the same notation as that of a default value in an input pool. Simply to say, the underline symbol represents a variable in a program while it is a default value in an input pool. See the default value example in Section 4.1.

4.8.2 System Variable

NCL's system variables make it easy for user to control the NCL engine. The following example gives readers a first idea about them.

Given the program:

```
'O' ⇒ (
    input = 'O',
    output = '@',
    terminate = '.',
),

@ (`input`      " = "    input      "\n"),
@ (`output`     " = "    output     "\n"),
@ (`terminate`  " = "    terminate  "\n\n"),

@ (`'O'`        " = "    'O'        "\n"),
@ (`'@'`        " = "    '@'        "\n"),
@ (`'.'`        " = "    '.'        "\n\n"),

@ (`'Work Directory'`    " = "    'Work Directory'    "\n\n"),
@ (`'Model Depth'`       " = "    'Model Depth'       "\n"),
@ (`'Solution Count'`    " = "    'Solution Count'    "\n"),
@ (`'Backtrack Count'`   " = "    'Backtrack Count'   "\n"),
@ (`'Global Time'`       " = "    'Global Time'       "\n"),
@ (`'Search Depth'`      " = "    'Search Depth'      "\n").
```

the answer is:

```
input       = T
output      = U
terminate   = U

'O'   = U
'@'   = T
'.'   = U

'Work Directory' = C:\Program Files\Poem\Test\

'Model Depth'       = 0
'Solution Count'    = 1
'Backtrack Count'   = 0
'Global Time'       = 0.271000
'Search Depth'      = 0
```

4.9 Predefined Function

4.9.1 Float Function

NCL provides user with a rich list of unary float functions including cosine, sine, tangent, arccosine, arcsine, arctangent, logarithm, exponential and square root.
   Given the program:

```
@ (`cos 1.0`       " = "    cos 1.0    "\n"),
@ (`sin 2.0`       " = "    sin 2.0    "\n"),
@ (`tan 1.0`       " = "    tan 1.0    "\n"),
@ (`cos 1`         " = "    cos 1    "\n"),
@ (`sin 2`         " = "    sin 2    "\n"),
@ (`tan 1`         " = "    tan 1    "\n"),

@ (`arccos 0.0`    " = "    arccos 0.0    "\n"),
@ (`arcsin 0.0`    " = "    arcsin 0.0    "\n"),
@ (`arctan -1.0`   " = "    arctan -1.0    "\n"),
@ (`arccos 1`      " = "    arccos 1    "\n"),
@ (`arcsin 1`      " = "    arcsin 1    "\n"),
@ (`arctan -1`     " = "    arctan -1    "\n"),

@ (`log 1.0`       " = "    log 1.0    "\n"),
@ (`log 1`         " = "    log 1    "\n"),
@ (`exp 1.0`       " = "    exp 1.0    "\n"),
@ (`exp 0.0`       " = "    exp 0.0    "\n"),
@ (`exp 1`         " = "    exp 1    "\n"),
@ (`exp 0`         " = "    exp 0    "\n"),
@ (` √1.0 `        " = "    √1.0    "\n"),
@ (` √0 `          " = "    √0    "\n"),
```

the answer is:

```
cos 1.0            = <0.5403022766113..0.5403023362160>
sin 2.0            = <0.9092974066734..0.9092974662781>
tan 1.0            = <1.5574076175690..1.5574077367783>
cos 1              = <0.5403022766113..0.5403023362160>
sin 2              = <0.9092974066734..0.9092974662781>
tan 1              = <1.5574076175690..1.5574077367783>

arccos 0.0         = <1.5707962512970..1.5707963705063>
arcsin 0.0         = 0.0000000000000
arctan -1.0        = <-0.7853981852531.. -0.7853981256485>
arccos 1           = 0.0000000000000
arcsin 1           = <1.5707962512970..1.5707963705063>
arctan -1          = <-0.7853981852531..- 0.7853981256485>

log 1.0            = 0.0000000000000
log 1              = 0.0000000000000

exp 1.0            = <2.7182817459106..2.7182819843292>
exp 0.0            = 1.0000000000000
exp 1              = <2.7182817459106..2.7182819843292>
exp 0              = 1.0000000000000
```

$\sqrt{1.0}$ = 1.0000000000000

$\sqrt{0}$ = 0.0000000000000

This program illustrates the numeric precision and the accuracy of logic reasoning over real numbers.

4.9.2 Aggregate Function

NCL provides user with conventional aggregate functions including minimum (min), maximum (max), sum (Σ), global conjunction ($\wedge$), global disjunction ($\vee$), global exclusive-or ($\oplus$), global intersection ($\cap$), global union ($\cup$) with a single index or two indices.

Given the program:

```
A = [1, 5],
B = {1, 2+3, 3+4},

C = {`1 = 2`, `2 > 4`, `1 ∈ [1, 4]`},
D = {`1`, `2+3`, `3+4`},
E = {`{1, 3, 5}`, `[7, 10]`, `{2, 4, 6}`},
F = {`2.0`, `-2E3`, `3.0×4.0`},

@(`min_{i ∈ A} i`    " = "    min_{i ∈ A} i    "\n"),
@(`max_{i ∈ A} i`    " = "    max_{i ∈ A} i    "\n"),
@(`Σ_{i ∈ A} i`      " = "    Σ_{i ∈ A} i      "\n\n"),
```

```
@(`min·ₓ·∈D x`    " = "   min·ₓ·∈D x   "\n"),
@(`max·ₓ·∈D x`    " = "   max·ₓ·∈D x   "\n"),
@(`∑·ₓ·∈D x`      " = "   ∑·ₓ·∈D x   "\n\n"),

@(`min·f·∈F f`    " = "   min·f·∈F f   "\n"),
@(`max·f·∈F f`    " = "   max·f·∈F f   "\n"),
@(`∑·f·∈F f`      " = "   ∑·f·∈F f   "\n\n"),

@(`∧·a·∈C a`      " = "   ∧·a·∈C a   "\n"),
@(`∨·a·∈C a`      " = "   ∨·a·∈C a   "\n"),
@(`⊕·a·∈C a`      " = "   ⊕·a·∈C a   "\n\n"),

@(`∩·i·∈E i`      " = "   ∩·i·∈E i   "\n"),
@(`∪·i·∈E i`      " = "   ∪·i·∈E i   "\n\n"),

∀ i ∈ A (
  xᵢ = i,
  fᵢ = i × 2.0,
  aᵢ = (i < 3),
  Aᵢ = {i},

  ∀ j ∈ A \ i (
    Yᵢ,ⱼ = i,
    gᵢ,ⱼ = i × 2.0,
    bᵢ,ⱼ = (i < 3),
    Bᵢ,ⱼ = {i},
  ),
),

@ (`minᵢ∈A xᵢ`    " = "   minᵢ∈A xᵢ   "\n"),
@ (`maxᵢ∈A xᵢ`    " = "   maxᵢ∈A xᵢ   "\n"),
@ (`∑ᵢ∈A xᵢ`      " = "   ∑ᵢ∈A xᵢ   "\n\n"),

@ (`minᵢ∈A,ⱼ∈A\i Yᵢ,ⱼ`    " = "   minᵢ∈A,ⱼ∈A\i Yᵢ,ⱼ   "\n"),
@ (`maxᵢ∈A,ⱼ∈A\i Yᵢ,ⱼ`    " = "   minᵢ∈A,ⱼ∈A\i Yᵢ,ⱼ   "\n"),
@ (`∑ᵢ∈A,ⱼ∈A\i Yᵢ,ⱼ`      " = "   ∑ᵢ∈A,ⱼ∈A\i Yᵢ,ⱼ   "\n\n"),

@ (`minᵢ∈A fᵢ`    " = "   minᵢ∈A fᵢ   "\n"),
@ (`maxᵢ∈A fᵢ`    " = "   maxᵢ∈A fᵢ   "\n"),
@ (`∑ᵢ∈A fᵢ`      " = "   ∑ᵢ∈A fᵢ   "\n\n"),

@ (`minᵢ∈A,ⱼ∈A\i gᵢ,ⱼ`    " = "   minᵢ∈A,ⱼ∈A\i gᵢ,ⱼ   "\n"),
@ (`maxᵢ∈A,ⱼ∈A\i gᵢ,ⱼ`    " = "   maxᵢ∈A,ⱼ∈A\i gᵢ,ⱼ   "\n"),
@ (`∑ᵢ∈A,ⱼ∈A\i gᵢ,ⱼ`      " = "   ∑ᵢ∈A,ⱼ∈A\i gᵢ,ⱼ   "\n\n"),
```

```
@ (`∧ᵢ∈A aᵢ`     " = "   ∧ᵢ∈A aᵢ   "\n"),
@ (`∨ᵢ∈A aᵢ`     " = "   ∨ᵢ∈A aᵢ   "\n"),
@ (`⊕ᵢ∈A aᵢ`     " = "   ⊕ᵢ∈A aᵢ   "\n\n"),

@ (`∧ᵢ∈A,ⱼ∈A\i bᵢ,ⱼ`   " = "   ∧ᵢ∈A,ⱼ∈A\i bᵢ,ⱼ   "\n"),
@ (`∨ᵢ∈A,ⱼ∈A\i bᵢ,ⱼ`   " = "   ∨ᵢ∈A,ⱼ∈A\i bᵢ,ⱼ   "\n"),
@ (`⊕ᵢ∈A,ⱼ∈A\i bᵢ,ⱼ`   " = "   ⊕ᵢ∈A,ⱼ∈A\i bᵢ,ⱼ   "\n\n"),

@ (`∩ᵢ∈A Aᵢ`     " = "   ∩ᵢ∈A Aᵢ   "\n"),
@ (`∪ᵢ∈A Aᵢ`     " = "   ∪ᵢ∈A Aᵢ   "\n\n"),

@ (`∩ᵢ∈A,ⱼ∈A\i Bᵢ,ⱼ`   " = "   ∩ᵢ∈A,ⱼ∈A\i Bᵢ,ⱼ   "\n"),
@ (`∪ᵢ∈A,ⱼ∈A\i Bᵢ,ⱼ`   " = "   ∪ᵢ∈A,ⱼ∈A\i Bᵢ,ⱼ   "\n\n").
```

the answer is:

```
minᵢ∈A i = 1
maxᵢ∈A i = 5
Σᵢ∈A i = 15

min`x`∈D x = 1
max`x`∈D x = 7
Σ`x`∈D x = 13

min`f`∈F f = -2000.000000
max`f`∈F f = 12.000000
Σ`f`∈F f = -1986.000000

∧`a`∈C a = F
∨`a`∈C a = T
⊕`a`∈C a = T

∩`i`∈E i = ∅
∪`i`∈E i = [1, 10]

minᵢ∈A xᵢ = 1
maxᵢ∈A xᵢ = 5
Σᵢ∈A xᵢ = 15

minᵢ∈A,ⱼ∈A\i yᵢ,ⱼ = 1
maxᵢ∈A,ⱼ∈A\i yᵢ,ⱼ = 5
Σᵢ∈A,ⱼ∈A\i yᵢ,ⱼ = 60
```

$$\min_{i \in A} f_i = 2.000000$$
$$\max_{i \in A} f_i = 10.000000$$
$$\sum_{i \in A} f_i = 30.000000$$

$$\min_{i \in A, j \in A \setminus i} g_{i,j} = 2.000000$$
$$\max_{i \in A, j \in A \setminus i} g_{i,j} = 10.000000$$
$$\sum_{i \in A, j \in A \setminus i} g_{i,j} = 120.000000$$

$$\bigwedge_{i \in A} a_i = F$$
$$\bigvee_{i \in A} a_i = T$$
$$\bigoplus_{i \in A} a_i = F$$

$$\bigwedge_{i \in A, j \in A \setminus i} b_{i,j} = F$$
$$\bigvee_{i \in A, j \in A \setminus i} b_{i,j} = T$$
$$\bigoplus_{i \in A, j \in A \setminus i} b_{i,j} = F$$

$$\bigcap_{i \in A} A_i = \emptyset$$
$$\bigcup_{i \in A} A_i = [1, \ 5]$$

$$\bigcap_{i \in A, j \in A \setminus i} B_{i,j} = \emptyset$$
$$\bigcup_{i \in A, j \in A \setminus i} B_{i,j} = [1, \ 5]$$

4.9.3 Transformation

Substring functions (str[n], str[n1..n2]) greatly facilitates the manipulation of strings. Similarly, element function (set[n]) and subset function (set[n1..n2]) evaluate respectively element and subset from a set.

4.9.4 Substring

Given the program:

```
y = "abc",
@ (`y`              " = "    y            "\n"),
@ (`# y`            " = "    # y          "\n"),
@ (`y[0]`           " = "    y[0]         "\n"),
@ (`y[1]`           " = "    y[1]         "\n"),
@ (`y[2]`           " = "    y[2]         "\n"),
@ (`y[3]`           " = "    y[3]         "\n"),
@ (`y[4]`           " = "    y[4]         "\n\n"),
@ (`y[-1]`          " = "    y[-1]        "\n"),
@ (`y[-2]`          " = "    y[-2]        "\n"),
@ (`y[-3]`          " = "    y[-3]        "\n"),
@ (`y[-4]`          " = "    y[-4]        "\n\n"),
@ (`y[1..2]`        " = "    y[1..2]      "\n"),
```

```
@ (`y[2..3]`      " = "      y[2..3]      "\n"),
@ (`y[-1..4]`     " = "      y[-1..4]     "\n"),
@ (`y[-2..-1]`    " = "      y[-2..-1]    "\n"),
@ (`y[-3..-2]`    " = "      y[-3..-2]    "\n"),
@ (`y[-3..0]`     " = "      y[-3..0]     "\n\n"),

z = "",
@ (`z`            " = \""    z            "\"\n"),
@ (`#z`           " = "      #z           "\n"),
@ (`z[0]`         " = "      z[0]         "\n"),
@ (`z[1]`         " = "      z[1]         "\n"),
@ (`z[2]`         " = "      z[2]         "\n"),
@ (`z[3]`         " = "      z[3]         "\n"),
@ (`z[4]`         " = "      z[4]         "\n\n"),
@ (`z[-1]`        " = "      z[-1]        "\n"),
@ (`z[-2]`        " = "      z[-2]        "\n"),
@ (`z[-3]`        " = "      z[-3]        "\n"),
@ (`z[-4]`        " = "      z[-4]        "\n\n"),
@ (`z[1..2]`      " = "      z[1..2]      "\n"),
@ (`z[2..3]`      " = "      z[2..3]      "\n"),
@ (`z[-1..4]`     " = "      z[-1..4]     "\n"),
@ (`z[-2..-1]`    " = "      z[-2..-1]    "\n"),
@ (`z[-3..-2]`    " = "      z[-3..-2]    "\n"),
@ (`z[-3..0]`     " = "      z[-3..0]     "\n\n").
```

the answer is:

```
y = abc
#y = 3
y[0] =
y[1] = a
y[2] = b
y[3] = c
y[4] =

y[-1] = c
y[-2] = b
y[-3] = a
y[-4] =

y[1..2]    = ab
y[2..3]    = bc
y[-1..4]   = c
y[-2..-1]  = bc
y[-3..-2]  = ab
y[-3..0]   =
```

```
z = ""
#z = 0
z[0]  =
z[1]  =
z[2]  =
z[3]  =
z[4]  =

z[-1]  =
z[-2]  =
z[-3]  =
z[-4]  =

z[1..2]  =
z[2..3]  =
z[-1..4]  =
z[-2..-1]  =
z[-3..-2]  =
z[-3..0]  =
```

4.9.5 Elements of a Set

Given the program:

```
A = [1,5],
@ (`A`          " = "    A          "\n"),
@ (`A[0]`       " = "    A[0]       "\n"),
@ (`A[1]`       " = "    A[1]       "\n"),
@ (`A[3]`       " = "    A[3]       "\n"),
@ (`A[5]`       " = "    A[5]       "\n"),
@ (`A[6]`       " = "    A[6]       "\n\n"),
@ (`A[-1]`      " = "    A[-1]      "\n"),
@ (`A[-3]`      " = "    A[-3]      "\n"),
@ (`A[-5]`      " = "    A[-5]      "\n"),
@ (`A[-6]`      " = "    A[-6]      "\n\n"),

@ (`A[0..5]`    " = "    A[0..5]    "\n"),
@ (`A[1..2]`    " = "    A[1..2]    "\n"),
@ (`A[1..5]`    " = "    A[1..5]    "\n"),
@ (`A[1..6]`    " = "    A[1..6]    "\n"),
@ (`A[3..5]`    " = "    A[3..5]    "\n"),
@ (`A[0..-1]`   " = "    A[0..-1]   "\n"),
@ (`A[-3..-1]`  " = "    A[-3..-1]  "\n\n").
```

the answer is:

```
A = [1, 5]
A[0] = 1
```

```
A[1] = 1
A[3] = 3
A[5] = 5
A[6] = 5

A[-1] = 5
A[-3] = 3
A[-5] = 1
A[-6] = 1

A[0..5] = [1, 5]
A[1..2] = [1, 2]
A[1..5] = [1, 5]
A[1..6] = [1, 5]
A[3..5] = [3, 5]
A[0..-1] = ∅
A[-3..-1] = [3, 5]
```

4.9.6 Date/Time Attribute

Given the program:

```
date = O: "yyyy-mm-dd",
@ date   : "mm/dd/yyyy",
@ "\n",

date = O: "yyyymmdd",
@ date : "dd/mm/yyyy",
@ "\n",

year = date["yyyy"],
month = date["mm"],
day = date["dd"],

@ ("year: " year " month: " month " day: " day "\n\n"),

datetime_m = O: "mm/dd/yyyy hh:mm",
date     = datetime_m["yyyy-mm-dd"],
time_m = datetime_m["hh:mm"],

datetime_s = O: "mm/dd/yyyy hh:mm:ss",
date     = datetime_s["yyyy-mm-dd"],
time_s = datetime_s["hh:mm:ss"],

@ (datetime_m "\n"),
@ (time_m "\n\n"),
@ (datetime_s "\n"),
```

```
@ (time_s "\n\n"),

Datetime :: Ø,
Datetime = O: "mm/dd/yyyy hh:mm",
Date = Datetime["mm/dd/yyyy"],
Time = Datetime["hh:mm"],
@ (Datetime "\n"),
@ (Date "\n"),
@ (Time "\n").
```

and given the input:

```
2000-01-01
20000101

01/01/2000 22:48
01/01/2000 22:48:00

{03/01/1800 22:48, 01/01/2000 00:00, 09/30/3004 22:48}
```

the answer is:

```
01/01/2000
01/01/2000
year: 2000 month: 1 day: 1

01/01/2000 22:48
22:48

01/01/2000 22:48:00
22:48:00

{03/01/1800 22:48, 01/01/2000 00:00, 09/30/3004 22:48}
{03/01/1800, 01/01/2000, 09/30/3004}
{00:00, 22:48}
```

4.9.7 Extraction

One strong feature of NCL is its extraction functions. It allows low-level access and control. Note that extraction does not reason logically; it is introduced for a temporal control.

Given the program:

```
@ "Bool extraction: \n\n",

a :: T,
@ (`a` " = " a "\n"),
@ (`a` " = " a "\n"),
@ (`a` " = " a "\n\n"),
```

```
@ "Float extraction: \n\n",

f ∈ [1.0, 2.0],
@ (`f` " = "     f    "\n"),
@ (`f` " = "     f      "\n"),
@ (`f` " = "     f     "\n\n"),
@ (`#f` " = "    #f    "\n\n"),

@ "Int extraction: \n\n",

x ∈ [1, 2],
@ (`x` " = "    x    "\n"),
@ (`x` " = "    x     "\n"),
@ (`x` " = "    x     "\n\n"),

@ "Set extraction: \n\n",

A ⊂ [1,5],
@ (`A` " = "    A    "\n\n"),
@ (`Δa` " = "    Δa    "\n"),
@ (`Δx` " = "    Δx    "\n"),
@ (`ΔA` " = "    ΔA    "\n\n"),
@ (`A` " = "    A    "\n"),
@ (`A` " = "    A     "\n\n"),
```

the answer is:

```
Bool extraction:

a = U
a = F
a = T


Float extraction:

f = <1.000000..2.000000>
f = 1.000000
f = 2.000000
#f = 1.000000


Int extraction:

x = <1..2>
x = 1
```

$\overline{x}$ = 2

Set extraction:

A = {<1..5>}

Δ a = [0, 1]
Δ x = [1, 2]
Δ A = [1, 5]

$\underline{A}$ = $\varnothing$
$\overline{A}$ = [1, 5]

4.9.8 Assignment

As a special kind of extraction, an assignment statement assigns the value of an expression to a variable. Here the assignment symbol (:=) is different from the equality relation (=) and Boolean equivalence (≡). Assignment is a simple unidirectional data transmission operation. As explained in Chapter 3, assignment is a "temporal control" statement; it does not conform to "declarative programming". That is to say, the value of an extraction function varies from time to time in the running process of the NCL engine. An assignment statement in a program can let a variable represent the value of an expression so as to facilitate the usage of this expression in the program. The following example illustrates the assignment functionality.

Given the program:

```
x ∈ [1, 6],
y := # Δ x,
x > 3,
@ y,  @ "\n".
```

the answer is:
    3

4.10 User-Defined Function

NCL supports logical functions of all types; a function can be used in any expression of its type. The definition of a function is by grouping an identifier with angle brackets, followed by a list of arguments grouped by parentheses.

4.10.1 Cotangent

The cotangent function is not predefined. However, it can be programmed as a user-defined function.

Given the program:

```
pi ∈ [3.0, 4.0],
sin pi = 0,

f ∈ [1.0, 2.0],
cotangent(f) = 0,

<cotangent>(f)
    cotangent = cos f / sin f,

@ (`pi`   " = "   pi   "\n"),
@ (`cotangent(pi/2)`   " = "   cotangent(pi/2)   "\n"),
@ (`f`   " = "   f   "\n").
```

the answer is:

```
pi = <3.1415925025940..3.1415927410126>
cotangent(pi/2) = <-0.0000000437114..0.0000000754979>
f = <1.5707962512970..1.5707963705063>
```

4.10.2 Global Variable in a Function

Given the program:

```
<f>(n)
(
    f ≥ n,
    f ≤ x
),

x ∈ [1, 3],

∀ i ∈ [1, 3]
    @ (`f(i)`   " = "   f(i)   "\n"),

@ (`x`   " = "   x   "\n").
```

the answer is:

```
f(1) = <1..3>
f(2) = <2..3>
f(3) = 3
x = 3
```

Note that the global variable x is instantiated after the function calls.

4.10.3 Query and Objective in a Function

Given the program:

```
A = [1,5],
```

```
∀ i ∈ A (
    ∀ j ∈ A
        x_i,j ∈ A,

    ∀ j ≠ k ∈ A
        x_i,j ≠ x_i,k,

    s_i = Σ_{j∈A} x_i,j,
),

<query>(i)
(
    ∀ j ∈ A → (min  #Δx_i,j)
        x_i,j = ?,

    max    s_i,
),

∀ i ∈ A → (min  #Δs_i)
    query(i),

obj = Σ_{i∈A} s_i,

max    obj,

∀ i ∈ A (
    ∀ j ∈ A (
        @ (x_i,j  "     "),
    @ "\n",
),

@ (`obj`  " = " obj  "\n").
```

the answer is:

```
1    2    3    4    5
1    2    3    4    5
1    2    3    4    5
1    2    3    4    5
1    2    3    4    5
obj = 75
```

The search is carried out locally to maximize the local objective s_i. Once the local optimums are all reached, the global optimum is reached.

4.10.4 Predicate

A predicate is a special Boolean function.

Given the program:

```
<predicate>(x, y, z)
    x ∈ [y, z],

@ predicate(1,2,3).
```

the answer is:

```
F
```

In this example, function identifier does not occur in the function body. The value of the function is false if a constraint in the function is violated; otherwise it is true.

If predicate(1,2,3) is stated as a tautology in the above program, the system will fail.

4.10.5 Recursive Function

A logical function can be defined recursively.

Given the program:

```
<factorial>(n)
    n ≤ 2 ⇒ (
        factorial = n ;
        factorial = n × factorial(n-1))
    ),

y = factorial(x),
x ∈ [1, 5],
y ∈ [100, 200],

∀ i ∈ [1, 5]
    @ (factorial(i) "\n"),

@ (`x`  " = "  x  "\n"),
@ (`y`  " = "  y  "\n").
```

the answer is:

```
1
2
6
24
120
x = 5
y = 120
```

In this example, recursive reasoning can successfully instantiate x and y.

4.10.6 Termination of a Recursion

The above example uses if-then-else to control the termination of a recursion. In fact, the factorial function can also be programmed using the system variable ' . ' to control the termination:

```
<factorial>(n)
(
    n ≤ 0 → '.',
    factorial = (n ≤ 2 ? n : n × factorial(n-1))
),
```

4.10.7 Tree

Tree structures can be represented by combining set programming and function. Given the program:

```
nbNode = O,
NODE   = [1, nbNode],

∀ i ∈ NODE (
    i = O,
    ChildNode_i = O
),

∀ i ∈ NODE (
    ParentNode_i ⊂ NODE,
    ∀ j ∈ NODE
        i ∈ ParentNode_j ≡ j ∈ ChildNode_i,
),

<Leaf>(node)
(
    node ∈ NODE,
    Child = ChildNode_node,
    Leaf = (Child = ∅ ? {node} : ∪_{i∈Child} Leaf(i))
),

<Root>(Node)
(
    Node ⊂ NODE,
    ∀ i ∈ Node
        RootNode_i = (
            ParentNode_i = ∅ ? {i} : Root(ParentNode_i)
        ),
    Root = ∪_{i∈Node} RootNode_i
),
```

```
7 ∈ Leaf(x),
x ∈ [2, 6],

∀ i ∈ NODE (
    @ (`Root({i})`  " = "  Root({i})   "\t"),
    @ (`Leaf(i)`   " = "  Leaf(i)    "\n")
),

@ (`Root([8,9])`  " = "  Root([8,9])   "\n"),
@ (`x`  " = "  x  "\t"  `Leaf(x)`  " = "  Leaf(x)   "\n").
```

and given the input:

```
%        1               2
%       / \             / \
%      3   4           5   6
%     / \               |
%    7   8              9
9
1   {3, 4}
2   {5, 6}
3   {7, 8}
4   {}
5   {9}
6   {}
7   {}
8   {}
9   {}
```

the answer is:

```
Root({1}) = {1}    Leaf(1) = {4, 7..8}
Root({2}) = {2}    Leaf(2) = {6, 9}
Root({3}) = {1}    Leaf(3) = [7, 8]
Root({4}) = {1}    Leaf(4) = {4}
Root({5}) = {2}    Leaf(5) = {9}
Root({6}) = {2}    Leaf(6) = {6}
Root({7}) = {1}    Leaf(7) = {7}
Root({8}) = {1}    Leaf(8) = {8}
Root({9}) = {2}    Leaf(9) = {9}
Root([8,9]) = [1, 2]
x = 3   Leaf(x) = [7, 8]
```

4.11 Selection Statement

4.11.1 Switch

Given the program:

```
true,

n = 5,
x :: 0,
x ∈ [1,3],

f ∈ [1.0, 3.0],

A ⊂ [1, n],
f = x,

inf B > 1,
sup B < 1,

@ "Mixed int/float/set switch:\n",

? f (
1.0: ? A (
     ∅          : B = ∅;
                 : ¬true
     ),
     A = ?, B = ?;

2.0: ? A (
     [1, 2]     : B = ∅;
                 : ¬true
     ),
     A = ?, B = ?;

   : ? A (
     ∅          : B = [1,n];
     {1, 3, 5} : B = ∅;
     [1, n]    : B = {1, 3, 5};
                 : A = B
   ),
   A = ?, B = ?
),
x = ?,

@ ("x ="x   "\tf = "f   "\tA=" A   "\tB=" B   "\n\n"),

@ "Set ref switch:\n",
∀ `i` ∈ {`[1,3]`,`{100}`,`∅`} (
    ? i (
        [1,3]   : C·i· = ∅;
```

```
              Ø        : C·i· = {1, 3, 5};
                       : C·i· = i
         ),

         @ (`C·i·`   "\t="   C·i·   "\n"),
    ),
    @ "\n\n\n".
```

the answer is:

```
Mixed int/float/set switch:
x = 1    f = 1.000000    A = Ø    B = Ø

Set ref switch:
C·[1,3]· = Ø
C· 100· = {100}
C·ø· = {1, 3, 5}

Mixed int/float/set switch:
x = 2    f = 2.000000    A = [1, 2]    B = Ø

Set ref switch:
C·[1,3]· = Ø
C·100· = {100}
C·ø· = {1, 3, 5}

Mixed int/float/set switch:
x = 3    f = 3.000000    A = {1, 3, 5}    B = Ø

Set ref switch:
C·[1,3]· = Ø
C·100· = {100}
C·ø· = {1, 3, 5}
```

Note that a branch (default or not) can be executed only when no earlier case is matched with the option part. NCL executes (only) the first branch for which the case is matched with the option.

4.11.2 If-Then-Else

If-then-else is a switch of at most two branches. If the option is true, the first branch will be executed. Otherwise it is the second branch that should be satisfied.

Given the program:

```
w ∈ [3, 5],
x ∈ [1, 4],

y > 5,
```

```
z > 2,

w > 3 ⇒ (
    y < 4 ;
    z > 3
),

x > 3 ⇒ (
    y > 4 ;
    z < 2
),

@ ("w = " w "\n"),
@ ("x = " x "\n").
```

the answer is:

```
w = 3
x = 4
```

4.12 Quantification

4.12.1 Existential Quantification

In the case of an existential quantifier, NCL will automatically launch a query over its variable.

Given the program:

```
n = 5,
x ∈ [1, n],

@ "Existential int quantification:\n",
∃ i < j ∈ [1,n](
    x = i × j,

    @ (`i × j` " = " x "\n\n"),
),

y ∈ [2, n×2],
x = 2 × y,

@ "Existential int ref quantification:\n",
∃ `i`<`j` ∈ {`x`, `y`}(
    i > 2,
    i × j = x × y,
    i = ?,
    j = ?,
```

```
        @(`i`" × "`j`" = "(i × j)"\n\n"),
    ),

    subject = "She",
    verb = "works",

    @ "Existential string quantification:\n",
    ∃ i ∈ {"He runs", "She works", "She sleeps"} (
        (subject " " verb) = i,

        @ (i "\n\n"),
    ),

    A ⊂ [1, 2],
    B ⊂ [3, 4],
    C ⊂ {10, -1, -100},
    #C = 2,

    @ "Existential set ref quantification:\n",
    ∃ `i` ∈ {`A`, `B`, `C`} (
        #i > 0,
        i ⊃ {-1},
        i = ?,

        @ (`i `    " = " i    "\n\n"),
    ),

    @ "Existential bool ref quantification:\n",
    ∃`i`,`j`∈{`1<2`,`[1,2]⊂ ∅`,`1.0<3`,`("abc" "d")="abcd"`} (
        i ⊕ j,

        @ ("(" `i` ")" " ⊕ " "(" `j` ")" " = "(i ⊕ j)"\n\n"),
    ),

    @ "\n".
```

the answer is:

```
Existential int quantification:
i × j = 4

Existential int ref quantification:
x × y = 8

Existential string quantification:
```

She works

Existential set ref quantification:
C = {-100, -1}

Existential bool ref quantification:
(1 < 2) ⊕ ([1, 2] ⊂ ∅) = T

Note that for the quantified references `i` and `j`, the existential queries are on the references, not on the referenced variables i and j. That is why queries i = ? and j = ? are added.

4.12.2 Universal Quantification

The following example illustrates the expressive power of NCL when universal quantification and referencing are combined.

Given the program:

```
A ⊂ [9, 11],
B ⊂ [3, 4],
C ⊂ {10, -1, -100},

@ "Universal set ref quantification:\n\n",
∀ `i`∈{`A`, `B`, `C`} (
        #i = 2,
        inf i ≥ -1,
        sup i < 11,

        @ (`i` " = " i "\n"),
),
@ "\n\n",

true,  ¬false,

@ "Universal bool ref quantification:\n\n",
∀`i`≠`j`∈{`1<2`,`[1,2]⊂∅`,`1.0<3`,`("abc" "d")="abcd"`}(
        i ⊕ j ⇒ (
                @ true: 8;
                @ false: 8
        ),
        @ ("("`i`")" " ⊕ " "(" `j` ")" " = " (i ⊕ j) "\n"),
),
@ "\n".
```

the answer is:

Universal set ref quantification:

A = [9, 10]

```
B = [3, 4]
C = {-1, 10}
```

Universal bool ref quantification:

```
T    (1<2) ⊕ ([1,2] ⊂ Ø)                 = T
F    (1<2) ⊕ (1.0<3)                      = F
F    (1<2) ⊕ (("abc" "d")="abcd")        = F
T    ([1,2] ⊂ Ø) ⊕ (1<2)                 = T
T    ([1,2] ⊂ Ø) ⊕ (1.0<3)               = T
T    ([1,2] ⊂ Ø) ⊕ (("abc" "d")="abcd")= T
F    (1.0<3) ⊕ (1<2)                      = F
T    (1.0<3) ⊕ ([1,2] ⊂ Ø)               = T
F    (1.0<3) ⊕ (("abc" "d")="abcd")      = F
F    (("abc" "d")="abcd") ⊕ (1<2)        = F
T    (("abc" "d")="abcd") ⊕ ([1,2] ⊂ Ø)= T
F    (("abc" "d")="abcd") ⊕ (1.0<3)      = F
```

4.13 Jump

The definition of jump (>> ID) is similar to that of a procedural language such as C. In NCL, all statement can be labeled by <ID>, where ID is an NCL identifier. When an NCL program is running, the Jump statement >> ID will lead the NCL engine to the statement labeled by <ID>.

All labeled statements and Jump statements must be at the output state ('@').

4.13.1 Exit from a Universally Quantified Statement

Given the input:

```
1    2    3    4    5    6    100    8    9    10
```

and with the program:

```
∀ i ∈ [1,10] (
     xᵢ = 0,
),

'@'  ⇒  (
     ∀ i ∈ [1, 10] (
          @ xᵢ,
          @ "\n",

          xᵢ = 100  ⇒  >> exit,
     ),

     <exit>
```

) .

the answer is:

```
1
2
3
4
5
6
100
```

Note that in the above program, it is an empty statement after the <exit> label which defines the exit for the universal quantification.

4.13.2 Exit from an Infinite Loop

Given the program:

```
'@' ⇒ (
     x := 1,

<loop>
     x := x + 1,
     x ≥ 100   ⇒   >> exit,
     >> loop,

<exit>
     @ ("x = "   x)
) .
```

the answer is:

```
x = 100
```

The Jump statement plays an important role in the design of an optimization script. For example, the above program tells how to design an infinite loop using the assignment and jump statements with a label <loop> and how to exit from the loop using Jump with a label <exit>.

"Jump" can also be used to design an iteration script, for example, for the Traveling Salesman Problem (see Chapter 8) .

4.14 Query and Search

4.14.1 Approximate Solution

Sometimes there is no need to give an accurate solution for a hard problem; an approximate one may be enough. This example illustrates the basic skill to do so.

Given the program:

```
'Search Depth' ≥ 7 ⇒ '@',
```

```
E = [1,10],
∀ i < j ∈ E   xᵢ ≠ xⱼ,

∀ i ∈ E (
     xᵢ ∈ E,
     xᵢ = ?,
),

∀ i ∈ E (
     @ i: 4, @ xᵢ, @ "\n",
),
@ "\n",

'Solution Count' ≥ 1 ⇒ '.'.
```

the answer is:

```
1    1
2    2
3    3
4    4
5    5
6    6
7    7
8    <8..10>
9    <8..10>
10   <8..10>
```

In the above result, NCL gives values for the top seven variables and domains (sets of possible values) for the rest. The temporal control of termination ('.') should be stated after all the output statements. Otherwise the output may be incomplete.

4.14.2 Search over a Float Domain

Given the program:

```
f ∈ [1, 5],
f > 0.1,
f = 1.0 ∨ f = 2.0 ∨ f = 4.0,

f = ?,
@ ("f = " f "\n").
```

the answer is:

```
f = 1.000000
f = 2.000000
f = 4.000000
```

Note that for a float query, by default its enumeration mode is lower-part-first binary-domain-splitting. See Section 3.1.7.

4.15 Optimization Objective

In NCL, a programmer can specify optimization objectives for float, integer and date/time expressions. The precedence relation follows their order in the program.

4.15.1 Single-Objective Optimization

Given the program:
```
n = 11,
A ⊂ [1,n],
A = [i,j],

∀ i ∈ [1,n]
  xᵢ = O,
  % from input: -3, 3, -1, 4, -1, 5, 9, -26, 5, 3, 5

#A = ? (←),
A = ?,

max    Σₖ∈ₐ xₖ,

@ ("A=" A "\n"),    @ (`Σₖ∈ₐ xₖ` "=" Σₖ∈ₐ xₖ "\n\n").
```
the answer is:
```
A = [1, 11]
Σₖ∈ₐ xₖ = 3

A = [2, 11]
Σₖ∈ₐ xₖ = 6

A = [1, 7]
Σₖ∈ₐ xₖ = 16

A = [2, 7]
Σₖ∈ₐ xₖ = 19
```

4.15.2 Multiple-Objective Optimization

Given the program:
```
x ∈ {1,3,7,15},
y ∈ [3,9],
z ∈ [6,18],
x ≥ y,
x ≤ z,

x = ? (→),
```

```
y = ? (→),
z = ? (←),

min  x,
min  y,
max  z,

@ ("x = "  x   "\n"),
@ ("y = "  y   "\n"),
@ ("z = "  z   "\n").
```

the answer is:

```
x minimized to 3
y minimized to 3
z maximized to 18
```

Multiple-objective optimization follows the natural order of occurrences of the objectives in the model. In this example, the optimization order is the lexicographic order of (x, y, z).

4.16 Custom Message

In an NCL program a custom message can be associated to a group of statements. It will replace standard NCL messages in case of a constraint failure.

Given the main program:

```
n = 7,
∀ i ∈ [1,n] (
    (`aᵢ` " must be equal to " (3.1 + i × 1.4):
        aᵢ = 3.1 + i × 1.4
    ),

    (`aᵢ` " must be greater than " (2 × i) ", but it's equal to " aᵢ:
        aᵢ > 2 × i
    ),

    (`aᵢ` " must be less than " (3 × i) ", but it's equal to " aᵢ:
        aᵢ < 3 × i
    ),
).
```

the following messages are given:

Warning C22: a_6 must be greater than 12 but it's equal to <11.4999990463257..11.5000009536743>
Warning C22: a_7 must be greater than 14 but it's equal to <12.8999986648560..12.9000015258789>
Warning C22: a_1 must be less than 3 but it's equal to <4.4999995231628..4.5000004768372>

In fact, without custom message, the standard message for the first warning is:

Warning C22: constraint ' $a_6 > 2*6$ ' (INTFLOATLT) fails

4.17 Soft Constraint

Sometimes soft constraints in the form of *(bool : statements)* may occur. In preference, user does not hope that they fail. But the failure of such constraints can be tolerated if the Boolean expression *bool* can be true.

Given the program:

```
E = [1, 10],
SoftFail ⊂ E,
#SoftFail ≤ 1,

∀ i ∈ E (
    xᵢ ∈ E,
    xᵢ ≠ i,

    (i ∈ SoftFail : xᵢ < xᵢ₊₁),

    xᵢ = ?,
    @ i : 4,    @ xᵢ,  @ "\n",
),
@ "\n",

∀ i < j ∈ E   xᵢ ≠ xⱼ.
```

the answer is:

```
1     2
2     3
3     4
4     5
5     6
6     7
7     8
8     9
9     10
10    1
```

4.18 Sub-Model

4.18.1 Sub-Model in a File

Given the main program "master.n":

```
% To collect all solution information from the sub-program.
INDEX    = [1,5],
INTERVAL = [1,4],
sol_count ∈ INDEX,
```

```
GLOBSOL ⊂ INTERVAL,

∀ i ∈ INDEX (
    GLOBSET_i    ⊂ INTERVAL,
    solution_i  :: 0,
    time_i      :: 0.0,
    backtrack_i :: 0,
    depth_i     :: 0
),

'O' ⇒ [["slave.n"], ["ncl.cfg"], 1],

@ ("The sub-program returns" sol_count " solutions.\n"),
@ ("The last one is: "  GLOBSOL "\n\n"),
@ ("The " sol_count" solutions are as below:\n\n"),

∀ i ∈ [1, sol_count](
    @ GLOBSET_i     : 10,
    @ solution_i    : 20,
    @ time_i        : 20,
    @ backtrack_i   : 20,
    @ depth_i       : 20,
    @ "\n",
).
```

and given the sub program "slave.n":

```
MySet ⊂ INTERVAL,
Σ_{i∈MySet} i = 6,
MySet = ?,

[ "slave.sol" ] ← '@',
'@' ⇒ (
  sol_count = 'Solution Count',

  ∀ i ∈ {sol_count} (
    GLOBSET_i    = MySet,
    solution_i   = 'Solution Count',
    time_i       = 'Global Time',
    backtrack_i  = 'Backtrack Count',
    depth_i      = 'Search Depth'
  ),

  @ ('Solution Count'   ":\t"
        MySet    "\t"
        'Global Time'    "\t"
```

```
        'Backtrack Count'   "\t"
        'Search Depth'   "\n"
  )
),

GLOBSOL = MySet.
```

the answer in "master.sol" is:

```
The sub-program returns 2 solutions.
The last one is:  {2, 4}

The 2 solutions are as below:

[1,3]   1   0.881000   0   1
{2,4}   2   1.131000   1   0
```

and the answer in "slave.sol" is:

```
1:   [1,3]   0.881000   0   1
2:   {2,4}   1.131000   1   0
```

This example illustrates how information can be communicated between master and slave models.

4.18.2 Sub-Model in a Buffer

Given the program:

```
OutputBuf1 :: "",
OutputBuf2 :: "",
OutputBuf3 :: "",

SlaveProg = "
    [\"SlaveOutput1\" : OutputBuf1] ← '@',
    @ (`'Model Depth'`       \" = \"     'Model Depth'),

    [\"SlaveOutput2\" : OutputBuf2] ← '@',
    @ (`'Solution Count'`   \" = \"     'Solution Count'),

    [\"SlaveOutput3\" : OutputBuf3] ← '@',
    @ (`'Global Time'` \" = \" 'Global Time').
",

'O'  ⇒  [["SlaveProg" : SlaveProg],  ["ncl.cfg"],  1],

@ (OutputBuf1  "\n"  OutputBuf2  "\n"  OutputBuf3  "\n").
```

the answer is:

```
'Model Depth'      = 1
'Solution Count'  = 1
'Global Time'      = 0.221000
```

This example illustrates the use of buffer pools. Note that both the slave program and the slave outputs are buffer pools.

4.18.3 Return Values of a Sub-Model

Given the program:

```
msg :: "",
true,
code V true,

'@' ⇒ (
   code = [["Slave.n"], ["ncl.cfg"], 1],
   msg = [["Slave.n"], ["ncl.cfg"], 1],

   @ ("code = "   code "\n"),
   @ ("msg =\""   msg   "\"\n"),
).
```

and given the sub program "slave.n":

```
("1 is not equal to 3" : 1 = 3).
```

the answer is:

```
code = F
msg = "1 is not equal to 3"
```

This example illustrates return values of different types (Boolean and string) from a sub-model.

4.18.4 Recursive Sub-Model

The following example illustrates how to control the depth of a sub-model. Given the program "recursive1.n":

```
'O' ⇒ (
   "recursive call fails due to stack overflow" :
    'Model Depth' < 2 ⇒ [["recursive1.n"],["ncl.cfg"],1]
),

@ ("Depth of recursive call: "  'Model Depth'  "\n").
```

the answer is:

```
Depth of recursive call: 2
Depth of recursive call: 1
Depth of recursive call: 0
```

4.18.5 Overflow in Calling a Sub-Model

A recursive call can only reach a limited depth. Exceeding this depth, NCL will give a warning message on stack overflow. Given the program "recursive2.n":

```
'O' ⇒ (
    "recursive call fails due to stack overflow":
    [["recursive2.n"], ["ncl.cfg"],1]
).
```

the answer is:

Warning C22: recursive call fails due to stack overflow

4.19 SQL Query

NCL supports standard database connection/disconnection, SQL queries (e.g., "SELECT", "DELETE", "UPDATE", "INSERT") and data reading from a database. All NCL data types can be processed through a database. For example, the data of a set can be stored as a string in a database table.

Suppose that a database is named DBTEST with empty user name and password. Its table is also named DBTEST with fields as follows:

```
id  int  string  ref  StrSet  RefSet  float  datetime  yesno
```

Initially the table has the following records

id	int	string	ref	StrSet	RefSet	float	datetime	yesno
1	11	student	`x`	{"A","B"}	{`y`,`w`}		2000-01-01 12:30	T
2	22	worker	`y`	{"hello"}	{`x`,`z`}	2	2008-11-11 00:30	T
3	33		`0`	{}				F
4	44		`w`	{"OK"}		1.1		T

Given the program:

```
% Declaring variables
x = 1,
y ∈ [1,5],
z = y,
w = x,

% CONNECTING DB
'O' ← ["DBTEST" : "" : ""],

% DELETION
'O' ⇒  (SQL: "DELETE * FROM DBTEST WHERE int < 0"),

% READING
'O' ⇒ (SQL:
    "SELECT id,int,string,ref,StrSet,RefSet,float,datetime,yesno FROM
    DBTEST"
```

```
    ),

    m = O,
    ∀ i ∈ [1,m]  (
        id_i              :: 0,
        int_i             :: 0,
        str_i             :: "",
        ref_i             :: `x`,
        StrSet_i          :: ∅,
        RefSet_i          :: ∅,
        float_i           :: 0.0,
        yesno_i           :: T,

        id_i              = O,
        int_i             = O,
        str_i             = O,
        ref_i             = O,
        StrSet_i          = O,
        RefSet_i          = O,
        float_i           = O,
        datetime_i        = O : "yyyy-mm-dd hh:mm",
        yesno_i           = O,

        @ id_i            : 3,
        @ int_i           : -10,
        @ (" " str_i)     : 10,
        @ (" " ref_i)     : 6,
        @ (" " StrSet_i)  : 16,
        @ (" " RefSet_i)  : 16,
        @ float_i         : -4,

        @ datetime_i      : -20,
        @ yesno_i         : -4,
        @ "\n",
    ),
    @ "\n\n",

    % INSERTION
    'O' ⇒ (
        ∀ i ∈ [m+1, m+2] (
            (SQL:
                "INSERT INTO DBTEST(id, int, string) VALUES (" i ", 0,'FUN')"
            ),
        ),
    ),

    % UPDATING
```

'O' $\Rightarrow$ (SQL: "UPDATE DBTEST SET DBTEST.string = 'OK' WHERE int $\leq$ 0"),

% DISCONNECTING DB
["DBTEST" : "" : ""] $\leftarrow$ 'O',

% RECONNECTING DB
'O' $\leftarrow$ ["DBTEST" : "" : ""],

% REREADING
'O' $\Rightarrow$ (SQL:
    "SELECT id, int, string, ref, StrSet, RefSet, float, datetime, yesno FROM
      DBTEST"
),

n = O,
("database insertion operation error": n = m+2),

$\forall$ i $\in$ [1,n] (
```
    str1ᵢ              :: "",
    ref1ᵢ              :: `x`,
    StrSet1ᵢ          :: ∅,
    RefSet1ᵢ          :: ∅,
    float1ᵢ           :: 0.0,
    yesno1ᵢ           :: T,

    id1ᵢ              = O,
    int1ᵢ             = O,
    str1ᵢ             = O,
    ref1ᵢ             = O,
    StrSet1ᵢ          = O,
    RefSet1ᵢ          = O,
    float1ᵢ           = O,
    datetime1ᵢ        = O : "yyyy-mm-dd hh:mm",
    yesno1ᵢ           = O,

    @ id1ᵢ            : 3,
    @ int1ᵢ           : -10,
    @ (" " str1ᵢ)     : 10,
    @ (" " ref1ᵢ)     : 6,
    @ (" " StrSet1ᵢ)  : 16,
    @ (" " RefSet1ᵢ)  : 16,
    @ float1ᵢ         : -4,
    @ datetime1ᵢ      : -20,
    @ yesno1ᵢ         : -4,
    @ "\n",
```
),

```
% DELETION
'O' ⇒ (SQL: "DELETE FROM DBTEST WHERE id > "  m).
```

the answer is:

```
1    11 student  x   {"A","B"}  {`y`,`w`}   0.00 2000-01-01 12:30  T
2    22 worker   y   {"hello"}  {`x`,`z`}   2.00 2008-11-11 00:30  T
3    33          0   {}         {}          0.00 2000-01-01 00:00  F
4    44          w   {"OK"}     {}          1.10 2000-01-01 00:00  T

1    11 student  x   {"A","B"}  {`y`,`w`}   0.00 2000-01-01 12:30  T
2    22 worker   y   {"hello"}  {`x`,`z`}   2.00 2008-11-11 00:30  T
3    33          0   {}         {}          0.00 2000-01-01 00:00  F
4    44          w   {"OK"}     {}          1.10 2000-01-01 00:00  T
5     0 OK       0   {}         {}          0.00 2000-01-01 00:00  F
6     0 OK       0   {}         {}          0.00 2000-01-01 00:00  F
```

4.20 OS Command

OS commands are embedded in NCL. User can directly call OS commands such as "type" and "copy" in an NCL program.

Given the program:

```
'O' ⇒ (
    x = (OS: "type *.n"),
    y = (OS: "type *.n", "copy string.n tmp.n"),
    z = (OS: "copy c:\\test.n c:\\test1.n"),
),

'@' ⇒ (
    @ ("type *.n"  " = "  x  "\n"),
    @ ("type *.n"  " copy string.n tmp.n"  " = "  y  "\n"),
    @ ("copy c:\\test.n c:\\test1.n"  " = "  z  "\n"),
).
```

the answer is:

```
type *.n = T
type *.n copy string.n tmp.n = F
copy c:\test.n c:\test1.n = F
```

This example shows that "type*.n" succeeds while "copy string.n" and "copy c:\\test.n c :\\test1.n" fails.

4.21 Expectation and Debugging

Expectation constraint plays a role of supervision over variable domains. User may need to trace the evolution of the domain of a variable so as to understand the logic relations between variables.

Below is an example program for expectation constraints.

```
?? inf A > 4,
?? #A < 3,

?? 5 ∈ A,
?? 7 ∉ A,

?? [6,10] ⊂ A,
?? A ∩ [1,4] = ∅,

A ⊂ [1, 10],
inf A = 4,
sup A = 7,

#A = 3,
5 ∉ A.
```

This test program means to check the evolution of set A with the following expectations:

- The infimum of A is expected to be superior to 4;
- The cardinality of A is expected to be inferior to 3;
- 5 is expected to be in A;
- 7 is expected to be out of A;
- [6,10] is expected to be subset of A;
- [1,4] is expected to be disjoint with A.

If any of the above expectations is not satisfied, NCL will release a warning message. For the above program, NCL delivers the following warning messages to facilitate the debugging.

Warning C22: debug at ' \inf{A} = 4' : {4} not expected for '\inf{A}'
break for ' ?? \inf{A} > 4'

Warning C22: debug at ' \sup{A} ' : {8..10} expected for ' A '
break for ' ?? [6,10] \subset A '

Warning C22: debug at ' #{A} = 3 ' : {3} not expected for '#{A}'
break for ' ?? #{A} < 3 '

Warning C22: debug at ' 5 \not\in A ' : {5} expected for ' A '
break for ' ?? 5 \in A '

Warning C22: debug at '\inf{A}' : {4} not expected for infimum of ' A '
break for ' ?? \inf{A} > 4 '

Warning C22: debug at ' #{A} ' : {3} not expected for cardinality of ' A '
break for ' ?? #{A} < 3 '

Warning C22: debug at ' #{A} ' : {7} not expected for ' A '
break for ' ?? 7 \not\in A '

Warning C22: debug at ' #{A} ' : {4} not expected for ' A '
break for ' ?? A \cap [1,4] = \emptyset '

5 The POEM Software Platform

POEM is a software platform based on the NCL language. It aims to support software engineering for developing industrial solutions.

This chapter presents POEM and its practical functionalities in eight parts: main interface, configuration of a project, model folder and model library, information tables, visualization and debugging, trace window and working modes, message management, and help on line. Finally, some information on POEM's components and server is also given.

5.1 Main Interface

The main user interface of POEM® is composed of six parts (Figure 5.1):
- ① Main Menu;
- ② Tool Bar;
- ③ TeX Bar;
- ④ Workspace;
- ⑤ Edit Window;
- ⑥ Trace Window.

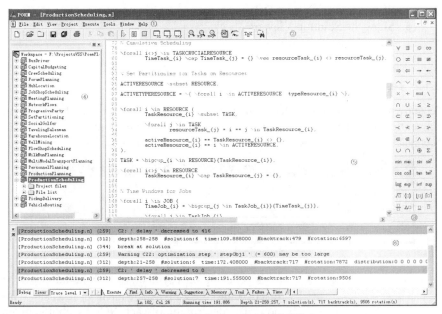

Figure 5.1 Main Interface of POEM

The main menu contains sub-menus for "File", "Edit", "View", "Project", "Execute", "Tools", "Window" and "Help". They all follow software conventions.

5.1.1 Tool Bar

Tool bar (Figure 5.2) includes the following facilities that are most frequently used (each of which can also be obtained from the main menu):

Figure 5.2 Tool Bar

1. Create a new text file, POEM project or workspace;
2. Open an NCL program, POEM project or workspace;
3. Show/Hide the Model Folder;
4. Save the current file;
5. Save the workspace (and all modified files);
6. Execute the active project;
7. Suspend/Resume the active project;
8. Stop the active project;
9. Show/Hide the table of Constants;
10. Show/Hide the table of Variables;
11. Show/Hide the table of Constraints;
12. Show/Hide the Quick Watch;
13. Show/Hide the Browser;
14. Show/Hide the Constraint Debugger;
15. Show/Hide the Visual Debugger;
16. Show the Solution Viewer;
17. Show/Hide the TeX Bar;
18. Show the "Find in files" window.

5.1.2 TeX Bar

As shown in Figure 5.3, TeX Bar displays all the NCL TeX symbols which are conventional mathematical notations. By moving the mouse onto a symbol, user gets its corresponding TeX notation for NCL keywords (Figure 5.4).

Figure 5.3 TeX Symbols

Figure 5.4 TeX Symbol

By clicking on a symbol, its TeX notation will be inserted into the current document in the Edit Window. The description of each NCL symbol is given in Chapter 2; some examples are given in Chapter 4. The TeX bar serves as an on-line memo for denoting mathematical symbols.

5.1.3 Workspace

POEM Workspace manages multiple projects (Figure 5.5). The active project, selected by "Set as active project" in the right-click menu, is in bold font.

A project consists of configuration, input, output, program, and trace files. A "File-list" can be added in order to attach some other files to the project.

Configuration of a project can be edited in the "Project settings" window. See Section 5.2.3.

5.1.4 Edit Window

User browses and edits a file in the Edit Window (Figure 5.6). The name of the current file is displayed on the top of the window.

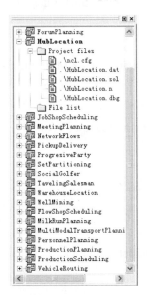

Figure 5.5 Workspace   **Figure 5.6** Edit Window

5.1.5 Trace Window

Trace Window displays messages in different options (Figure 5.7).

Figure 5.7 Trace Window

All the messages are available in Tab Execute. They will also be saved to the trace file if it exists. Trace options and working modes of this window will be explained in detail in Section 5.6.

5.2 Configuration of a Project

5.2.1 Data Pools for a Project

For a project, there are six files or data pools: configuration, input, output, program, trace and view.

Config File

User can set up a Config File for NCL to initialize basic reasoning parameters. The default postfix of a configuration file is .cfg.

Program File

An NCL program is submitted to the interpreter through a Program File. The default postfix of a program file is .n.

Input Pool

Data are fed to an NCL engine from Input Pools. The default postfix of an input file is .dat.

Output Pool

Solutions or any kind of output information can be written into Output Pools. The default postfix of an output file is .sol.

Trace File

All trace information across the running of an NCL program can be saved to a Trace File. The default postfix of a trace file is .dbg.

View File

In addition, user can create View Files for the purpose of debugging using Visual Debugger or displaying solutions using Solution Viewer. The default postfix of a view file is .view.

5.2.2 NCL Parameters

NCL parameters are saved in a .cfg configuration file. They have the following signification and default values (Table 5.1) .

Table 5.1 NCL Parameters

Parameter	Meaning	Default
TrueInput	string representation for input of True	T
FalseInput	string representation for input of False	F
TrueOutput	string representation for output of True	T
FalseOutput	string representation for output of False	F
FuzzyOutput	string representation for output of Fuzzy	U

Continued

Parameter	Meaning	Default
BoolDefault	default Boolean from null input	F
IntDefault	default integer from null input	0
FloatDefault	default float from null input	0.0
SetDefault	default set from null input	{}
StrDefault	default string from null input	
BoolRefDefault	default Boolean reference from null input	`F`
IntRefDefault	default integer reference from null input	`0`
FloatRefDefault	default float reference from null input	`0.0`
SetRefDefault	default set reference from null input	`{}`
DateDefault	default date from null input	01/01/2000
TimeMMDefault	default time in minutes from null input	00:00
TimeSSDefault	default time in seconds from null input	00:00:00
DateTimeMMDefault	default date-time in minutes from null input	01/01/2000 00:00
DateTimeSSDefault	default date-time in seconds from null input	01/01/2000 00:00:00
SqlLoginTimeOut	time-out in seconds for DB connection	30
SqlQueryTimeOut	time-out in seconds for SQL query	1000
BoolTrailSize	size of the Boolean trail	300000
IntTrailSize	size of the integral trail	200000
SetTrailSize	size of the set trail	150000
FloatTrailSize	size of the float trail	100000
ChoiceStackSize	size of the choice-point stack	10000
VariableTableSize	size of the table of variables	2000
StatisticsFrequency	statistics frequency in search nodes	200
StatisticsDepth	maximum statistics depth of search	10
NaturalDateTimeOutput	Natural format for output of date/time?	T
UniformSetOutput	Uniform format for output of sets?	F
TraceAllSolutions	Trace all solutions?	T
NoSolutionExists	no-solution at termination	"no solution exists"

		Continued
Parameter	Meaning	Default
AllSolutionsFound	all-solutions-found at termination	"all solutions found"
OptimalSolutionProved	optimal-solution-proved at termination	"optimal solution proved"
ApproximateSolutionFound	approximate-solution-found at termination	"approximate solution found"
StoppedWithoutSolution	stopped without-solution at termination	"stopped without solution"
StoppedWithSolution	stopped with-solution at termination	"stopped with solution"

Boolean Parameters

TrueInput and *FalseInput* tell the coding of Boolean constants "true" and "false" in an input pool. By default they are "T" and "F".

User also needs to define different coding for the output format of Boolean values. This can be done by setting parameters *TrueOutput*, *FalseOutput* and *FuzzyOutput* which by default are "T", "F" and "U". In particular, *FuzzyOutput* represents the non-instantiated value for a Boolean variable.

Default Values

When an NCL program reads data from a data pool, there should be a possibility of dealing with default values. For example, the field of a database record may be empty. For such an empty record, an NCL program reads it as a "default value".

For types of Boolean, float, integer, string, Boolean reference, float reference, integer reference, set reference, date, time, date-time and set, corresponding default-value parameters are *BoolDefault, FloatDefault, IntDefault, StrDefault, BoolRefDefault, FloatRefDefault, IntRefDefault, SetRefDefault, DateDefault, TimeDefault, DateTimeDefault* and *SetDefault*.

Database Connection and SQL Time-Out

SQL is embedded in NCL. Time-out parameters for Login and Query are initialized in parameters *SqlLoginTimeOut* and *SqlQueryTimeOut*.

Sizes of Trails

The search for solutions needs trails for storing domains of Boolean, float, integer and set variables. At backtracking, variable domains will be restored from the trails to keep the search sound and complete. The initial sizes of the trails are controlled by the parameters *BoolTrailSize, IntTrailSize, SetTrailSize,* and *FloatTrailSize*. Of course, NCL can automatically reallocate the trails whenever necessary.

Size of the Choice-Point Stack

Choice-points are stored in the Choice-Point stack. Its size corresponds to the maximum depth of the search tree. The initial size of the stack is parameterized by *ChoiceStackSize*. Of course, NCL can automatically resize the stack whenever necessary.

Size of the Variables Table

A look-up table for all variables is maintained to facilitate the consultation of variable names and addresses, etc. The initial size of the table is parameterized by *VariableTableSize*. Of course, NCL can automatically resize the table whenever necessary.

Parameters for Search Statistics

NCL displays search statistics during its running. Such statistics are about the range of search (minimum depth of backtracking and maximum depth of search), number of solutions already found, global running time, local running time (when a sub-model is called from a parent model, local time is part of the global one), number of backtracks, number of rotations of the NCL engine, and the distribution of numbers of backtracks. Two tags in the .cfg configuration file determine the statistics parameters:

- *StatisticsFrequency* controls the frequency for NCL to give statistics on the search. For example, if *StatisticsFrequency* = 200, then NCL will display search statistics each time 200 search nodes are explored.
- *StatisticsDepth* controls the maximum depth of the search tree within which NCL gives statistics. For example, if *StatisticsDepth* = 10, then NCL will display search statistics over the range from depth 0 to depth 9.

Output Format for a Date/Time

With *NaturalDateTimeOutput* set to be true, NCL will print Date/Time in a natural format; otherwise an integer format will be output. In some cases, integer format for a date/time can facilitate the debugging of an NCL model.

Output Format for a Set

With *UniformSetOutput* set to be true, NCL will print all sets in the format of $\{d_{11}..d_{1n}, \ldots, d_{m1}..d_{mn}\}$. In such a format, an interval $[d_1, d_2]$ is printed as $\{d_1..d_2\}$. For example, the following set output is legal:

$\{1\}$ $\{4..6\}$ $\{7, 9..10, 16, 20..30\}$

Parameter for Tracing Solutions or Errors

With *TraceAllSolutions* set to be true, NCL will trace all solutions or errors (if there is no solution) to the output file. In other words, if user only hopes to keep the last solution, *TraceAllSolutions* should be set to "false". In the case that there is no solution, if user hopes to trace all error messages before the system terminates, he should set *TraceAllSolutions* to be true; otherwise the system will terminate at the first error.

This parameter is especially useful when user wants to design an error checking model, for example, used to check data consistency for a problem. See Section 6.1.2.

Termination Messages

When user solves a problem, he may hope to obtain the solution status at the termination of the NCL engine. In the Boolean context, he gets TRUE or FALSE which signifies "there is a solution" or "there is no solution". In the string (message) context, he gets more detailed information about NCL's termination status. By default, they are:

- "no solution exists", if there is no solution;
- "all solutions found", if all solutions are found;
- "optimal solution proved", if optimal solution is found and its optimality is proved;
- "approximate solution found", if approximate solution is found; e.g., optimization step is greater than 1 in the integer objective case or optimization step is greater than 0 in the float objective case;
- "stopped without solution", if no solution is found before the NCL engine is stopped;
- "stopped with solution", if at least one solution is found before the NCL engine is stopped.

The above messages can be customized in NCL's configuration file to meet specific requirements.

5.2.3 Project Settings

This window is divided into three sub-windows: "Project", "Solver" and "Execute".

Tab Project

Tab Project gives general information about a project (Figure 5.8). The project name and thread priority can be changed. For the priority, user can choose among lowest, below, normal (default setting), above and highest.

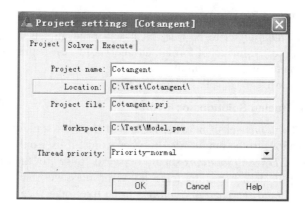

Figure 5.8 Project Settings: Tab Project

Tab Solver

In Tab Solver, the paths of all the files used in a project can be edited (Figure 5.9). Work directory which specifies the relative path of the project is also given. The content of the "Config file" is explained in Section 5.2.2.

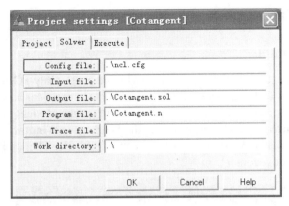

Figure 5.9 Project Settings: Tab Solver

Tab Execute

In Tab Execute, the seven options (Figure 5.10) have the following functionalities:

- Debug: It activates viewers and debuggers (Quick Watch, Browser, Constraint Debugger, and Visual Debugger) and model diagnosing (warnings and suggestions) for the parser;
- Timer: It activates the timer for constraints and the memory statistics on the dynamic allocation for the trails;
- Trace level: It defines the information level of parsing and search. Trace Level ranges from 0 to 3 (in an order from lower to higher);
- Break at end of parsing: It generates a break point for the NCL engine at the end of parsing;
- Break at solution: It generates a break point for the NCL engine when a solution is found;
- Break at termination: It generates a break point at the termination of the NCL engine;
- Break after search node: It generates a break point if the number of search nodes (search depth + number of backtracks) exceeds the given value.

Figure 5.10 Project Settings: Tab Execute

5.3 Model Management

5.3.1 Model Folder

Model Folder contains POEM applications (Figure 5.11). Only POEM workspaces, POEM projects, text and .exe files are displayed. In practice, a double click (or click and open) on an object (.pmw, .prj, .n, .exe) in the Model Folder will load a workspace (.pmw) or a project (.prj) into the Workspace Window, or will open an NCL file in the Edit Window, or will launch a .exe file. The Update button can refresh the window content.

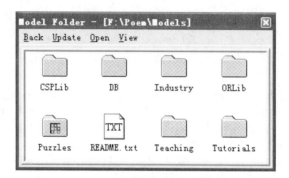

Figure 5.11 Model Folder

5.3.2 Model Library

Provided in any version of POEM, user always possesses a Model Library containing directories such as:
- Tutorials (tutorial programs)
- Puzzles (puzzles modeled and solved in NCL)

Beginners are advised to start learning POEM by using the Model Folder to explore the Model Library. The Tutorials directory contains NCL tutorial programs. They are specially prepared for beginners to learn the NCL syntax. After reading the tutorial programs, user should be able to acquire basic NCL programming skills.

5.4 Information Tables

Information tables provide user with necessary facilities to observe each project's running information.

An NCL project may have a series of sub-models hierarchically called from a main program. User may need to view the general running state about a project at all moment (parsing, pre-search reasoning and search). For this purpose, the information table of Running Models is offered. A double click on any line of the table will locate the cursor to the program line at which the NCL program is running.

Moreover, attached to each model of an NCL project, three information tables (Constants, Variables and Constraints) are available at all running moment. If user right clicks on a record of a table, through the pop-out menu some facilities such as Quick Watch and Browser can be activated to visualize the corresponding object.

Upon a break point event, all active information tables will be updated.

5.4.1 Running Models

The table of running models gives information about the running states of all NCL models of a project (Figure 5.12).

Status	Program	P.	Config	Input	Output	Trace	Work directory
Main	F:\ACC\AccScheduleMain.n	84	F:\ACC\ncl.cfg	F:\ACC\Acc.dat	F:\ACC\Acc.sol	F:\ACC\Acc.dbg	
Submodel	F:\ACC\AccSchedule1.n	92	F:\ACC\ncl.cfg	F:\ACC\Acc.dat	F:\ACC\Acc.sol	F:\ACC\Acc.dbg	

Figure 5.12 Running Models

For each model, the table contains the following information:
- Status: main or sub-model
- Program: path of a Program pool
- Parse line: program line at which the parse cursor is positioned
- Config: path of a Config pool
- Input: path of an Input pool
- Output: path of an Output pool
- Trace: path of a Trace pool
- Work directory: Work Directory of a model

5.4.2 Constants

All constants in the memory can be consulted in the table of constants (Figure 5.13). Each record of the table contains the following information:
- Name: name of a constant
- Type: Boolean, float, integer, string, or set etc.
- Dimension: dimension of an array constant
- #Constraint: number of constraints over a constant
- #Cell: number of cells allocated to a constant
- %Cell: percentage in terms of cells to all constants
- #Byte: number of bytes allocated to a constant
- %Byte: percentage in terms of bytes to all constants
- #Trail: meaningless for constants
- %Trail: meaningless for constants
- #Update: meaningless for constants
- %Update: meaningless for constants

- Ln1:   starting line of a constant object
- Col1:   starting column of a constant object
- Ln2:   ending line of a constant object
- Col2:   ending column of a constant object
- Pool: program pool of a constant

Name	Type	Dimension	#Constraint	#Cell	%Cell	#Byte	%Byte	#Trail	%Trail	#Update	%Update	Ln1	Col1	Ln2	Col2	Pool
nbTruck	int	0	0	1	0	24	0	0	0	0	43	1	43	7 [F:\P
capacity	int	0	0	1	0	24	0	0	0	0	44	1	44	8 [F:\P
nbOrder	int	0	0	1	0	24	0	0	0	0	45	1	45	7 [F:\P
depot	int	0	0	1	0	24	0	0	0	0	47	1	47	5 [F:\P
TRUCK	int-set	0	1	1	0	54	0	0	0	0	49	1	49	5 [F:\P
SOURCE	int-set	0	1	1	0	54	0	0	0	0	50	1	50	6 [F:\P

Figure 5.13 Constants

A right-click on a line will activate a pop-out menu which offers standard facilities such as *Quick Watch, Browser,* and table of *Constraints.* For example, if user selects *Quick Watch*, the value of the constant will be displayed.

5.4.3 Variables

All variables of an NCL model can be consulted in the table of variables (Figure 5.14). Each record of the table contains the following information:

- Name: name of a variable
- Type: Boolean, float, integer, string, or set etc.
- Dimension: dimension of an array variable
- #Constraint: number of constraints over a variable
- #Cell: number of cells allocated to a variable
- %Cell: percentage in terms of cells to all variables
- #Byte: number of bytes allocated to a variable
- %Byte: percentage in terms of bytes to all variables
- #Trail: number of trailing for a variable
- %Trail: percentage in terms of trailing to all variables
- #Update: number of updating over a variable
- %Update: percentage in terms of updating to all variables
- Ln1:   starting line of a variable object
- Col1:   starting column of a variable object
- Ln2:   ending line of a variable object
- Col2:   ending column of a variable object
- Pool: program pool of a variable

In the table of variables the "#Constraint" field is very useful. It tells the number of constraints over a variable. This information is helpful for designing the search strategy (e.g., querying first on the most-constrained variable).

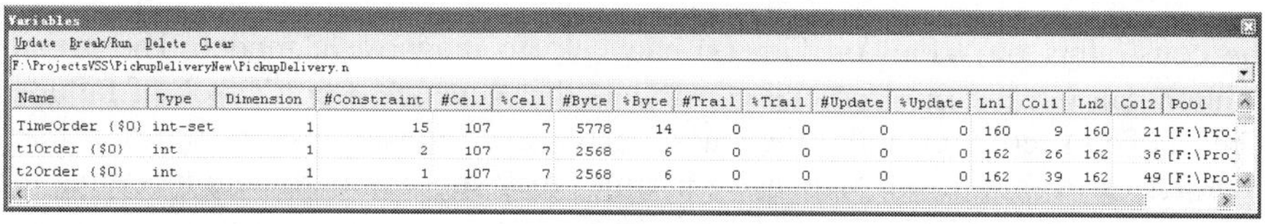

Variables

Update Break/Run Delete Clear

F:\ProjectsVSS\PickupDeliveryNew\PickupDelivery.n

Name	Type	Dimension	#Constraint	#Cell	%Cell	#Byte	%Byte	#Trail	%Trail	#Update	%Update	Ln1	Col1	Ln2	Col2	Pool
TimeOrder {$0}	int-set	1	15	107	7	5778	14	0	0	0	0	160	9	160	21	[F:\Pro;
t1Order {$0}	int	1	2	107	7	2568	6	0	0	0	0	162	26	162	36	[F:\Pro;
t2Order {$0}	int	1	1	107	7	2568	6	0	0	0	0	162	39	162	49	[F:\Pro;

Figure 5.14 Variables

As for the table of constants, a right-click on a line will activate a pop-out menu which offers visualization facilities. They are useful for programmers. For example, if user selects *Constraints*, the table of constraints over the variable will be displayed.

5.4.4 Constraints

All constraints can be consulted in the table of constraints (Figure 5.15). Each record of the table contains the following information:

- Name: constraint name
- ID: constraint id (type)
- #Cell: number of cells allocated to the variables of a constraint
- %Cell: percentage in terms of cells to all constraints
- #Byte: number of bytes allocated to the variables of a constraint
- %Byte: percentage in terms of bytes to all constraints
- #Fail: number of failures
- %Fail: percentage in terms of failure to all constraints
- Time(s): time consumption in seconds
- %Time: percentage in terms of time to all constraints
- #Update: number of updating over a constraint
- %Update: percentage in terms of updating to all constraints
- #Quantifier: number of universal quantifiers over a constraint
- Ln1: starting line of a constraint object
- Col1: starting column of a constraint object
- Ln2: ending line of a constraint object
- Col2: ending column of a constraint object
- Pool: program pool of a constraint

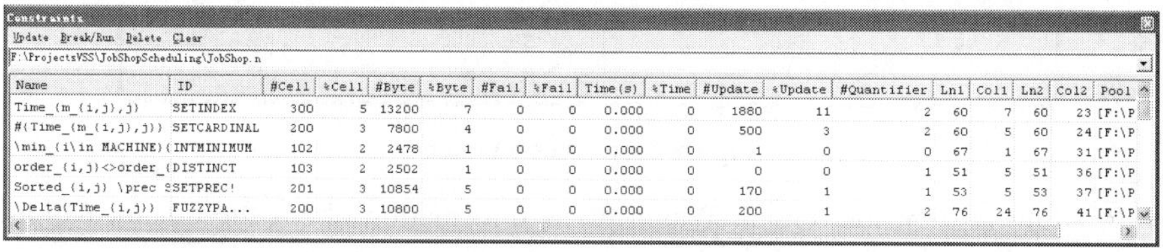

Constraints

Update Break/Run Delete Clear

F:\ProjectsVSS\JobShopScheduling\JobShop.n

Name	ID	#Cell	%Cell	#Byte	%Byte	#Fail	%Fail	Time(s)	%Time	#Update	%Update	#Quantifier	Ln1	Col1	Ln2	Col2	Pool
Time_{m_{i,j},j}	SETINDEX	300	5	13200	7	0	0	0.000	0	1880	11	2	60	7	60	23	[F:\P
#{Time_{m_{i,j},j}}	SETCARDINAL	200	3	7800	4	0	0	0.000	0	500	3	2	60	5	60	24	[F:\P
\min_{i\in MACHINE}{	INTMINIMUM	102	2	2478	1	0	0	0.000	0	1	0	0	67	1	67	31	[F:\P
order_{i,j}<>order_{	DISTINCT	103	2	2502	1	0	0	0.000	0	0	0	1	51	5	51	36	[F:\P
Sorted_{i,j} \prec S	SETPREC!	201	3	10854	5	0	0	0.000	0	170	1	1	53	5	53	37	[F:\P
\Delta(Time_{i,j})	FUZZYPA...	200	3	10800	5	0	0	0.000	0	200	1	2	76	24	76	41	[F:\P

Figure 5.15 Constraints

The columns #Cell, %Cell, #Byte, and %Byte provide important static statistics; while #Fail, %Fail, Time(s), and %Time are dynamic statistics. Sorting the constraints on #Fail or Time(s) can help to diagnose a model. The #Fail column can tell the most crucial constraints that generate a bottleneck of failure. The Time(s) column tells the most expensive constraints in time. Either "bottleneck of failure" or "expensive in time" may suggest inefficient modeling of a problem or inefficient coding of a constraint.

User should set Timer mode to activate #Update, %Update, Time(s) and %Time.

User can "Set Focus for Debug" to concentrate the debugging on the focused constraint while neglecting the failure of all other constraints.

5.5 Visualization and Debugging

It is better to use POEM's visualization and debugging facilities at break points. This is because user needs reliable (relatively stable) information, but variable evolution is constant during the constraint reasoning phase.

5.5.1 Quick Watch

The Quick Watch window allows user to watch the value of an expression when an NCL project is running (Figure 5.16). By selecting an expression in an Edit Window, in a table of constants or in a table of variables, a Quick Watch window can be activated through the right-click menu. The value of the selected object will be displayed. User can watch its values by modifying the index (subscripts) of the expression.

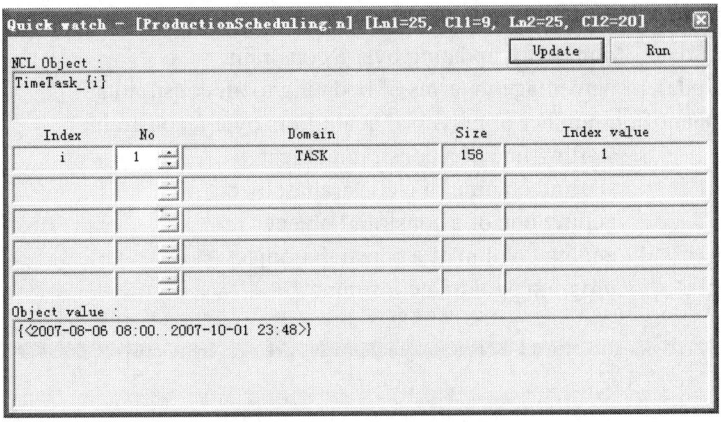

Figure 5.16 Quick Watch

In addition to value, Quick Watch gives information about the quantification domain and the size for each object.

5.5.2 Browser

Browser is a more powerful viewer (Figure 5.17). It can visualize more than one variable and provides an interesting browsing functionality: User can simultaneously watch the values of a list of cells of an array variable. Furthermore, after selecting a constraint in the table of constraints, through the right-click menu user can fetch all the variables of the constraint into a Brower window.

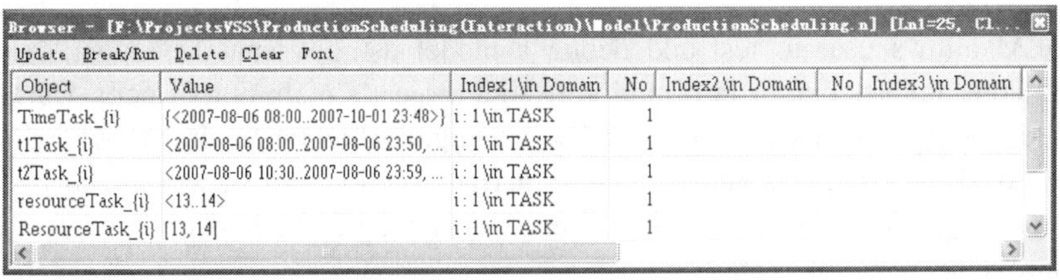

Object	Value	Index1 \in Domain	No	Index2 \in Domain	No	Index3 \in Domain
TimeTask_{i}	{<2007-08-06 08:00..2007-10-01 23:48>}	i : 1 \in TASK	1			
t1Task_{i}	<2007-08-06 08:00..2007-08-06 23:50, ...	i : 1 \in TASK	1			
t2Task_{i}	<2007-08-06 10:30..2007-08-06 23:59, ...	i : 1 \in TASK	1			
resourceTask_{i}	<13..14>	i : 1 \in TASK	1			
ResourceTask_{i}	[13, 14]	i : 1 \in TASK	1			

Figure 5.17 Browser

Each record in a Browser window contains the following fields:
- Object: variable object
- Value: variable value
- Index i \in Domain: value and domain of the i-th subscript or index
- No: number of the subscript or index in the domain

5.5.3 Constraint Debugger

Constraint Debugger allows user to debug a constraint when it fails. By default, all subscripts (indices) of an expression are fixed in accordance with the quantifier indices at the moment of failure.

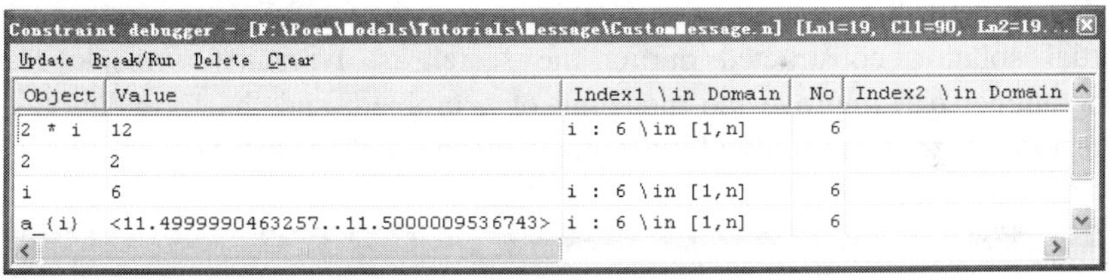

Object	Value	Index1 \in Domain	No	Index2 \in Domain
2 * i	12	i : 6 \in [1,n]	6	
2	2			
i	6	i : 6 \in [1,n]	6	
a_(i)	<11.4999990463257..11.5000009536743>	i : 6 \in [1,n]	6	

Figure 5.18 Constraint Debugger

Figure 5.18 illustrates the use of Constraint Debugger for the tutorial example of "Custom Message" in Section 4.16. The debugger displays the values of relevant arguments of the constraint ($a_i > 2 \times i$): For quantified variable $i = 6$; $2 \times i = 12$, $a_i = <11.499990463257..11.5000009536743>$. This explains why the constraint fails:

<11.499990463257..11.5000009536743> is not greater than $2 \times i = 12$.

The fields of each record in the table have the same signification as those of a Browser.

To activate the Constraint Debugger user should set Debug mode and set Trace Level to at least 1; if it is for debugging a constraint which fails during the search, Trace Level should be at least 2.

If the flag "Set Focus for Debug" is added to a constraint in the table of constraints, the debugger will concentrate on the constraint and neglect other constraints.

5.5.4 Visual Debugger

POEM allows user to test and debug a model using Visual Debugger. Visual Debugger fetches output information from a project's main output pool. During a search process, everything printed by @, targeting to the main output, will be displayed in Visual Debugger. Thus a partial solution can be visualized for the programmer. This functionality is useful for a programmer to observe, test and improve his solution strategy.

Visual Debugger supports 2 modes of visualization: ①*Text*, if the main output file is a .sol file; ②*Graphics*, if the main output file is a .view file.

In the *Text* mode, user can display run-time information for Boolean, float, integer, and set expressions by printing variable domains. This helps to trace the running of an NCL engine. For example:

```
A ⊂ [1,4],

#A = 2,

@("A = " A "\n"),

A = ?.
```

With Trace Level set to be 3, at each search node the domain evolution of the set variable A will be displayed in the Visual Debugger window.

Figure 5.19 illustrates the visual debugging of the Golf Tournament model. A partial solution constructed during the search is dynamically displayed. A programmer can improve the modeling of a problem and the formulation of a constraint through the study of the domain evolution of variables.

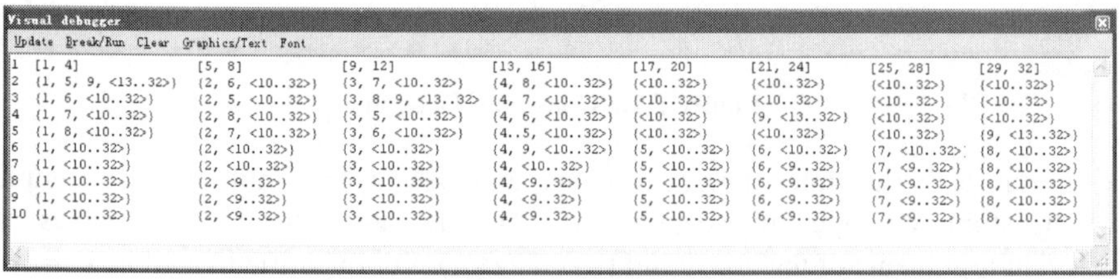

Figure 5.19 Visual Debugger (Text Mode)

The visual debugging, in the *Graphics* mode, of the Pick-up and Delivery model (see Chapter 6) is illustrated in Figure 5.20. A partial solution constructed during the search is displayed. User can trace the pick-up and delivery of different vehicles in the graphical window. This is useful for the programmer to "feel" directly about his search strategy.

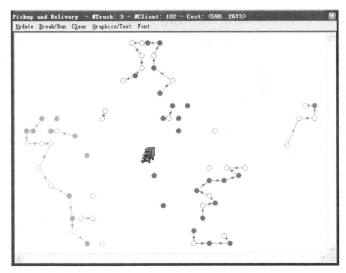

Figure 5.20 Visual Debugger (Graphics Mode)

5.5.5 Solution Viewer

When a solution is found, user can visualize it using Solution Viewer. If a .view file is specified for an output pool, then everything printed by @ into the pool will be displayed in Solution Viewer. The visualization of a solution of the Job-shop model (see Chapter 6) is displayed in Figure 5.21.

A File-list is used to attach related files such as data or view files. So if an NCL project has more than one .view file, they can be added to the File-list. User can select any file in the File-list and visualize it in Solution Viewer.

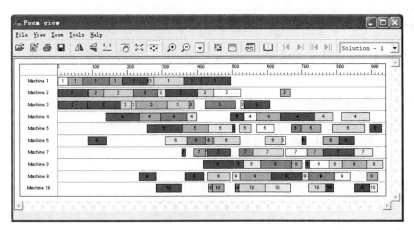

Figure 5.21 Solution Viewer

This book will concentrate on the logic and optimization aspects of POEM. Detailed presentation of POEM's visualization functionalities will be provided in additional documents.

5.6 Trace Window and Working Modes

Trace Window provides the functionalities of information tracing, diagnosis and analysis. As shown in Figure 5.22, the three working modes of POEM are:

- Debug: It activates the visualization facilities of Quick Watch and Browser and the functionality of model diagnosing (especially warnings and suggestions) of the parser;
- Timer: It activates the timer for constraints and the trail statistics for variables;
- Trace level: It ranges from 0 to 3 (in an order from lower to higher) for tracing the parsing and the search.

Figure 5.22 Options of Trace Window

Other options concerning diagnosis and statistics have the following functionalities:

- Execute: It displays the messages in the running process of a model;
- Find: It displays the search results by "Find in files" (   );
- Info: It collects "info" messages from the Execute window;
- Warning: It collects "warning" messages from the Execute window;
- Suggestion: It collects suggestion messages from the Execute window to help user to improve his model;
- Memory: It displays the statistics on the static memory of variables;
- Trail: In Timer mode it displays trail statistics on the updating of variables;
- Failure: It displays the statistics on the failure of constraints;
- Time: In Timer mode it displays the statistics on the time consumption of constraints.

Note that a trail is a stack for "trailing" domains of variables during the search for solutions.

5.6.1 Debug Mode

If Debug mode is set active, the system will take the following controls:

- To facilitate the consultation of variables (Quick Watch and Browser), all NCL variables will be kept in memory (no modeling optimization and garbage release) until the complete shut-down of an NCL engine;
- More importantly, the system provides help messages for modeling (Warning and Suggestion) if the mode is activated before parsing.

5.6.2 Timer Mode

Timer mode coordinates the "Update/Time" statistics of variables and constraints:

- Statistics on the time consumption by parsing and data input will come into effect;

- The fields of #Trail, %Trail, #Update, %Update of the table of variables and the fields of #Update, %Update, Time(s), %Time of the table of constraints will be active. In Timer mode, the running of the NCL engine may be very time costly. But it gives useful statistics (quantity and percentage) of updating and time consumption of all active constraints and variables.

Once reset inactive, the fields of #Update, %Update, Time(s), and %Time will all be cleared to 0.

5.6.3 Trace Level

Trace Level is used to control the tracing of NCL information. The trace information is given in accordance with the following levels in a progressive manner:

- Trace Level 0: Only termination notification is given at the end of the running of an NCL model;
- Trace Level 1: Messages such as help messages (Warning/Suggestion) for modeling, end of parsing, end of search, solution found, and inference statistics are given;
- Trace Level 2: Detailed warning and information messages of parsing, enumeration, search and the failure of a constraint are given;
- Trace Level 3: Detailed information at the beginning and end of each search depth is given.

5.6.4 Options for Diagnosis

Trace Window has optional windows for diagnosis purposes. They sort model diagnosis during parsing and search into three message windows: information (Tab Info), warning (Tab Warning) and suggestion (Tab Suggestion).

For a programmer, warning messages imply possible defects in a model, while suggestion messages provide advices for the improvement of the modeling.

5.6.5 Options for Statistics

Trace Window has optional windows for statistics purposes. They sort static and dynamic statistics on memory allocation, constraint failure and time consumption during the running process into four message windows: Memory (static memory), Trail (dynamic memory by trails), Failure (failure of constraints) and Time (time consumption). They will respectively help a programmer to identify the most memory-costly expression, the most critical constraint and the most time-costly constraint:

- In the case of insufficient memory, a programmer should consult the messages in the "Memory" and "Trail" options to sort out the expressions that are the most expensive in static memory and trails. He then needs to find a solution to reduce the memory consumption of his model;
- In the case of frequent constraint failure, a programmer should consult the messages in the "Failure" option to sort out the constraints that generate the

most of failure in the reasoning. He then needs to find a solution to avoid the bottleneck of constraint failure;

- In the case of excessive execution time, a programmer should consult the messages in the "Time" option to sort out the expressions that are the most expensive in time. He then needs to find a solution to save time for his model.

5.6.6 Recommended Diagnosis Mode

A standard diagnosing mode is recommended as below:
- Debug = active;
- Timer = active;
- Trace Level = 1, if it's not necessary to activate Constraint Debugger upon each failure;
- Trace Level = 2, if it's necessary to activate Constraint Debugger upon a failure of a constraint during the search;
- Trace Level = 3, if more detailed diagnosis at each search depth is needed. A break point is generated at each search depth to allow user to do a debugging.

In addition, user can program break points in his NCL program by using the system variable '' (empty between two single quotes) to facilitate the debugging. For more advanced debugging, user should resort to programmed debugging with expectation constraints.

5.6.7 Recommended Working Mode

A normal working mode is recommended as below:
- Debug = inactive;
- Timer = inactive;
- Trace Level = 0, if it's necessary to search for many solutions. For example, there are many solutions for the Queens problem (see Chapter 6). At Trace Level 0, messages of "Solution Found" will not be sent upon a solution;
- Trace Level = 1, if only an optimal solution is the target or a few good solutions (normally only one) are searched for.

5.7 Message Management

NCL communicates to user all kinds of information through messages. On the POEM platform, such messages can be viewed in its Trace Window; for a programmer, such messages can be obtained through a message interface in Visual Basic, Visual C++, C#, Java, Asp.net, etc.; for an NCL project, messages can be viewed in its trace file.

5.7.1 Message Levels

There are six message levels in POEM:
- Trivial: trivial information

- Special: special information
- Info: ordinary information
- Warning: warning
- Error: system error
- Exception: system exception

A project will crash at the Exception level. User may need to deal with the message carefully to solve such a system problem.

5.7.2 Message Types

There are seven message types for "Info", "Warning", "Error" and "Exception":

- Parse: related to syntax
- i/o: related to input and output
- Memory: related to memory
- Data: related to data
- Typing: related to data types
- Range: related to all kinds of ranges (e.g., of subscripts)
- Inference: related to reasoning

5.7.3 Message Codes

The list of message codes is given in Table 5.2.

Table 5.2 Message Codes

Code	ID	Text
0	NCL_TRIVIAL_MESSAGE	trivial message
1	NCL_BREAKPOINT	break point
2	NCL_SOLUTION_FOUND	solution found
3	NCL_NO_SOLUTION_EXISTS	no solution found
4	NCL_ALL_SOLUTIONS_FOUND	all solutions found
5	NCL_OPTIMAL_SOLUTION_PROVED	optimal solution proved
6	NCL_APPROXIMATE_SOLUTION_FOUND	approximate solution found
7	NCL_STOPPED_WITHOUT_SOLUTION	Stopped without solution
8	NCL_STOPPED_WITH_SOLUTION	stopped with solution
9	NCL_PARSE_INFO	parse info
10	NCL_IO_INFO	i/o info
11	NCL_DATA_INFO	data info
12	NCL_TYPING_INFO	typing info
13	NCL_RANGE_INFO	range info
14	NCL_MEMORY_INFO	memory info
15	NCL_INFERENCE_INFO	inference info
16	NCL_PARSE_WARNING	parse warning
17	NCL_IO_WARNING	i/o warning

Continued

Code	ID	Text
18	NCL_DATA_WARNING	data warning
19	NCL_TYPING_WARNING	typing warning
20	NCL_RANGE_WARNING	range warning
21	NCL_MEMORY_WARNING	memory warning
22	NCL_INFERENCE_WARNING	inference warning
23	NCL_PARSE_ERROR	parse error
24	NCL_IO_ERROR	i/o error
25	NCL_DATA_ERROR	data error
26	NCL_TYPING_ERROR	typing error
27	NCL_RANGE_ERROR	range error
28	NCL_MEMORY_ERROR	memory error
29	NCL_INFERENCE_ERROR	inference error
30	NCL_PARSE_EXCEPTION	parse exception
31	NCL_IO_EXCEPTION	i/o exception
32	NCL_DATA_EXCEPTION	data exception
33	NCL_TYPING_EXCEPTION	typing exception
34	NCL_RANGE_EXCEPTION	range exception
35	NCL_MEMORY_EXCEPTION	memory exception
36	NCL_INFERENCE_EXCEPTION	inference exception

5.7.4 Message Handler

To communicate with the NCL engine in an application through NCL messages, user can program a message interface to coordinate NCL with his application program. The message handling method in C++ is explained below.

The Message Handler is a procedure of the following form:

```
typedef void NclMsg (long lCode,  LPCTSTR szMsg);
```

Here **lCode** represents the message codes and **szMsg** represents the message text.

User should define in the message handler his actions upon receipt of an NCL message. Note that in the process of the message handler, NCL is suspended till the message handler accomplishes its task and hands the control over to the NCL engine. In its body, a switch structure that reacts to important messages is to be programmed. For example, messages about solution can be handled as below:

```
switch (lCode)  {
case NCL_SOLUTION_FOUND:
        /* A solution is found. Actions for processing this event.*/
        break;

case NCL_NO_SOLUTION_EXISTS:
        /* NCL informs that there exists no solution. Actions before termination.*/
```

```
        break;

case NCL_ALL_SOLUTIONS_FOUND:
        /* NCL informs that all solutions are found. Actions before termination.*/
        break;

case NCL_OPTIMAL_SOLUTION_PROVED:
        /* NCL informs that optimal solution is found. Actions before termination.*/
        break;

case NCL_APPROXIMATE_SOLUTION_FOUND:
        /* NCL informs that approximate solution is found. Actions before termination.*/
        break;

case NCL_STOPPED_WITHOUT_SOLUTION:
        /* NCL informs that no solution is found. Actions before termination. */
        break;

case NCL_STOPPED_WITH_SOLUTION:
        /* NCL informs that one solution is found so far. Actions before termination.*/
        break;
}
```
See Appendix 2 for more information.

5.7.5 Termination Status

NCL's termination notification includes 6 NCL messages as explained below.

For a complete solving of a problem:

- NCL_NO_SOLUTION_EXISTS: upon receipt of this message user knows that there is no solution. The search is complete.
- NCL_ALL_SOLUTIONS_FOUND: upon receipt of this message user knows that all solutions to the problem are found. The search is complete.
- NCL_OPTIMAL_SOLUTION_PROVED: upon receipt of this message user knows that the optimal solution to the optimization problem is concluded. The search is complete.

For an incomplete solving of a problem:

- NCL_APPROXIMATE_SOLUTION_FOUND: upon receipt of this message user knows that an approximate solution is found. The search is incomplete.
- NCL_STOPPED_WITHOUT_SOLUTION: upon receipt of this message user knows that the NCL engine is terminated without any solution. The search is incomplete.
- NCL_STOPPED_WITH_SOLUTION: upon receipt of this message user knows that the NCL engine is terminated with a solution. The search is incomplete.

One of the 6 messages will be sent in all cases, that is to say, user will always be informed about the termination of an NCL model.

The texts of the termination messages can be customized in a configuration file.

5.8 Help on Line

POEM provides an on-line help. It includes standard help information and the "Find" functionality. For example, user can quickly find information about NCL keywords.

By selecting a keyword such as \forall in the Edit Window and clicking on "Help" as shown in Figure 5.23, POEM's help in an appropriate heading will be opened.

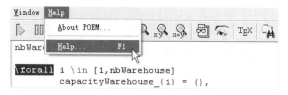

Figure 5.23 Help on Line: Search for Keywords

5.9 Component and Server

In addition to the development toolkit, the POEM platform includes computation component ComPoem (see Appendix 2), visualization component ComView and computation server PoemServer.

In an application, ComView is deployed to each client to provide visualization service locally and PoemServer is deployed to a server to provide computation and optimization services for clients.

For more details, readers are referred to Appendix 2 and handbooks on software components and computation server of POEM.

The POEM software package is commercialized by ENGINEST (www.enginest.com).

6 Modeling and Solving

This chapter presents the methodology of modeling and solving using NCL.

Section 6.1 proposes some general principles on software development in NCL. Some advices on development process are given.

Section 6.2 studies some abstract mathematical models that are usually used in formulating constraint satisfaction problems. Though only a few, these models frequently occur in industrial problems: distinct integers, disjoint sets, sorting, set covering, packing, sum, cumulation, etc.

Section 6.3 continues to illustrate problem modeling and problem solving with some puzzles.

Section 6.4 presents the solutions to some harder problems such as Job-Shop Scheduling and Pick-up and Delivery with Time Windows.

6.1 Development Principles

Only by software engineering can large-scale applications of NCL become possible. Only with clarity and readability can software engineering become feasible. Thus, object-oriented analysis and design (Booch 2007) is fundamental for software engineering in NCL.

6.1.1 Generality

For a constraint satisfaction problem which is NP-hard, there is hardly algorithm for solving it in polynomial time. On this subject, readers are referred to the complexity theory (Garey and Johnson 1979; Lenstra and Rinnooy Kan 1979). To successfully deal with NP-hard problems, the following steps are recommended:

- Requirement analysis with an effort on problem simplification;
- Decomposing a problem into simpler sub-problems, if possible, in accordance with the principles presented in Section 8.2;
- Analysis on conceptual models of the problem and its sub-problems;
- Data modeling based on conceptual models with object-oriented analysis (Creating a highly clear data model is fundamental for solving an NP-hard problem);
- Modeling constraints and objectives in accordance with the principles presented in Section 6.2;
- Modeling queries by exhaustively experimenting on query criteria and enumeration modes in accordance with the principles presented in Section 6.1.4;
- Benchmarking and refinement on problem modeling by studying NCL's help messages, by consulting the tables of Constants, Variables and Constraints, by analyzing the statistics in Trace Window options of "Memory", "Trail", "Failure" and "Time". See Sections 6.1.5 and 6.1.6;

- If the quality of a solution is still not satisfactory after the above efforts, local optimization based on relaxation techniques should be adopted to improve the solution. See Section 8.1.

6.1.2 Data Modeling

An efficient constraint model reposes on a highly clear and simple data model. In fact, a problem model can be straightforwardly written by describing the relations within a data model using the description language NCL.

Known/Unknown Analysis

Given a problem, user should first analyze what is known and what is unknown. For those which are known, they are organized as input data and are considered "constants" in the data model. For those unknown, they are organized as output data (for a solution) and are considered "variables" in the data model. The relations will be described over constants and variables in the modeling of constraints and objectives; see Section 6.1.3. The unknown to be computed by NCL needs to be expressed in the queries over the critical variables; see Section 6.1.4.

Once the known/unknown analysis is completed, user is advised to use the following naming conventions for the purpose of keeping clarity in the development of a project.

Rules for Naming Data and Variables

Well known to programmers, data and variable naming is critical for the readability and clarity of a program. This is even more important for mathematical modeling.

For an industrial problem that concerns hierarchical concepts, multiple modules and complex constraints, there is no doubt that software engineering must be adopted in developing a solution to the problem. To support the development of an industrial solution, efficient modeling conventions that facilitate a software co-development should be used.

For NCL, the following naming convention is proposed:

- The name of a variable, of set type or not, is always written in singular (not plural), for example, CLIENT, $idOrder_i$, $OrderClient_i$;
- The name of a set variable is always started with a capital letter, for example, $OrderClient_i$;
- For a data class, its name is entirely in capital letters, for example, CLIENT;
- The name of a variable of any other type (numeric, date/time, string, reference, or Boolean, etc.) is always started with a small letter, for example, $idOrder_i$, $activeOrder_i$.

Some abbreviations are adopted by all developers in order to make it easy to coordinate a collaborative team work. For example, for a data class its attributes can be named as below:

- id: identifier
- nb: number

- min: minimum
- max: maximum
- idx: index
- t0:   initial time
- t1:   start time
- t2:   completion time

For example:

```
nbCity = 0,                        % number of the cities
CITY   = [1, nbCity],              % data class of cities written in capital
∀ i ∈ CITY(
    idCity_i = 0,                  % identifier of city i

    ClientCity_i ⊂ CLIENT,         % clients of city i

),
```

Rules for Naming Tables and Fields

If the development is based on a database, data modeling can follow some rules. This is because usually the design of a database respects the object-oriented principle, that is, every table is a well defined object. The following principles can be borrowed in data modeling:

- Encapsulation: encapsulating a data class in a table;
- Least Redundancy: simplifying the concept for each field and avoiding redundancy between fields;
- Inheritance: information is inherited through keys (identifiers of the tables) between tables.

Based on a database, the technical conventions for naming a variable/constant are:

- Each table corresponds to a data class. Its name is written entirely in capital letters and in singular (not plural). For example, CLIENT and TRUCK represent respectively the client table and the truck table.
- A constant or a variable corresponding to a field/attribute of a table is introduced by concatenating the field/attribute name and the table name. Concretely the naming convention is: 1) If the attribute is a set, the first letter of its name should be in capital; otherwise a small letter is used; 2) The first letter of the table name should be in capital. For example, constant $idTruck_i$ (string type) represents the identifier of truck i; variable $activeTruck_i$ (Boolean type) signifies whether truck i works or not; variable $Order Truck_i$ (set type) corresponds to the set of orders assigned to truck i.
- A constant or a variable that is related to an attribute and to more than one table is introduced by concatenating the attribute name and the names of the tables. Concretely the naming convention is: 1) If the attribute is a set, the first letter of its name should be in capital; otherwise a small letter is used; 2) The first letters of the table names should be all in capital; the rest of the letters of the names should be small letters; 3) The subscripts of the constant/variable are sorted in a reverse order of the table names. For example,

the Personnel Planning model (see Chapter 7) involves three important data classes: PROFILE, DATE and SHIFT. If a constant should be introduced to represent the number of employees of the profile p, on the date d and at the shift i, then the constant can be named nbStaffShiftDatePro-file$_{p,d,i}$, which is the concatenation of the attribute name nbStaff (the number of employees) and the table names SHIFT, DATE and PROFILE. The subscripts p,d,i are sorted in a reverse order of data classes SHIFT, DATE and PROFILE.

Checking Data Consistency

In an industrial application, the work on data can be very long and hard. As an important step of data modeling, user is advised to design an NCL program to check data consistency in accordance with his data model. This investment can be very beneficial in a real-world project. It is advised to do so in the following way:

- Creating a data checking project and attaching an output file to it;
- Setting the NCL parameter *TraceAllSolutions* in the .cfg file to be true (see Section 5.2.2);
- Modeling all the constraints of the problem (see Section 6.1.3);
- Adding custom messages to those constraints that require special checking for the input (see Section 3.1.5 for custom message).

When a constraint fails on an input, a corresponding message (a personalized explanation about the failure) will be printed to the output file. At the termination of the model, a report of all errors will be available in the output.

6.1.3 Modeling Constraints and Objectives

A good definition of a problem can lead to efficient modeling. A good NCL model should formulate compactly constraints and objectives of the problem and should account for efficient search. If user has a big trouble in modeling, he should re-check the problem definition. For compactly modeling, readers are referred to Section 6.2 for modeling abstraction.

6.1.4 Modeling Queries

Search strategy is important for exploring the solution space. It should be designed to fully exploit the combinatorial structure of the problem. Usually, with an inappropriate strategy, a combinatorial problem can be intractable; while being careful with the search, user may get his problem magically solved. Note especially that a small difference in a search heuristic (Query Criteria and Enumeration Modes) may result in a great difference in efficiency.

Principles for Designing Criteria

In NCL, there are five general principles for designing a query criterion.

Sequential Search

It aims to respect the problem structure to keep the solution space as convex as possible, for example, by enumerating first the query variables (e.g., resource and execution time) of a production task which has the earliest release time. See the Production Scheduling problem in Chapter 7.

Least Slack

It aims to identify a query variable with the least uncertainty in the search. If the slack (uncertainty of a variable) is the least, possibility of failure is hopefully minimized.

Greatest Slack

If the slack (uncertainty of a variable) is the greatest, branching may result in the greatest cutting of the solution space. This criterion is useful in solving problems over the floating-point numbers.

Least Regret

Usually, based on an optimization objective, a regret function can be defined to measure the easiness of choice-making in the branching at a query variable. Generally, the least-regret criterion is used together with a greedy-search criterion; the least regret implies the easiest choice for the greedy search.

For example, the optimization objective of the Traveling Salesman Problem (see Chapter 8) is to minimize the total distance of the travel. A regret function (for the choice of a successor) based on node-to-node distances can be defined to represent the easiness on the choice of a successor. For the detailed method, readers are referred to the Pick-up and Delivery problem in Section 6.4.7 and the Traveling Salesman Problem in Chapter 8.

Greedy Search

Locally, toward optimization objectives the search can be as greedy as possible. This criterion is usually used as the last one.

Criticality of a Query Variable

Query criteria are designed to select critical variables used in the queries. In general, user should always take into consideration the following critical variables:

- Most-Constrained Variable: This strategy, which conforms to the least-slack query criterion, selects a variable that is the most constrained (e.g., in terms of the number of constraints). See the solving of the Calculs d'Enfer problem in Section 6.3.9;

- Smallest-Domain Variable (e.g., $\rightarrow$ (min $\# \Delta x_i$)): This strategy complies with the least-slack criterion. If the size of the variable domain is the smallest, hopefully the fewest choice points will be generated, and failure or solution can be concluded earlier. See the solving of the Magic Square problem in Section 6.3.5;

- Greatest-Domain Variable (e.g., $\rightarrow$ (max $\# \Delta x_i$)): In accordance with the greatest-slack criterion, this strategy aims to cause the greatest change to the constraint system so that the greatest cutting of the solution space may be achieved. See the solving of the Magic Sequence problem in Section 6.3.7 and Heat Exchanger problem in Section 6.4.6.

6.1.5 Test and Benchmarking

Test and Benchmarking for model refinement may be the most time-costly phase in a development process.

Space Complexity and Time Complexity

During the test, space and time complexity should be studied in order to improve the model in response to statistics and messages of NCL. Useful sources of information are:

- Tables of constants, variables and constraints;
- Help messages (re-organized into "Info", "Warning" and "Suggestion" in the Trace Window) ;
- Statistics on space complexity ("Memory" and "Trail" in the Trace Window);
- Statistics on time complexity ("Failure" and "Time" in the Trace Window).

Stability and Scalability

Benchmarking on test data aims to improve the stability and scalability of a model. Stability means that the solver can always find a solution with few backtracks. Scalability means that as the size of the problem increases, the solver can still stably find a feasible solution.

Benchmarking work should be started first on small-size problems. This facilitates diagnosing the modeling of constraints, objectives and queries. Progressively user can test the scalability over large-scale problems after the model is stabilized over small data.

6.1.6 Diagnosing a Model

Some approaches to conducting a diagnosis on space and time complexity are presented below.

Analysis Based on Static Statistics

At the end of parsing, user should consult the tables of constants, variables and constraints to study the efficiency of a model. Additional information in the "Memory" option of the Trace Window can be also helpful.

In the table of constraints, the fields of "#Cell", "%Cell", "#Byte" and "%Byte" provide important statistics concerning the space complexity of a constraint. If a constraint costs heavily in %Cell (percentage in variable cells) or %Byte (percentage in bytes), it may suggest an inefficient formulation of the constraint. In the "Memory" option of the Trace Window, information on static memory allocated to expressions is also displayed. User can try to improve the formulation of the constraints which are the most time expensive.

In the table of variables, the field "#Constraint" provides crucial information useful for the design of a search strategy. Usually, the most constrained variables should take place in query criteria; it may be important for reducing the time complexity of a model.

Analysis Based on Dynamic Statistics

After the analysis of static information on the model, at the end of search user can analyze the dynamic statistics in the "Trail" field of the table of variables and in the fields of "#Fail", "%Fail", "Time(s)" and "%Time" of the table of constraints. User can also analyze the statistics in the options of "Trail", "Failure" and "Time" of the Trace Window.

On the aspect of space complexity, user should consult in the "Trail" option the expressions that are the most memory-costly. For the stability and the scalability of the model, the formulation of such expressions may need to be improved to reduce the memory consumption.

On the aspect of time complexity, consulting the "Failure" and "Time" options in the Trace Window or sorting the constraints on #Fail (number of constraint failures) and on Time(s) (execution time in seconds) can reveal crucial information about a model. The number of failures (#Fail) usually tells the most critical constraints that generate a bottleneck of failure; the information on execution time (Time(s)) usually tells the most time-costly constraints. Either "a bottleneck of failure" or "expensive in time" may suggest inefficient modeling of a problem or inefficient formulation of a constraint. User should then try to simplify the formulation of the constraint or improve search rules by adding or adjusting least-slack criteria on critical variables in the constraint.

Diagnosing with Help Messages

NCL is an intelligent modeling language. Its help messages (e.g., warning and suggestion) for modeling will be activated in the Debug mode at a trace level no less than 1. In particular, warning messages of parsing may suggest defective programming.

On the aspect of space complexity, special attention should be paid to "memory insufficient" exceptions or warnings. If such a message is communicated, user should carefully study the corresponding constraints which produce the trouble and try to simplify the formulation of the constraints. In particular, the number of quantified variables and the ranges of domains of discourse for the expressions must be limited; they should not be too memory expensive.

On the aspect of time complexity, special attention should be paid to "try modeling" suggestions. If such a message is communicated, user should carefully study the corresponding constraints which generate bottlenecks of failure and try to simplify the formulation of the constraints. Moreover, least-slack (global or local) criteria on critical variables for a failure-bottleneck constraint can be used in the search rules to improve the stability and scalability of the model.

Diagnosing with Viewers and Debuggers

The POEM platform provides user with flexible viewing and debugging facilities such as Quick Watch, Browser, Constraint Debugger and Visual Debugger.

Quick Watch and Browser can be used to consult the domain of a variable which gives information about the evolution of the constraint system. User should carry out a study on the cutting of variable domains. If the domain of a variable seems not to be cut enough, he should try to improve the formulation of the constraints over it.

Upon the failure of a constraint, Constraint Debugger allows user to study why such a failure happens by providing information about the domains of all the variables of the constraint. Such information can help to identify the defects in modeling. To facilitate debugging a constraint, programmed break can be added to the model before the constraint so that user can observe the evolution of the variable domains before the constraint fails.

More effective diagnosis method may be using Visual Debugger in its text or graphics mode. To do so, an output file should be specified for the project and user should add print statements in the model so that Visual Debugger can display printed information from the output. Visual Debugger is especially useful for tracing the search and for improving the solution strategy. See Section 5.5 for more detailed presentation.

Finally, as presented in "Expectation and Debugging" of Section 3.1.6, user can also program an advanced debugging by using expectation constraints to supervise the domain evolution of a variable.

6.2 Modeling Abstraction

A basic distinction of NCL from some existing constraint/logic programming languages/systems such as Prolog II (Colmerauer 1982), CLP(R) (Jaffar and Lassez 1987), CHIP (Dincbas et al. 1988), Prolog III (Colmerauer 1990), Prolog IV (Colmerauer 1995), Ilog Solver (Puget 1994), Oz (Smolka 1995) and Eclipse (Apt and Wallace 2007) lies in NCL's parser which understands natural problem formulation in mathematical logic and submits abstract models to embedded algorithms for efficiently solving problems.

More precisely, compared to other problem-solving systems, one contribution of NCL is the design of the Semantic Parser and higher level mathematical logic abstraction of problem modeling. A common point of NCL and other systems is the design and implementation of embedded algorithms. However, no specific predicates such as *Sort, Alldisjoint, Alldifferent, Cumulative, Cycle/Path, Global Cardinality/Among/Distribute*, etc. (Aggoun and Beldiceanu 1993; Régin 1994; Zhou 1997; Bleuzen-Guernalec and Colmerauer 2000) are introduced in NCL, though algorithms for solving related problems exist internally in NCL.

In fact, without Semantic Parser to recognize a problem's natural formulation, NCL has to introduce built-in predicates (global constraints) to provide user with a specific logical interface. The problem is: There are several tens of global algorithms in NCL. If global constraints are explicitly defined, too many specific names and concepts will be introduced in NCL and must be carefully explained in its user's manual. In that case, user would be drowned by hundreds of new concepts. It's imaginable how "clumsy" it would be for a programmer to program in NCL.

At an abstract level, this section tries to classify the modeling of a large scope of constraint satisfaction problems into naive mathematical logic models. After understanding these basic models, user will understand what underlies the solving of a combinatorial problem.

The presentation here is not exhaustive. Only a part of NCL abstract models will be illustrated. It should also be noted that even for each model, lots of variants may exist.

To facilitate the presentation, the following convention for naming variables and constants is adopted:

- Boolean variables: a, b, c
- Float variables: f, g, h
- Integer variables: x, y, z, w
- Set variables: A, B, C, D
- Integer constants: n, d

6.2.1 Distinct Integers

For solving combinatorial problems, constraints related to "distinctness" are almost indispensable. Many problems such as Queens and Knight in this chapter are related to the constraint of "distinct integers" ("all-different") (Hall 1935; Régin 1994; Zhou 1997) which in its nature states that $x_1, ..., x_n$ are distinct integers. Such constraint, which may have a lot of variants, is basically expressed as follows:

$$\forall\, i \neq j \in [1, n]$$
$$x_i \neq x_j,$$

6.2.2 Disjoint Sets

By analogy to "distinct integers", in the context of sets user will need the disjointness relation expressed as follows:

$$\forall\, i \neq j \in [1, n]$$
$$A_i \cap A_j = \varnothing,$$

"Disjoint Integers" and "Disjoint Sets" are combinatorial constraints. The algorithms designed for these constraints underlie the solution to most of the combinatorial optimization problems, and are especially useful for solving resource allocation problems.

6.2.3 Sorting

The sorting models introduce the "sorting" concepts into NCL at the logical programming level. It is well known to programmers that "sorting" is a fundamental algorithm in computer science. Especially in an NCL program, "set sorting" is fundamental for modeling scheduling and routing problems. In this section, logical sorting models and their variants are illustrated.

Sorting with 3 Tuples of Variables

Integer Sorting

A tuple of n integers $(z_1, ..., z_n)$ is an ascending sorting of $(y_1, ..., y_n)$, with $(x_1, ..., x_n)$ being order variables for $(y_1, ..., y_n)$ to be permuted to $(z_1, ..., z_n)$.

$$\forall\ i \in [1, n]\ ($$
$$\quad x_i \in [1, n],$$
$$\quad y_i = z_{x_i}$$
$$),$$

$$\forall\ i < j \in [1, n]\ ($$
$$\quad x_i \neq x_j,$$
$$\quad z_i \leq z_j$$
$$),$$

The integer sorting model is illustrated in Figure 6.1. The tuple z of 5 integers: $(1,\ 3,\ 5,\ 8,\ 9)$ is an ascending sorting of y: $(8,\ 5,\ 9,\ 3,\ 1)$. Here x: $(4,\ 3,\ 5,\ 2,\ 1)$ is the tuple indicating the order for y to be permuted to z in accordance with the integer sorting relation.

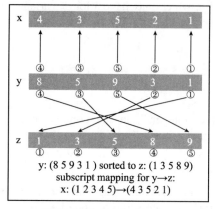

y: (8 5 9 3 1) sorted to z: (1 3 5 8 9)
subscript mapping for y→z:
x: (1 2 3 4 5)→(4 3 5 2 1)

Figure 6.1 Integer Sorting

Set Sorting

A tuple of n sets $(B_1, ..., B_n)$ is an ascending sorting of $(A_1, ..., A_n)$, with $(x_1, ..., x_n)$ being the order variables for $(A_1, ..., A_n)$ to be permuted to $(B_1, ..., B_n)$.

$$\forall\ i \in [1, n]\ ($$
$$\quad x_i \in [1, n],$$
$$\quad A_i = B_{x_i}$$
$$),$$

$\forall\, i < j \in [1, n]\, ($

$\qquad x_i \neq x_j,$

$\qquad B_i \prec B_j$

$),$

The set sorting model is illustrated in Figure 6.2.

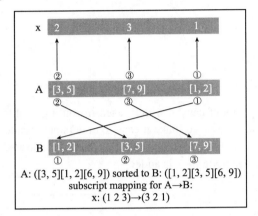

Figure 6.2 Set Sorting With 3 Tuples of Variables

The tuple B of 3 sets: $([1, 2]\ [3, 5]\ [7, 9])$ is an ascending sorting of A: $([3, 5]\ [7, 9]\ [1, 2])$. Here x: $(2, 3, 1)$ is the tuple indicating the order for A to be permuted to B in accordance with the set sorting relation. See the solving of the Job-shop Scheduling problem in this chapter for an explanatory note.

Sorting with 2 Tuples of Variables

Integer Sorting

A tuple of n integers $(z_1, ..., z_n)$ is sorted in an ascending order by successor indicators $(x_1, ..., x_{n-1})$. To facilitate the presentation, 1 is fixed as the entry and n is fixed as the exit for the chain of the successor indicators.

$\forall\, i \in [1, n-1]\, ($

$\qquad x_i \in [2, n],$

$\qquad z_i \leq z_{x_i}$

$),$

$\forall\, i \neq j \in [1, n-1]$

$\qquad x_i \neq x_j,$

This Integer Sorting model can be used to model the precedence relation in Production Scheduling problems.

Set Sorting

A tuple of n sets $(B_1, ..., B_n)$ is sorted in an ascending order by successor indicators $(x_1, ..., x_{n-1})$. To facilitate the presentation, 1 is fixed as the entry and n is fixed as the exit for the chain of the successor indicators.

$$\forall\ i \in [1, n-1]\ ($$
$$\quad x_i \in [2, n],$$
$$\quad B_i \prec B_{x_i}$$
$$),$$
$$\forall\ i \neq j \in [1,\ n-1]$$
$$\quad x_i \neq x_j,$$

This Set Sorting model can be widely used in routing problems (e.g., Pick-up and Delivery) (Zhou 2009). To make it easy to understand, readers can regard 1 as the source and n+1 as the sink for the routing model illustrated in Figure 6.3, in which case a fictitious node n+1 is added.

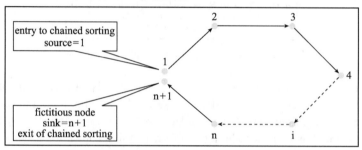

Figure 6.3 Set Sorting With 2 Tuples of Variables

6.2.4 Set Covering

For solving placement and assignment problems, constraints related to "set covering" are frequently used. For example, "C is the union of sets $A_1, ..., A_n$" can be expressed mathematically as below:

$$C = \bigcup_{i \in [1, n]} A_i,$$

Set Partitioning

If $A_1, ..., A_n$ are disjoint sets, then $(A_1, ..., A_n)$ is a partition of C, that is:

$$C = \bigcup_{i \in [1, n]} A_i,$$
$$\forall\ i \neq j \in [1, n]$$
$$\quad A_i \cap A_j = \emptyset,$$

Interval Sequence

A special case of set partition is the partition with a sequence of intervals. That is,

it segments the elements of a set into a sequence of separated intervals and the
gaps between the intervals are all greater than 0.

```
n = #C,
∀ i ∈ [1, n] (
        Bᵢ = [xᵢ, yᵢ],
        Bᵢ ⊂ C,
),

w ∈ [0, n],
∀ i ∈ [1, w]
        Bᵢ ≠ ∅,

C = ∪ᵢ∈[1, w]Bᵢ,

∀ i < j ∈ [1, n]
        Bᵢ ≺ Bⱼ,

∀ i ∈ [1, n - 1]
        (xᵢ₊₁ - yᵢ) > 1,
```

For example, the model of interval sequence (Figure 6.4) can be used in the
Personnel Planning problem (see Chapter 7) to formulate complex constraints
such as maximum number of consecutive working days, minimum number of rest
days, etc. In Chapter 8, interval sequence model is used to decompose and group
jobs for solving large-scale Production Scheduling problems.

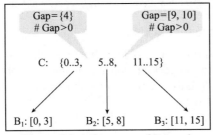

Figure 6.4 A Sequence of Intervals

6.2.5 Packing

Packing with Integers

```
∀ i ≠ j ∈ [1, n]
        xᵢ ≠ xⱼ ∨ yᵢ ≠ yⱼ,
```

Packing with Sets

```
∀ i ≠ j ∈ [1, n]
        Bᵢ ∩ Bⱼ = ∅ ∨ Cᵢ ∩ Cⱼ = ∅,
```

Packing with Integers and Sets

$$\forall \, i \neq j \in [1, n]$$
$$x_i \neq x_j \ \lor \ C_i \cap C_j = \varnothing,$$

The above packing models and their variants occur in a lot of combinatorial problems such as Square Packing, Progressive Party and Ship Loading problems in this Chapter.

Examples of packing with set variables can be found in the models of Square Packing and Ship Loading problems.

More practically, packing of integers and sets is the kernel model that usually dominates the Production Scheduling problem (see Chapter 7). The abstract model in Figure 6.5 uses dates/times as the abscissa axis and resources as the ordinate axis of a Gantt chart: integer variable x_i represents the resource taken by task i and set variable C_i represents the date/time interval of task i.

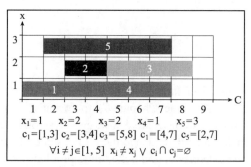

Figure 6.5 Packing with Integers and Sets

2-Dimensional Capacity for Packing

A scarce resource allocation problem involves the 2-dimensional capacity constraint in addition to the packing constraint; see the problem of Ship Loading. For example, the constraint of capacity in 2 dimensions for a set packing model can be expressed as below:

$$\forall \, i \in [1, n] \ ($$
$$A_i \subset D_1,$$
$$B_i \subset D_2,$$
$$\#A_i \times \#B_i = d_i$$
$$),$$

$$\forall \, i \neq j \in [1, n]$$
$$A_i \cap A_j = \varnothing \ \lor \ B_i \cap B_j = \varnothing,$$

D_1 and D_2 represent sets of scarce resources. The multiplication $\#A_i \times \#B_i$ represents the capacity of packing for the set variables A_i and B_i.

6.2.6 Sum

The *Sum* relation is a general constraint that occurs in many constraint satisfaction problems. Over domains of real numbers, integers, and Booleans, the concept of sum makes a significant sense. They are especially useful in the formulation of optimization objectives; see for example Set Partitioning and Pick-up and Delivery problems in this chapter.

Sum of Real Numbers

$$f = \sum_{i \in A} g_i,$$

Sum of Integers

$$y = \sum_{i \in A} x_i,$$

Sum of Booleans

$$y = \sum_{i \in A} a_i,$$

The relation of *Sum of Booleans* is a bit special. The definition domain is mapped from {false, true} to {0, 1} so that the sum makes sense.

Increment

$$\forall\, i \in [1, n-1]\,($$
$$\quad x_i \in [2, n],$$
$$\quad z_{x_i} = z_i + w_{x_i}$$
$$),$$

When a sum relation is formulated in the form of successive addition, it is an *increment* relation. The *Increment* model can be used in routing problems for modeling the incremental load constraints (see the Pick-up and Delivery problem in this chapter).

6.2.7 Cumulation

The cumulation model states that, for any i taken from set D, the number of its occurrences in the sets C_j's (for all j in A) equals y_i:

$$\forall\, i \in D$$
$$\quad y_i = \sum_{j \in A} (i \in C_j),$$

There can be a lot of variants for the cumulation model. In general, weights (w_j) can be associated to the arguments in the sum function:

$$\forall\, i \in D$$
$$\quad y_i = \sum_{j \in A} (i \in C_j) \times w_j,$$

A related work is the global cumulative constraint (Aggoun and Beldiceanu 1993). Such constraints often occur in Personnel Planning problems (see Chapter 7).

For creating compact models, the cumulation relation requires sets $C_1, ..., C_n$ to be intervals. Space complexity of the model requires special attention. The modeling precision for set D must be carefully studied to ensure that memory can be sufficient for running the model.

Let's use an example to explain the above formulation. If A represents the set of employees, and D is a time slot, and C_j represents the working time interval of employee j, and y_i represents the number of persons working at time i, then the above constraint states that the number of employees of A working at any time i of the time slot D should equal to y_i. Figure 6.6 illustrates the cumulation relation.

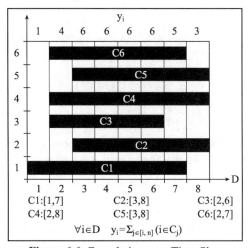

Figure 6.6 Cumulation over Time Slots

A special case of cumulation is the global cardinality constraint (Régin 1996): When for all j in A each C_j is a singleton, the cumulation model can be simplified as:

$$\forall \ i \in D$$
$$y_i = \Sigma_{j \in A} (x_j = i) ,$$

6.3 Solving Puzzles

6.3.1 Send More Money

This is a classic cryptarithmetic puzzle (Dudeney 1924). It requires finding out the values for the letters of words SEND, MORE and MONEY so that:

- SEND + MORE = MONEY;
- All letters take different values.

Program:
```
SENDMORY = {`S`,`E`,`N`,`D`,`M`,`O`,`R`,`Y`},

∀ `i` ∈ SENDMORY
    i ∈ [0,9],
```

```
∀ `i` ≠ `j` ∈ SENDMORY
   i ≠ j,
                    S × 1000 + E × 100 + N × 10 + D
                  + M × 1000 + O × 100 + R × 10 + E
   = M × 10000 + O × 1000 + N × 100 + E × 10 + Y,


S ≠ 0,
M ≠ 0,


∀ `i` ∈ SENDMORY
   i = ?,

@ ("SEND    = " S E N D    "\n"),
@ ("MORE    = " M O R E    "\n"),
@ ("MONEY   = " M O N E Y  "\n\n").
```

A solution given by NCL is:
```
SEND    = 9567
MORE    = 1085
MONEY   = 10652
```

6.3.2 Primes

The Primes problem requires calculating all the primes contained in [2,n] for a given integer n.

This book does not encourage user to solve the Primes problem using NCL; the proposed solution is not efficient. However, this is an excellent example to illustrate the concept of descriptive modeling, which is different from a procedural method.

Program:
```
Prime ⊂ [2, 100],


∀ i ≤ j ∈ [2, 100 ÷ 2]
   (i × j) ∉ Prime,


@("Primes = " ‾Prime‾).
```

The set of primes is defined as a set of numbers that cannot be the result of the multiplication of any 2 integers which are different from 1. In the above model, Prime is a set variable. Prime being subset of [2,100], it is sufficient to state that no composite number can be in Prime. Thus with all composite numbers eliminated from Prime, the rest ($\overline{\text{Prime}}$) is the set of primes.

A solution given by NCL is:
```
Primes =
{2..3,5,7,11,13,17,19,23,29,31,37,41,43,47,53,59,61,67,71,73,79,83,89,97}
```

6.3.3 Integer Sorting

The Integer Sorting problem requires sorting a sequence of integers. The model of integer sorting with 2 tuples of variables is used to sort $(x_1, ..., x_n)$ in an ascending order. Here it is assumed that for the successor indicators 1 is the entry and that n+1 is the exit. This restricts that the first input takes the minimum value.

Program:

```
n = 5,
∀ i ∈ [1, n]
  xᵢ = 0,

∀ i ∈ [1, n] (
  nextᵢ ∈ [2, n+1],

  xᵢ < x_nextᵢ,
),

∀ i ≠ j ∈ [1, n]
  nextᵢ ≠ nextⱼ,

∀ i ∈ [1, n]
  @(nextᵢ "\t").
```

The model introduces a successor variable $next_i$, the domain of which is $[2, n+1]$.

For example, with input data:

1	3	5	4	2

A solution given by NCL is:

5	4	6	3	2

6.3.4 Queens

This well known problem consists in placing n queens on an n × n chessboard so that the queens do not attack each other.

Program:

```
n = 16,

∀ i ≠ j ∈ [1, n]  xᵢ      ≠ xⱼ,

∀ i ≠ j ∈ [1, n]  xᵢ - i ≠ xⱼ - j,

∀ i ≠ j ∈ [1, n]  xᵢ + i ≠ xⱼ + j,

∀ i ∈ [1, n] → (min    # Δ xᵢ) (

  xᵢ ∈ [1, n],

  xᵢ = ? (→)
).
```

Because there are n queens, n rows and n columns, each queen must have its own row and its own column. So x_i is introduced to represent the row of the queen on column i. The constraint "the queens do not attack each other" requires that there is at most one queen on each row, at most one on each column and at most one on each diagonal. These constraints are formulated by the following relations:

$\forall \; i \ne j \in [1, n] \; x_i \ne x_j,$

% no two queens on a same row

$\forall \; i \ne j \in [1, n] \; x_i-i \ne x_j-j,$

% no two queens on a same diagonal from left-bottom to right-top

$\forall \; i \ne j \in [1, n] \; x_i+i \ne x_j+j,$

% no two queens on a same diagonal from right-bottom to left-top

The search strategy is simple: NCL selects a queen on column i for which the fewest candidate rows are available; next, the solver adopts lower-bound first bound enumeration on variable x_i, which is in fact the default enumeration mode for integer variables.

A solution is given in Figure 6.7.

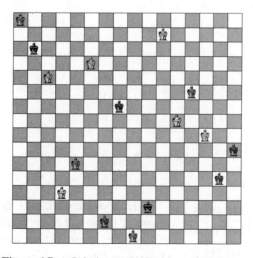

Figure 6.7 A Solution to the Problem of 16 Queens

6.3.5 Magic Square

The problem consists in filling distinct integers in an n × n big square so that the sums of all rows, columns and diagonals are equal (Andrews 1960).

Program:

```
n = 7,
m = ((n × n + 1) × n) / 2,
```

$\forall$ i,j $\in$ [1, n]

   $x_{i,j}$ $\in$ [1, n $\times$ n],

$\forall$ `i` $\neq$ `j` $\in$ {$\forall$i,j $\in$ [1, n]`$x_{i,j}$`}

   i $\neq$ j,

$\forall$ i $\in$ [1, n] (

   m = $\Sigma_{j \in [1, n]}$ $x_{i,j}$,

   m = $\Sigma_{j \in [1, n]}$ $x_{j,i}$

),

m = $\Sigma_{i \in [1, n]}$ $x_{i,i}$,

m = $\Sigma_{i \in [1, n]}$ $x_{i, n-i+1}$,

$x_{1,1}$ < $x_{1,n}$,   % (1)

$x_{1,n}$ < $x_{n,1}$,   % (2)

$x_{1,1}$ < $x_{n,n}$,   % (3)

l = (n + 1)/2,

$x_{1,1}$ = ?($\Rightarrow$),

$\forall$ i $\in$ [1, n] $\rightarrow$ (min   # Δ $x_{i,i}$)

   $x_{i,i}$ = ?($\Rightarrow$),

$\forall$ i $\in$ [1, n] $\rightarrow$ (min   # Δ $x_{i, n-i+1}$)

   $x_{i,n-i+1}$ = ?($\Rightarrow$),

$\forall$ i,j $\in$ [1, n] $\rightarrow$ (min   # Δ $x_{i,j}$)

   $x_{i,j}$ = ?($\Rightarrow$).

2	6	37	41	42	43	4
28	3	31	39	29	5	40
21	33	25	32	30	19	15
34	38	20	1	11	35	36
18	23	44	16	47	13	14
26	45	8	24	7	48	17
46	27	10	22	9	12	49

Figure 6.8 A solution to a Magic Square Instance

In the above model, n is the width of the big square, l is the half of the width and m is the sum of a row. $x_{i,j}$ are distinct integers ranging over [1, n×n] and the sum of any row, any column and any diagonal is m. Note also that in the model, the constraints (1), (2) and (3) are used to eliminate symmetric solutions.

The query criterion respects the least-slack principle. The enumeration mode is the lower-part-first binary-domain splitting. The $x_{i,j}$ variables for both diagonals are instantiated first.

A solution is given in Figure 6.8.

6.3.6 Sudoku

Sudoku is a combinatorial number-placement puzzle (Smith 2005). The problem requires filling in a 9×9 grid with digits so that each column, each row, and each of the nine 3×3 sub-grids that compose the grid contains distinct digits from 1 to 9. An additional constraint is that the digits already filled in the grid should be fixed (Figure 6.9).

	2	8	4	7	6	3		
			8	3	9		2	
7			5	1	2		8	
		1	7	9			4	
3								
		9				1		
	5			8				
		6	9	2				5
		2	6	4	5			8

Figure 6.9 A Sudoku Instance

Problem:
```
nbDigit = 9,
DIGIT = [1, nbDigit],

∀ i,j ∈ DIGIT(
    digit_{i,j} ∈ DIGIT,

    given_{i,j} = 0,
    given_{i,j} > 0 ⇒ digit_{i,j} = given_{i,j}
),

∀ i ∈ DIGIT
∀ j ≠ k ∈ DIGIT(
    digit_{i,j} ≠ digit_{i,k},
    digit_{j,i} ≠ digit_{k,i}
),

∀ i ∈ DIGIT(
    RefDigit_i = {∀j ∈ DIGIT
        `digit`_{((i-1)÷3)×3+(j-1)÷3+1, ((i-1)mod 3)×3+(j-1)mod 3+1}
    },

    ∀ `j` ≠ `k` ∈ RefDigit_i
        j ≠ k
),
```

```
∀ i,j ∈ DIGIT → (
    min     # Δ digit_{i,j},
    max     digit_{i,j},
)
digit_{i,j} = ?.
```

DIGIT is the set of the digits from 1 to 9. The constant $given_{i,j}$ represents the digit already fixed at (i,j) if its value is greater than 0. The objective is to fill in those cells where $given_{i,j} = 0$. The program introduces digit variable $digit_{i,j}$ to represent the unknown digit.

The numbers filled in each row and those in each column are distinct:

```
∀ i ∈ DIGIT
∀ j ≠ k ∈ DIGIT (
    digit_{i,j} ≠ digit_{i,k},
    digit_{j,i} ≠ digit_{k,i}
),
```

From top to bottom and from left to right, the 9×9 grid is decomposed to nine 3×3 sub-grids; every 3×3 sub-grid is numbered from 1 to 9. The references (`digit_{j,k}`) to the digit variables $digit_{j,k}$ in each sub-grid i are collected in the reference set $RefDigit_i$:

```
∀ i ∈ DIGIT
RefDigit_i = {∀ j ∈ DIGIT
    `digit_{((i-1)÷3)×3+(j-1)÷3+1, ((i-1) mod 3)×3+(j-1) mod 3+1}`
},
```

Distinct digits are filled in each sub-grid:

```
∀ i ∈ DIGIT
∀ `j` ≠ `k` ∈ RefDigit_i
    j ≠ k,
```

The search strategy is: first, select a column and a row in the lexicographic order of (fewest candidate digits, maximum lower bound of the candidate digits); next, enumerate the variable $digit_{i,j}$ with the default integer enumeration mode.

A solution is given in Figure 6.10.

9	2	8	4	7	6	3	5	1
5	1	4	8	3	9	6	2	7
7	6	3	5	1	2	9	8	4
2	8	1	7	9	3	5	4	6
3	7	5	1	6	4	8	9	2
6	4	9	2	5	8	1	7	3
4	5	7	3	8	1	2	6	9
8	3	6	9	2	7	4	1	5
1	9	2	6	4	5	7	3	8

Figure 6.10 A Solution to the Sudoku Instance

6.3.7 Magic Sequence

Given integer n, the Magic Sequence problem consists in finding all sequences of the form $(x_0, \ldots, x_{n-1})$ such that each x_i is the number of occurrences of i (Colmerauer 1990).

Program:

n = 10,

$\forall \ i \in [0, \ n-1] ($

   $x_i \geq 0$,

   $x_i = \Sigma_{j \in [0, n-1]} (x_j = i)$

),

n = $\Sigma_{i \in [0, n-1]} \ x_i$,   % (1)

n = $\Sigma_{i \in [0, n-1]} \ x_i \times i$,   % (2)

$\forall \ i \in [0, \ n-1] \rightarrow (\max \quad \# \Delta x_i)$

   $x_i = ? (\Rightarrow)$.

Two redundant constraints (1) and (2) are added so as to solve the problem faster. Though logically redundant, they are useful in cutting the solution space.

The query criterion is to select an integer variable x_i in accordance with the greatest-slack principle. The enumeration mode is binary-domain-splitting and lower-part-first.

When n = 10, a solution given by NCL is:

$x_0 = 6$	$x_1 = 2$	$x_2 = 1$	$x_3 = 0$	$x_4 = 0$	$x_5 = 0$
$x_6 = 1$	$x_7 = 0$	$x_8 = 0$	$x_9 = 0$		

6.3.8 Einstein's Quiz

There are 5 houses in 5 different colors. In each house lives a person with a different nationality. These 5 owners drink a certain beverage, smoke a certain brand of cigar and keep a certain pet. No owners have the same pet, smoke the same brand of cigar or drink the same drink. In addition, the following constraints must be respected:

- The British lives in the red house
- The Swede keeps dogs as pets
- The Dane drinks tea
- The green house is on the left of the white house
- The green homeowner drinks coffee
- The person who smokes Pall Mall keeps birds
- The owner of the yellow house smokes Dunhill
- The man living in the center house drinks milk
- The Norwegian lives in the first house
- The man who smokes Blend lives next to the one who keeps cats

- The man who keeps the horse lives next to the man who smokes Dunhill
- The owner who smokes Bluemaster drinks beer
- The German smokes prince
- The Norwegian lives next to the blue house
- The man who smokes Blend has a neighbor who drinks water

The question is: Who owns the fish?

Program:

```
IDENTITY = [1, 5],

COLOR = {`white`,`green`,`blue`,`red`,`yellow` },
NATIONALITY =
   {`British`,`Swede`,`Dane`,`Norwegian`,`German`},
DRINK = {`tea`,`water`,`milk`,`beer`, `coffee` },
CIGAR = {`PallMall`,`Dunhill`,`Blend`,`Bluemaster`,`Prince`},
PET = {`fish`,`cat`,`dog`,`bird`,`horse`},

∀ `i` ∈ COLOR ∪ NATIONALITY ∪ DRINK ∪ CIGAR ∪ PET
   i ∈ IDENTITY,

∀ `i` ≠ `j` ∈ COLOR        i ≠ j,
∀ `i` ≠ `j` ∈ NATIONALITY  i ≠ j,
∀ `i` ≠ `j` ∈ DRINK        i ≠ j,
∀ `i` ≠ `j` ∈ CIGAR        i ≠ j,
∀ `i` ≠ `j` ∈ PET          i ≠ j,

British = red,
Swede = dog,
Dane = tea,
green = white-1,
green = coffee,
PallMall = bird,
yellow = Dunhill,
milk = 3,
Norwegian = 1,
|Blend-cat| = 1,
|horse-Dunhill| = 1,
Bluemaster = beer,
German = Prince,
|Norwegian-blue| = 1,
|Blend-water| = 1,

∃ `someone` ∈ NATIONALITY(
   someone = fish,
   @(`someone` "owns the fish")
).
```

An abstract set of identities is labeled by IDENTITY = [1, 5]. The program identifies the 5 houses by numbers ranging over IDENTITY. To each house 5 set constants and the corresponding integer variables referenced in the sets are introduced as below:

- COLOR: white, green, blue, red, yellow
- NATIONALITY: British, Swede, Dane, Norwegian, German
- DRINK: tea, water, milk, beer, coffer
- CIGAR: PallMall, Dunhill, Blend, Bluemaster, Prince
- PET: fish, cat, dog, bird, horse

The reference set constants COLOR, NATIONALITY, DRINK, CIGAR, PET represent respectively the sets of colors, nationalities, drinks, cigars and pets. Each variable takes a distinct value in IDENTITY:

```
∀ `i` ≠ `j` ∈ COLOR        i ≠ j,
∀ `i` ≠ `j` ∈ NATIONALITY  i ≠ j,
∀ `i` ≠ `j` ∈ DRINK        i ≠ j,
∀ `i` ≠ `j` ∈ CIGAR        i ≠ j,
∀ `i` ≠ `j` ∈ PET          i ≠ j,
```

The following constraints must hold:

```
British = red,
Swede = dog,
Dane = tea,
green = white-1,
green = coffee,
PallMall = bird,
yellow = Dunhill,
milk = 3,
Norwegian = 1,
|Blend-cat| = 1,
|horse-Dunhill| = 1,
Bluemaster = beer,
German = Prince,
|Norwegian-blue| = 1,
|Blend-water| = 1,
```

NCL can solve this constraint system easily using query through existential quantification:

```
∃ `someone` ∈ NATIONALITY
   someone = fish,
```

A solution given by NCL is:

```
German owns the fish
```

6.3.9 Calculs d'Enfer

This problem is taken from (Stewart 1994). It requires assigning distinct integers to the 26 letters (from a to z) so that each number (from 0 to 12) equals to the sum of the letter values of its corresponding words (from zero to twelve). The objective is to minimize the maximum of the absolute values for the letters.

Program:

```
Refset = {
    `a`,`b`,`c`,`d`,`e`,`f`,`g`,`h`,`i`,`j`,`k`,`l`,`m`,
    `n`,`o`,`p`,`q`,`r`,`s`,`t`,`u`,`v`,`w`,`x`,`y`,`z`
```

```
},

∀ `i` ≠ `j` ∈ Refset
    i ≠ j,

z + e + r + o                       = 0,
o + n + e                           = 1,
t + w + o                           = 2,
t + h + r + e + e                   = 3,
f + o + u + r                       = 4,
f + i + v + e                       = 5,
s + i + x                           = 6,
s + e + v + e + n                   = 7,
e + i + g + h + t                   = 8,
n + i + n + e                       = 9,
t + e + n                           = 10,
e + l + e + v + e + n               = 11,
t + w + e + l + v + e               = 12,

min    max·ᵢˋ∈Refset |i|,

e = ?(→),  n = ?(→),  i = ?(→),  o = ?(→),  t = ?(→),

∀ `i` ∈ Refset → (min  #Δ i)(
    i ∈ [-100, 100],
    i = ?(→)
).
```

The model uses references to letters. The referencing mechanism makes it easy for a programmer to use universal quantification over variables with various names. The above model uses a reference set Refset to collect all the references to the 26 letter variables. With Refset as the domain of discourse for quantifiers, constraints of distinct integers, query criteria and optimization objectives can all be flexibly expressed.

The search strategy is: Using the least-slack principle to select a letter variable and instantiating it by lower-bound-first enumeration.

The idea is to instantiate the most constrained variables e, n, i, o, t first, then to instantiate the rest in a smallest-domain-first order.

The objective is to minimize the maximum of the absolute values of variables referenced in Refset.

A solution given by NCL is:

```
a = -13
b = -12
c = -11
d = -10
e = -5
f =  6
g = -8
```

```
h = 7
i = 4
j = -7
k = -3
l = 9
m = -2
n = 5
o = 1
p = -1
q = 3
r = -4
s = 0
t = 10
u = 13
v = 12
w = -9
x = 2
y = 6
z = 8
```
$\max_{i \in \text{Refset}} |i| = 13$

6.3.10 Square Packing

The Square Packing problem consists in placing a collection of squares with fixed dimensions into one big square (Bouwkamp and Duijvestijn 1992). A related research work can be found in (Gambini 1999).

Program:

```
d = 112,
n = 21,
∀ i ∈ [1,n] (
    sᵢ = 0,
    Xᵢ ⊂ [1, d],
    Yᵢ ⊂ [1, d],
    Xᵢ = [xᵢ, xᵢ + (sᵢ - 1)],
    Yᵢ = [yᵢ, yᵢ + (sᵢ - 1)],
),

∀ i ≠ j ∈ [1,n]
    Xᵢ ∩ Xⱼ = ∅ ∨ Yᵢ ∩ Yⱼ = ∅,

∀ i ∈ [1,n] → (min   xᵢ)
    Xᵢ = ?,
∀ i ∈ [1,n] → (min   yᵢ)
    Yᵢ = ?.
```

The sides of the small squares are given in constants s_i (data from input: 50, 42, 37, 35, 33, 29, 27, 25, 24, 19, 18, 17, 16, 15, 11, 9, 8, 7, 6, 4, 2). Because all squares do not overlap, the model uses the set packing model to express the problem. For each small square i, an interval variable X_i and an interval variable Y_i are introduced to represent the set of abscissas and the set of ordinates of square i. So two squares must have their abscissas or ordinates disjoint:

$$\forall \ i \neq j \in [1, \ n]$$
$$X_i \cap X_j = \varnothing \lor Y_i \cap Y_j = \varnothing,$$

The search strategy is: The solver searches for the abscissas of the squares by placing the biggest squares with lowest-abscissa first (because there may be less possibility) and then the solver searches for the ordinates of theses squares.

All 8 solutions are instantly found after a complete exploration of the solution space. A solution is given in Figure 6.11.

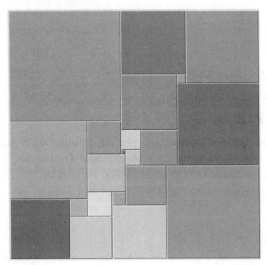

Figure 6.11 A Solution to the Square Packing Problem

6.3.11 Knight

The knight has to visit once and only once all squares of an n × n chessboard and it returns to its starting point, forming a Hamiltonian circuit (Conrad et al. 1994).

Program:

```
n = 12,
nbStep = n × n,

REFSTEP = {∀ i,j ∈ [1,n] `step_i,j`},

∀ `i` ≠ `j` ∈ REFSTEP
   i ≠ j,

step_1,1 = 1,
step_2,3 = 2,
```

$$\text{step}_{3,2} = \text{nbStep},$$

$$\forall\ i,j \in [1,\ n]\ ($$

$$\quad \text{step}_{i,j} \in [1,\ \text{nbStep}],$$

$$\quad \text{EntryRef}_{i,j} = \{$$

$$\quad\quad `\text{step}_{i+1,j+2}-\text{step}_{i,j} = -1`,\quad `\text{step}_{i+1,j-2}-\text{step}_{i,j} = -1`,$$

$$\quad\quad `\text{step}_{i-1,j+2}-\text{step}_{i,j} = -1`,\quad `\text{step}_{i-1,j-2}-\text{step}_{i,j} = -1`,$$

$$\quad\quad `\text{step}_{i+2,j+1}-\text{step}_{i,j} = -1`,\quad `\text{step}_{i+2,j-1}-\text{step}_{i,j} = -1`,$$

$$\quad\quad `\text{step}_{i-2,j+1}-\text{step}_{i,j} = -1`,\quad `\text{step}_{i-2,j-1}-\text{step}_{i,j} = -1`,$$

$$\quad\quad `\text{step}_{i,j} = 1`$$

$$\quad \},$$

$$\quad \text{ExitRef}_{i,j} = \{$$

$$\quad\quad `\text{step}_{i+1,j+2}-\text{step}_{i,j} = +1`,\quad `\text{step}_{i+1,j-2}-\text{step}_{i,j} = +1`,$$

$$\quad\quad `\text{step}_{i-1,j+2}-\text{step}_{i,j} = +1`,\quad `\text{step}_{i-1,j-2}-\text{step}_{i,j} = +1`,$$

$$\quad\quad `\text{step}_{i+2,j+1}-\text{step}_{i,j} = +1`,\quad `\text{step}_{i+2,j-1}-\text{step}_{i,j} = +1`,$$

$$\quad\quad `\text{step}_{i-2,j+1}-\text{step}_{i,j} = +1`,\quad `\text{step}_{i-2,j-1}-\text{step}_{i,j} = +1`,$$

$$\quad\quad `\text{step}_{i,j} = \text{nbStep}`$$

$$\quad \},$$

$$\quad \Sigma`k` \in \text{EntryRef}_{i,j}\ k = 1,$$

$$\quad \Sigma`k` \in \text{ExitRef}_{i,j}\ k = 1,$$

$$),$$

$$\forall\ i,j \in [1,\ n]\ \to\ ($$

$$\quad \min\ \underline{\text{step}_{i,j}}$$

$$)$$

$$\text{step}_{i,j} = ?(\to).$$

The idea is to introduce an integer variable $\text{step}_{i,j}$ corresponding to the order of knight's visit on column i and row j of the $n\times n$ chessboard. The model introduces a reference set REFSTEP which contains the references to step variables. The step variables take values in $[1, n\times n]$ and respect the constraint of "distinct integers":

$$\forall\ `i` \neq `j` \in \text{REFSTEP}$$

$$\quad i \neq j,$$

Logical pointers (references) are useful for expressing the chaining of knight's steps on the chessboard. Considering that at each square (i,j) the knight has only one entry step and one exit step, 8 possible neighboring steps at (i,j) are:

$$(i + 1, j + 2) \quad (i - 1, j + 2) \quad (i + 2, j + 1) \quad (i - 2, j + 1)$$
$$(i + 1, j - 2) \quad (i - 1, j - 2) \quad (i + 2, j - 1) \quad (i - 2, j - 1)$$

In accordance with the above idea, data modeling can be done as follows:

- Entry constraints: Whether a neighboring step is an entry is judged by whether the difference between $\text{step}_{i,j}$ and its neighboring step is -1. The constraints over entries are expressed as:

$$\text{step}_{i+1,j+2} - \text{step}_{i,j} = -1, \quad \text{step}_{i+1,j-2} - \text{step}_{i,j} = -1,$$
$$\text{step}_{i-1,j+2} - \text{step}_{i,j} = -1, \quad \text{step}_{i-1,j-2} - \text{step}_{i,j} = -1,$$
$$\text{step}_{i+2,j+1} - \text{step}_{i,j} = -1, \quad \text{step}_{i+2,j-1} - \text{step}_{i,j} = -1,$$
$$\text{step}_{i-2,j+1} - \text{step}_{i,j} = -1, \quad \text{step}_{i-2,j-1} - \text{step}_{i,j} = -1,$$

- Exit constraints: Whether a neighboring step is an exit is judged by whether the difference between $\text{step}_{i,j}$ and its neighboring step is $+1$. The constraints over exits are expressed as:

$$\text{step}_{i+1,j+2} - \text{step}_{i,j} = +1, \quad \text{step}_{i+1,j-2} - \text{step}_{i,j} = +1,$$
$$\text{step}_{i-1,j+2} - \text{step}_{i,j} = +1, \quad \text{step}_{i-1,j-2} - \text{step}_{i,j} = +1,$$
$$\text{step}_{i+2,j+1} - \text{step}_{i,j} = +1, \quad \text{step}_{i+2,j-1} - \text{step}_{i,j} = +1,$$
$$\text{step}_{i-2,j+1} - \text{step}_{i,j} = +1, \quad \text{step}_{i-2,j-1} - \text{step}_{i,j} = +1,$$

- For the first and last steps of a knight tour, their constraints are represented by the following Boolean expressions:

$$\text{step}_{i,j} = 1, \quad \text{step}_{i,j} = \text{nbStep},$$

Up to now, for a square (i, j) the set $\text{EntryRef}_{i,j}$ is introduced to collect the references of entry constraints:

$$\text{EntryRef}_{i,j} = \{$$
$$`\text{step}_{i+1,j+2} - \text{step}_{i,j} = -1`, \quad `\text{step}_{i+1,j-2} - \text{step}_{i,j} = -1`,$$
$$`\text{step}_{i-1,j+2} - \text{step}_{i,j} = -1`, \quad `\text{step}_{i-1,j-2} - \text{step}_{i,j} = -1`,$$
$$`\text{step}_{i+2,j+1} - \text{step}_{i,j} = -1`, \quad `\text{step}_{i+2,j-1} - \text{step}_{i,j} = -1`,$$
$$`\text{step}_{i-2,j+1} - \text{step}_{i,j} = -1`, \quad `\text{step}_{i-2,j-1} - \text{step}_{i,j} = -1`,$$
$$`\text{step}_{i,j} = 1`$$
$$\},$$

Similarly, for a square (i, j) the set $\text{ExitRef}_{i,j}$ is introduced to collect the references of exit constraints:

$$\text{ExitRef}_{i,j} = \{$$
$$`\text{step}_{i+1,j+2} - \text{step}_{i,j} = +1`, \quad `\text{step}_{i+1,j-2} - \text{step}_{i,j} = +1`,$$
$$`\text{step}_{i-1,j+2} - \text{step}_{i,j} = +1`, \quad `\text{step}_{i-1,j-2} - \text{step}_{i,j} = +1`,$$
$$`\text{step}_{i+2,j+1} - \text{step}_{i,j} = +1`, \quad `\text{step}_{i+2,j-1} - \text{step}_{i,j} = +1`,$$
$$`\text{step}_{i-2,j+1} - \text{step}_{i,j} = +1`, \quad `\text{step}_{i-2,j-1} - \text{step}_{i,j} = +1`,$$
$$`\text{step}_{i,j} = \text{nbStep}`$$
$$\},$$

$\text{EntryRef}_{i,j}$ and $\text{ExitRef}_{i,j}$ are defined to manage the links between steps:

- Except for the starting square, at each square there is only one entry step:
$$\sum{}^{\backslash}k^{\backslash}{}_{\in EntryRef_{i,j}} k = 1$$

- Except for the ending square, at each square there is only one exit step:
$$\sum{}^{\backslash}k^{\backslash}{}_{\in ExitRef_{i,j}} k = 1$$

Note that a variable will be invalid if any of its subscripts leaks from its range and a reference over an invalid variable will be an empty pointer. Since NCL protects against subscript leak, user does not need to care about the bound of the chessboard. A variable $step_{i,j}$ is simply considered invalid and its reference `$step_{i,j}$` is an empty reference if subscript i or subscript j is out of range.

For example:
$EntryRef_{1,8} = \{$

    `$step_{1+1,8+2}-step_{1,8} = -1$`,   `$step_{1+1,8-2}-step_{1,8} = -1$`,

    `$step_{1-1,8+2}-step_{1,8} = -1$`,   `$step_{1-1,8-2}-step_{1,8} = -1$`,

    `$step_{1+2,8+1}-step_{1,8} = -1$`,   `$step_{1+2,8-1}-step_{1,8} = -1$`,

    `$step_{1-2,8+1}-step_{1,8} = -1$`,   `$step_{1-2,8-1}-step_{1,8} = -1$`,

    `$step_{1,8} = 1$`

$\}$

becomes in fact:
$EntryRef_{1,8} = \{$

    `F`,

    `$step_{1+1,8-2}-step_{1,8} = -1$`,

    `$step_{1+2,8-1}-step_{1,8} = -1$`,

    `$step_{1,8} = 1$`

$\}$

Thus in the reasoning the validity of knight's steps is not a problem.

For the search strategy, the query criterion of sequential search is used. The NCL engine always enumerates a step variable whose lower bound is the minimal among others. The instantiation is lower-bound-first enumeration.

A solution by NCL is given in Figure 6.12.

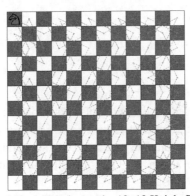

Figure 6.12 A Solution to the 12×12 Knight Problem

6.4 Solving Hard Problems

The models presented in this section are for tutorial purposes. Due to consideration of scalability, methods such as decomposition and relaxation are often employed to tackle industrial problems. In practice, NCL is not only a solver but also a computer language to program the solving of complex problems. See Chapter 8 for practical programming techniques in NCL.

6.4.1 Set Partitioning

The Set Partitioning problem requires selecting some subsets to form a partition for a given set. The test bed for this problem is cited from (Hoffman and Padberg 1993). Its NCL program is:

```
nbTask  = 0,      % number of tasks
nbShift = 0,      % number of shifts

TASK        = [1, nbTask],
SHIFT       = [1, nbShift],
∀ i ∈ SHIFT (
   costShift_i = 0,             % cost of shift i
   TaskShift_i = 0,             % set of tasks of shift i
),

Partition ⊂ SHIFT,

∪_{i∈Partition} TaskShift_i = TASK,    % set partitioning constraint

∀ i ≠ j ∈ Partition
   TaskShift_i ∩ TaskShift_j = ∅,


∀ i ∈ SHIFT → (
   min    inf TaskShift_i,       % sequential search

   min    costShift_i,           % greedy search

   max    #TaskShift_i,

)
i ∈ Partition?,

min    Σ_{i∈Partition} costShift_i.
```

Here $nbTask$ represents the number of tasks; $nbShift$ represents the number of shifts. For each shift i, a set of tasks $TaskShift_i$ and its cost $costShift_i$ are given. NCL needs to compute Partition (set variable) which is a subset of SHIFT such that the union of tasks of all shifts indexed by elements of Partition equals to TASK.

The query aims to decide whether a shift should be selected.

Three criteria are used in the lexicographic order of (least task index, minimum cost, biggest shift). The criterion (min   inf TaskShift$_i$) selects a shift i with the least task index; the criterion (min   costShift$_i$) selects a shift i with the minimum cost; the criterion (max   #TaskShift$_i$) selects a shift i with the greatest number of tasks.

The query "i∈Partition?" triggers the branching: first, try to assign shift i to Partition; next, try the inverse logic.

The objective is to minimize the total cost of all the shifts in Partition:

$$\Sigma_{i \in Partition} costShift_i$$

On this problem, NCL's computation results are interesting: Without any problem-specific pre-processing or symmetry breaking, a subset of the problems (Hoffman and Padberg 1993) can be solved completely (with proof of optimality). Solutions are:

nw19: $\Sigma_{i \in Partition} cost_i = 10898$

    Partition = {62, 134, 484, 942, 1543, 2126, 2699}

nw09: $\Sigma_{i \in Partition} cost_i = 67760$

    Partition = {3, 10, 18, 27, 42, 108, 210, 424, 810, 1217, 1306,1929,2170, 2581, 2651, 2904}

nw06: $\Sigma_{i \in Partition} cost_i = 7810$

    Partition = {4, 136, 200, 421, 874, 1538, 2901, 3845}

nw07: $\Sigma_{i \in Partition} cost_i = 5476$

    Partition = {23, 88, 591, 1943, 3017, 5150}

nw11: $\Sigma_{i \in Partition} cost_i = 116256$

    Partition = {9, 52, 135, 221, 333..334, 368, 2414, 2960, 3638,4077, 6286, 6940, 7380, 7511, 8438, 8696, 8753, 8819}

What merits attention is that data format of (Hoffman and Padberg 1993) is tailored for linear solvers. In practice, data modeling can be refit to NCL for better solving the problem.

6.4.2 Golf Tournament

The Golf Tournament problem states that in a golfer club, there are 32 social golfers each of whom play golf once a week and always in groups of 4. The club coordinator would like to generate a schedule for these golfers, to last as many weeks as possible, such that no golfer plays in the same group with any other golfer on more than one occasion (Harvey and Winterer 2005).

The NCL program is:

```
nbWeek     = 9,
nbPlayer   = 32,
sizeTeam   = 4,
nbTeam     = nbPlayer ÷ sizeTeam,
PLAYER     = [1, nbPlayer],
WEEK       = [1, nbWeek],
```

```
TEAM      = [1, nbTeam],

nbActiveWeek ∈ WEEK,
ACTIVEWEEK = [1, nbActiveWeek],

∀ i ∈ WEEK (
  ∀ j ∈ TEAM (
    PlayerTeamWeek_{i,j} ⊂ PLAYER,

    #PlayerTeamWeek_{i,j} = sizeTeam,

  ),
  RefTeamWeek_i = {∀ j ∈ TEAM `PlayerTeamWeek_{i,j}`},
),

∀ i ∈ ACTIVEWEEK (
  ∀ `j` ≠ `k` ∈ RefTeamWeek_i

    j ∩ k = ∅,

  ∪`k`∈RefTeamWeek_i k = PLAYER,      % each golfer once a week
),

REFTEAM = {∀ i ∈ WEEK, j ∈ TEAM `PlayerTeamWeek_{i,j}`},

PLAYER = ∪`i`∈REFTEAM i,  % set covering constraint over players

∀ `i` ≠ `k` ∈ REFTEAM
  #(i ∩ k) ≤ 1,
               % every 2 foursomes have at most 1 common player

∀ i ∈ TEAM                  % fix the foursomes of first week
  PlayerTeamWeek_{1,i} = [(i-1)×sizeTeam+1, i×sizeTeam],

nbActiveWeek = ?, % first query on number of weeks to plan

∀ k ∈ PLAYER → (
  min   k,                     % one player after another
)
∀ i ∈ ACTIVEWEEK
∀ j ∈ TEAM → (
  min   #Δ PlayerTeamWeek_{i,j},   % least slack

)
k ∈ PlayerTeamWeek_{i,j} ?,

max   nbActiveWeek.
```

This example illustrates the use of set programming for a sports scheduling problem. For each week i, the program introduces $PlayerTeamWeek_{i,j}$ to place golfers to each team j, its corresponding set reference is $RefTeamWeek_j$. Integer variable $nbActiveWeek$ and set variable $ACTIVEWEEK$ respectively represent the number of active weeks and the set of active weeks to be planned. For an active week i, each golfer plays once. This constraint can be formulated by set partitioning:

$\forall\ i\ \in\ ACTIVEWEEK\ ($
  $\forall\ `j`\ \neq\ `k`\ \in\ RefTeamWeek_i$
    $j \cap k = \varnothing,$

  $\cup_{`k`\in RefTeamWeek_i}\ k = PLAYER,$
$),$

References to variables $PlayerTeamWeek_{i,j}$ (set of players of team j in week i) are collected in $REFTEAM$. Thus the constraint "No golfer plays in the same team with any other golfer on more than one occasion" can be expressed by a set covering constraint:

$PLAYER\ =\ \cup_{`i`\in REFTEAM}\ i,$

$\forall\ `i`\ \neq\ `k`\ \in\ REFTEAM$
  $\#(i \cap k) \leq 1,$

In order to cut the solution space, the following constraint fixes golfers to the first-week teams corresponding to their indices from 1 to $sizeTeam$:

$\forall\ i\ \in\ TEAM$
  $PlayerTeamWeek_{1,i} = [(i-1)\times sizeTeam+1,\ i\times sizeTeam],$

The search requires instantiating the integer variable $nbActiveWeek$ (number of active weeks) and the set variables (of players) $PlayerTeamWeek_{i,j}$. The search strategy is: NCL selects the golfer with the least index k by the sequential-search criterion ($\min\ k$). Next, NCL selects a $PlayerTeamWeek_{i,j}$ such that its uncertain part is the least: ($\min\ \#\Delta$ $PlayerTeamWeek_{i,j}$).

The query "$k\ \in\ PlayerTeamWeek_{i,j}$?" triggers the branching: first, try to constrain player k to be in $PlayerTeamWeek_{i,j}$; next, try the inverse logic.

A solution for 9 weeks given by NCL is:

```
w1:[1,  4]        [5,  8]        [9,  12]       [13,  16]
   [17, 20]       [21, 24]       [25, 28]       [29, 32]
w2:{1,5,9,13}     {2,6,10,14}    {3,7,11,15}    {4,8,12,16}
   {17,21,25,29}  {18,22,26,30}  {19,23,27,31}  {20,24,28,32}
w3:{1,6,11,16}    {2,5,12,15}    {3,8..9,14}    {4,7,10,13}
   {17,22,27,32}  {18,21,28,31}  {19,24..25,30} {20,23,26,29}
w4:{1,7,17,23}    {2,8,18,24}    {3,5,19,21}    {4,6,20,22}
   {9,15,25,31}   {10,16,26,32}  {11,13,27,29}  {12,14,28,30}
```

```
w5:{1,8,19,22}     {2,7,20..21}   {3,6,17,24}    {4..5,18,23}
   {9,16,27,30}    {10,15,28..29}{11,14,25,32}  {12..13,26,31}
w6:{1,10,18,25}    {2,9,17,26}    {3,12,20,27}   {4,11,19,28}
   {5,14,22,29}    {6,13,21,30}   {7,16,24,31}   {8,15,23,32}
w7:{1,12,21,32}    {2,11,22,31}   {3,10,23,30}   {4,9,24,29}
   {5,16..17,28}   {6,15,18,27}   {7,14,19,26}   {8,13,20,25}
w8:{1,14,20,31}    {2,13,19,32}   {3,16,18,29}   {4,15,17,30}
   {5,10,24,27}    {6,9,23,28}    {7,12,22,25}   {8,11,21,26}
w9:{1,15,24,26}    {2,16,23,25}   {3,13,22,28}   {4,14,21,27}
   {5,11,20,30}    {6,12,19,29}   {7,9,18,32}    {8,10,17,31}
```

6.4.3 Progressive Party

The problem of Progressive Party is to organize a party for n yacht teams at a regatta (Smith et al. 1996). Some of the teams act as hosts and have an available capacity ranging from 4 to 10 guests on their boat at each hour. The constraints to be respected are the boat capacity, that two teams meet only once and that every team visits a new boat each hour. The optimization objective is to minimize the number of host boats.

The NCL program is:

```
nbHour   = 0,
nbBoat   = 0,
HOUR     = [1, nbHour],
BOAT     = [1, nbBoat],

HOSTBOAT = [1, nbHostBoat],
HOSTBOAT ⊂ BOAT,

∀ i ∈ BOAT(
   capacityBoatᵢ = 0,
   SeatBoatᵢ = [1, capacityBoatᵢ],
),

nbGuest = 0,
GUEST    = [1,nbGuest],
∀ i ∈ GUEST
   sizeGuestᵢ = 0,

∀ i ∈ HOUR(
   ∀ j ∈ GUEST(
      boatGuestHourᵢ,ⱼ ∈ HOSTBOAT,

      SeatGuestHourᵢ,ⱼ =
            [seat1GuestHourᵢ,ⱼ, seat2GuestHourᵢ,ⱼ],

      SeatGuestHourᵢ,ⱼ ⊂ SeatBoat_boatGuestHourᵢ,ⱼ,
```

```
      #SeatGuestHour_{i,j} = sizeGuest_j,
   ),

   ∀ j ∈ BOAT(
      GuestBoatHour_{i,j} ⊂ GUEST,

      ∀ k ∈ GUEST
         k∈GuestBoatHour_{i,j} ≡ boatGuestHour_{i,k} = j,

      loadBoatHour_{i,j} = Σ_{k∈GuestBoatHour_{i,j}} sizeGuest_k,
      loadBoatHour_{i,j} ≤ capacityBoat_j,
   ),

   ∀ j ≠ k ∈ BOAT
      GuestBoatHour_{i,j} ∩ GuestBoatHour_{i,k} = ∅,
),

∀ k ∈ GUEST
∀ i ≠ j ∈ HOUR
   boatGuestHour_{i,k} ≠ boatGuestHour_{j,k},

∀ i ≠ j ∈ GUEST
   Σ_{k∈HOUR}(boatGuestHour_{k,i} = boatGuestHour_{k,j}) ≤ 1,

∀ i ∈ HOUR
∀ j ≠ k ∈ GUEST
   boatGuestHour_{i,j} ≠ boatGuestHour_{i,k} ∨

   SeatGuestHour_{i,j} ∩ SeatGuestHour_{i,k} = ∅,

HOSTBOAT = ?,

∀ i ∈ HOUR
∀ j ∈ HOSTBOAT → (
   max    loadBoatHour_{i,j}
)
∀ k ∈ GUEST → (
   min    # Δ boatGuestHour_{i,k},

   min    boatGuestHour_{i,k},

   max    sizeGuest_k
)
boatGuestHour_{i,k} = j?,
```

$\forall\ i\ \in\ \text{HOUR}$
$\quad \forall\ j\ \in\ \text{GUEST}$
$\qquad \text{seat1GuestHour}_{i,j}\ =\ ?,$

$\min\quad \#\text{HOSTBOAT}.$

HOUR represents the set of hours for the regatta. HOSTBOAT is the set of all host teams, and GUEST represents the set of all guest teams. Each host boat i has a capacity of capacityBoat_i. Its space is modeled using a set variable $\text{SeatBoat}_i\ =\ [1,\ \text{capacityBoat}_i]$.

For the data model, it is important to represent the following fact: at any hour i, each guest team j should be assigned to a host boat. So a boat selection (integer) variable $\text{boatGuestHour}_{i,j}$ is introduced to represent the host boat for guest j at hour i. The guest team j consists of sizeGuest_j people. A set variable $\text{SeatGuestHour}_{i,j}$ is introduced to represent all the seats for guest j at hour i. To make the data model compact, $\text{SeatGuestHour}_{i,j}$ is defined to be an interval $[\text{seat1GuestHour}_{i,j}, \text{seat2GuestHour}_{i,j}]$. Apparently, $\text{SeatGuestHour}_{i,j}$ should be a subset of $\text{SeatBoat}_{\text{boatGuestHour}_{i,j}}$.

$\forall\ i\ \in\ \text{HOUR}$
$\quad \forall\ j\ \in\ \text{GUEST}$
$\qquad \text{SeatGuestHour}_{i,j}\ \subset\ \text{SeatBoat}_{\text{boatGuestHour}_{i,j}},$

With this data model, the mathematical model of the problem becomes simple to write. Each team visits a new boat at each hour:

$\forall\ k\ \in\ \text{GUEST}$
$\quad \forall\ i\ \neq\ j\ \in\ \text{HOUR}$
$\qquad \text{boatGuestHour}_{i,k}\ \neq\ \text{boatGuestHour}_{j,k},$

Every two teams meet at most once:

$\forall\ i\ \neq\ j\ \in\ \text{GUEST}$
$\quad \Sigma_{k \in \text{HOUR}}(\text{boatGuestHour}_{k,i}\ =\ \text{boatGuestHour}_{k,j})\ \leq\ 1,$

Each seat on a boat can only accommodate one guest. So if two teams meet together, either they are on different boats or they must have different seats on a boat:

$\forall\ i\ \in\ \text{HOUR}$
$\quad \forall\ j\ \neq\ k\ \in\ \text{GUEST}$
$\qquad \text{boatGuestHour}_{i,j}\ \neq\ \text{boatGuestHour}_{i,k}\ \vee$

$\qquad \text{SeatGuestHour}_{i,j}\ \cap\ \text{SeatGuestHour}_{i,k}\ =\ \varnothing,$

Corresponding to the boat selection variable $\text{boatGuestHour}_{i,j}$ for each team j at hour i, the set variable $\text{GuestBoatHour}_{i,j}$ is introduced to represent the set of guest teams for boat j at hour i, satisfying the following constraints:

$\forall\ i\ \in\ \text{HOUR}\,($
$\quad \forall\ j\ \in\ \text{BOAT}$
$\quad \forall\ k\ \in\ \text{GUEST}$
$\qquad k\ \in\ \text{GuestBoatHour}_{i,j}\ \equiv\ \text{boatGuestHour}_{i,k}\ =\ j,$

$\forall\ j \neq k \in$ BOAT

    GuestBoatHour$_{i,j}$ $\cap$ GuestBoatHour$_{i,k}$ = $\varnothing$,

),

The variable loadBoatHour$_{i,j}$ represents the loading of boat i at hour j which is expressed as follows:

loadBoatHour$_{i,j}$ = $\Sigma_{k \in \text{GuestBoatHour}_{i,j}}$ sizeGuest$_k$,

At hour i boat j's capacity should not be exceeded:

loadBoatHour$_{i,j}$ $\leq$ capacityBoat$_j$,

To solve the problem, the following search rules are used:
- Since the objective is to minimize the number of host boats, NCL starts to instantiate nbHostBoat before instantiating the boat selection variable boatGuestHour$_{i,k}$ for each guest team k at each hour i;
- With the greedy search strategy, the model first chooses an hour i and a host boat j on which the greatest number of guests are present by the criterion (max   loadBoatHour$_{i,j}$). In order to choose a guest team k, three criteria in the lexicographic order are used: First, the domain Δ boatGuestHour$_{i,k}$ of the boat selection variable boatGuestHour$_{i,k}$ is expected to be the smallest (min   # Δ boatGuestHour$_{i,k}$) so that the uncertainty of boat selection is the minimum. Second, guest team k is expected to have possibly the least boat index (min   boatGuestHour$_{i,k}$). Third, with the greedy-search criterion, guest team k is expected to have the biggest team size sizeGuest$_k$;
- The query "boatGuestHour$_{i,k}$ = j?" triggers the branching: first, try to assign boat j to guest k at hour i; next, try the inverse logic.

The test data is below:
```
% nbHour
7

% nbBoat
13

% capacityBoat
10 10 9 8 8 8 8 8 8 7 6 4 4

% nbGuest
29

% sizeGuest
7 6 5 5 5 4 4 4 4 4 4 4 4 3 3 2 2 2 2 2 2 2 2 2 2 2 2 2 2
```

The problem of 13 hosts/29 guests/7 hours is solved completely (with proof of optimality). An optimal solution is shown as below.
- The numbers of the boats (boatGuestHour$_{i,j}$) for the 29 guests during 7 hours are:

```
1  7  6  4  5  2  2  9  3  11  12  13  3  1  10  10  4  6  2  5  7  10  8  11  8  8  9  8  9
2  1  7  5  6  9  3  4  8  4  10  8  13  5  2  1  1  3  7  11  11  6  9  9  12  11  10  3  12
3  2  1  1  7  8  5  11  10  8  9  4  6  2  13  3  6  7  11  9  5  9  4  12  5  10  6  12  4
4  3  2  6  2  5  13  10  1  7  1  12  7  9  3  8  9  5  8  8  6  11  10  1  9  5  11  11  8
5  4  3  7  1  11  8  2  2  10  6  6  9  3  1  9  11  4  1  7  12  13  12  8  13  9  8  2  10
6  5  4  2  3  10  11  12  13  9  8  1  8  10  4  2  3  2  5  1  3  7  11  7  1  7  1  9  7
7  6  5  3  4  1  9  1  9  2  2  10  11  4  8  5  8  8  3  6  1  3  2  10  11  12  12  13  13
```

- The sets of seats on the boats (SeatGuestHour$_{i,j}$) for the 29 guests during 7 hours are:

[1,7] [1,6] [1,5] [1,5] [1,5] [1,4] [5,8] [1,4] [1,4] [1,4] [1,4] [1,4] [5,8] [8,10] [1,3] [4,5] [6,7] [6,7] [9,10] [6,7] [7,8] [6,7] [1,2] [5,6] [3,4] [5,6] [5,6] [7,8] [7,8]

[1,7] [1,6] [1,5] [1,5] [1,5] [1,4] [1,4] [1,4] [1,4] [5,8] [1,4] [5,8] [1,4] [6,8] [8,10] [7,8] [9,10] [5,6] [6,7] [1,2] [3,4] [6,7] [5,6] [7,8] [1,2] [5,6] [5,6] [7,8] [3,4]

[1,7] [1,6] [1,5] [6,10] [1,5] [1,4] [1,4] [1,4] [1,4] [5,8] [1,4] [1,4] [1,4] [7,9] [1,3] [8,9] [5,6] [6,7] [5,6] [5,6] [5,6] [7,8] [5,6] [1,2] [7,8] [5,6] [7,8] [3,4] [7,8]

[1,7] [1,6] [1,5] [1,5] [6,10] [1,4] [1,4] [1,4] [1,4] [1,4] [5,8] [1,4] [5,8] [1,3] [7,9] [1,2] [4,5] [5,6] [3,4] [5,6] [6,7] [1,2] [5,6] [9,10] [6,7] [7,8] [3,4] [5,6] [7,8]

[1,7] [1,6] [1,5] [1,5] [1,5] [1,4] [1,4] [1,4] [5,8] [1,4] [1,4] [5,8] [1,4] [6,8] [6,8] [5,6] [5,6] [7,8] [9,10] [6,7] [1,2] [1,2] [3,4] [5,6] [3,4] [7,8] [7,8] [9,10] [5,6]

[1,7] [1,6] [1,5] [1,5] [1,5] [1,4] [1,4] [1,4] [1,4] [1,4] [1,4] [1,4] [5,8] [5,7] [6,8] [6,7] [6,7] [8,9] [7,8] [5,6] [8,9] [1,2] [5,6] [3,4] [7,8] [5,6] [9,10] [5,6] [7,8]

[1,7] [1,6] [1,5] [1,5] [1,5] [1,4] [1,4] [5,8] [5,8] [1,4] [5,8] [1,4] [1,4] [6,8] [1,3] [6,7] [4,5] [6,7] [6,7] [7,8] [9,10] [8,9] [9,10] [5,6] [5,6] [1,2] [3,4] [1,2] [3,4]

6.4.4 Ship Loading

A set of tasks have to be accomplished by some workers. Demand for man-hours of each task and precedence relations between tasks are given. The problem requires scheduling the tasks so as to minimize the makespan of all tasks (Faure 1991).

The NCL program is:

```
nbTask    = O,              % number of tasks
nbWorker  = O,              % number of workers
nbHour    = O,              % number of hours
TASK      = [1, nbTask],
WORKER    = [1, nbWorker],
HOUR      = [1, nbHour],


∀ i ∈ TASK(
  SuccTask_i = O,           % tasks to be scheduled after task i

  TimeTask_i ⊂ HOUR,        % time interval of task i

  TimeTask_i = [t1Task_i, t2Task_i],

  WorkerTask_i ⊂ WORKER,    % workers allocated to task i

  WorkerTask_i = [worker1Task_i, worker2Task_i],
                            % interval of worker numbers
  #TimeTask_i × #WorkerTask_i = O

                            % man-hour requirement of task i
),

∀ i ∈ TASK
```

$\forall\ j\ \in\ \text{SuccTask}_i$

    $\text{TimeTask}_i\ \prec\ \text{TimeTask}_j,\ \%$ precedence constraint

$\forall\ i\ \neq\ j\ \in\ \text{TASK}$ $\%$ task placement constraint
   $\text{TimeTask}_i\ \cap\ \text{TimeTask}_j\ \neq\ \varnothing\ \rightarrow$

   $\text{WorkerTask}_i\ \cap\ \text{WorkerTask}_j\ =\ \varnothing,$

$\forall\ i\ \in\ \text{TASK}\ \rightarrow\ ($
   $\min$ $\#\Delta\text{t1Task}_i,$ $\%$ task with least slack first

   $\min$ $\underline{\text{t1Task}_i}\ ,$ $\%$ earliest start time first

   $\max$ $\#\text{TimeTask}_i\times\#\text{WorkerTask}_i$

                $\%$ greatest man-hour first
$)$
$($

   $\#\text{TimeTask}_i\ =\ ?,$ $\%$ query on task duration
   $\text{t1Task}_i\ =\ ?$ $\%$ query on start time

$),$

$\forall\ i\ \in\ \text{TASK}\ \rightarrow\ ($
   $\min$ $\#\Delta\text{worker1Task}_i,\ \%$ task with fewest-candidates first

   $\min$ $\underline{\text{worker1Task}_i}$ $\%$ lowest worker index first

$)$
$\text{worker1Task}_i\ =\ ?,$ $\%$ query on first worker

$\min$ $\max_{i\in\text{TASK}}\text{t2Task}_i.$ $\%$ optimization objective

In the above model, nbTask represents the number of tasks; nbWorker represents the number of workers and nbHour represents the maximum time to accomplish all the tasks. For each task i, SuccTask_i is the set of all tasks which must be scheduled after task i.

For task i, WorkerTask_i represents the set of workers who accomplish task i during its working time TimeTask_i. To make the data model compact, WorkerTask_i is defined to be an interval of indices of workers. For each task i, the product ($\#\text{TimeTask}_i \times \#\text{WorkerTask}_i$) corresponds to the man-hour requirement of task i:

   $\forall\ i\ \in\ \text{TASK}$

      $\#\text{TimeTask}_i\ \times\ \#\text{WorkerTask}_i\ =\ 0$

Every two tasks must be executed either by different workers or during different time intervals:

$$\forall\ i \neq j \in \text{TASK}$$
$$\text{TimeTask}_i \cap \text{TimeTask}_j \neq \varnothing \rightarrow$$
$$\text{WorkerTask}_i \cap \text{WorkerTask}_j = \varnothing,$$

The search rules are as below:

- For each task i, the model first instantiates its time interval TimeTask_i, then its set of workers WorkerTask_i;
- Instantiation of TimeTask_i is done by instantiating the cardinality of $\#\text{TimeTask}_i$ and its start time t1Task_i (infimum of TimeTask_i);
- When querying on the start time variable t1Task_i, three criteria in the lexicographic order are used: First, the domain of the start time variable t1Task_i is expected to be the smallest (min $\#\Delta\text{t1Task}_i$) so that the uncertainty of the start time is the minimum. Second, task i is expected to have possibly the earliest start time (min t1Task_i). Third, with the greedy-search criterion, task i is expected to have the greatest requirement of man-hours $\#\text{TimeTask}_i \times \#\text{WorkerTask}_i$;
- When querying on variable WorkerTask_i, its infimum variable worker1Task_i (first worker) is queried instead. Two criteria in the lexicographic order are used: First, the domain of the first-worker variable worker1Task_i is expected to be the smallest so that the uncertainty is the minimum (min $\#\Delta\text{worker1Task}_i$). Second, with the sequential-search criterion (min worker1Task_i), task i is expected to have possibly the least index for its first worker.

The objective is to minimize the makespan: $\max_{i \in \text{TASK}}\text{t2Task}_i$.

The test data is shown as below:
```
%nbTask
34

%nbWorker
8

%nbHour
1000
```

%SuccTask	%Man-Hours
{2,4}	12
{3}	16
{5,7}	12
{5}	24
{6}	25
{8}	10

{8}	12
{9}	12
{10,14}	12
{11,12}	16
{13}	12
{13}	10
[15,16]	4
{15}	15
{18}	6
{17}	9
{18}	12
[19,21]	14
{23}	4
{23}	4
{22}	4
{23}	8
{24}	28
{25}	40
{26,30..32}	16
{27}	3
{28}	3
{29}	12
{}	8
{28}	9
{28}	6
{33}	3
{34}	6
{}	6

This instance of the ship-loading problem is solved completely (with proof of optimality). An optimal solution with the cost of 55 hours is shown in the following solution(Figure 6.13):

```
Task 1 : TimeTask_{1} = [1,2] WorkerTask_{1} = [1,6]
Task 2 : TimeTask_{2} = [3,4] WorkerTask_{2} = [1,8]
Task 3 : TimeTask_{3} = [8,9] WorkerTask_{3} = [1,6]
Task 4 : TimeTask_{4} = [5,7] WorkerTask_{4} = [1,8]
Task 5 : TimeTask_{5} = [10,14] WorkerTask_{5} = [1,5]
Task 6 : TimeTask_{6} = [15,16] WorkerTask_{6} = [1,5]
Task 7 : TimeTask_{7} = [10,13] WorkerTask_{7} = [6,8]
Task 8 : TimeTask_{8} = [17,18] WorkerTask_{8} = [1,6]
Task 9 : TimeTask_{9} = [19,20] WorkerTask_{9} = [1,6]
Task 10: TimeTask_{10} = [21,22] WorkerTask_{10} = [1,8]
Task 11: TimeTask_{11} = [23,24] WorkerTask_{11} = [1,6]
Task 12: TimeTask_{12} = [25,26] WorkerTask_{12} = [1,5]
Task 13: TimeTask_{13} = [27,27] WorkerTask_{13} = [1,4]
Task 14: TimeTask_{14} = [25,29] WorkerTask_{14} = [6,8]
```

```
Task 15: TimeTask_{15} = [30,32] WorkerTask_{15} = [7,8]
Task 16: TimeTask_{16} = [28,30] WorkerTask_{16} = [1,3]
Task 17: TimeTask_{17} = [31,32] WorkerTask_{17} = [1,6]
Task 18: TimeTask_{18} = [33,34] WorkerTask_{18} = [1,7]
Task 19: TimeTask_{19} = [35,35] WorkerTask_{19} = [1,4]
Task 20: TimeTask_{20} = [37,37] WorkerTask_{20} = [1,4]
Task 21: TimeTask_{21} = [35,35] WorkerTask_{21} = [5,8]
Task 22: TimeTask_{22} = [36,36] WorkerTask_{22} = [1,8]
Task 23: TimeTask_{23} = [38,41] WorkerTask_{23} = [1,7]
Task 24: TimeTask_{24} = [42,46] WorkerTask_{24} = [1,8]
Task 25: TimeTask_{25} = [47,48] WorkerTask_{25} = [1,8]
Task 26: TimeTask_{26} = [49,49] WorkerTask_{26} = [1,3]
Task 27: TimeTask_{27} = [52,52] WorkerTask_{27} = [1,3]
Task 28: TimeTask_{28} = [53,54] WorkerTask_{28} = [1,6]
Task 29: TimeTask_{29} = [55,55] WorkerTask_{29} = [1,8]
Task 30: TimeTask_{30} = [50,52] WorkerTask_{30} = [4,6]
Task 31: TimeTask_{31} = [49,51] WorkerTask_{31} = [7,8]
Task 32: TimeTask_{32} = [49,49] WorkerTask_{32} = [4,6]
Task 33: TimeTask_{33} = [50,51] WorkerTask_{33} = [1,3]
Task 34: TimeTask_{34} = [52,54] WorkerTask_{34} = [7,8]
```

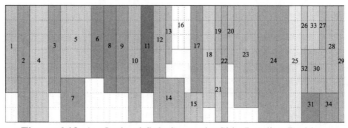

Figure 6.13 An Optimal Solution to the Ship-Loading Problem

6.4.5 Job-Shop Scheduling

Given n jobs each consisting of m tasks that have to be processed on m machines, the Job-Shop Scheduling problem consists in scheduling the jobs on the machines so as to minimize the makespan subject to precedence, duration and disjunctive constraints (Muth and Thompson 1963).

(Muth and Thompson 1963) includes 3 Job-Shop Scheduling problem instances: MT06, MT20 and MT10. The famous MT10 instance had remained an open problem since 1963 until it was completely solved by French researchers Jacques Carlier and Eric Pinson (Carlier and Pinson 1989).

The NCL program is:

```
nbJob       = O,           % number of jobs
nbMachine   = O,           % number of machines
TIME        = [1, O],      % time horizon

JOB         = [1, nbJob],
```

```
MACHINE    = [1, nbMachine],
IDXJOB     = [1, #JOB],
IDXMAC     = [1, #MACHINE],
∀ i ∈ MACHINE
∀ j ∈ JOB(
  TimeJobMac_{i,j} = [t1JobMac_{i,j}, t2JobMac_{i,j}],

  TimeJobMac_{i,j} ⊂ TIME,
),                      % time interval of job j on machine i


∀ j ∈ JOB(
  ∀ i ∈ IDXMAC(
    macIdxJob_{j,i} = O + 1,

    #TimeJobMac_{macIdxJob_{j,i},j} = O,
  ),            % machine scheduled i-th for job j is known


  ∀ i < k ∈ IDXMAC(
    TimeJobMac_{macIdxJob_{j,i},j} ≺ TimeJobMac_{macIdxJob_{j,k},j},
  )            % machine precedence relation for job j
),

∀ i ∈ MACHINE(
  ∀ j ∈ IDXJOB(
    TimeIdxMac_{i,j} = [t1IdxMac_{i,j}, t2IdxMac_{i,j}],

    TimeIdxMac_{i,j} ⊂ TIME,
  ),        % time interval for job scheduled j-th on machine i

  ∀ j ∈ JOB(
    idxJobMac_{i,j} ∈ IDXJOB,   % order of job j on machine i
    TimeJobMac_{i,j} = TimeIdxMac_{i,idxJobMac_{i,j}}
  ),                      % sorting relation

  ∀ j < k ∈ JOB
    idxJobMac_{i,j} ≠ idxJobMac_{i,k},

  ∀ j < k ∈ IDXJOB
    TimeIdxMac_{i,j} ≺ TimeIdxMac_{i,k},
                % precedence constraint over scheduled tasks
),
```

$\forall\ i\ \in\ \text{MACHINE}\ \rightarrow\ ($

   $\min\quad \Sigma_{k \in \text{IDXJOB}} \# \Delta \text{TimeIdxMac}_{i,k},\quad$ % most saturated machine

$)$

$\forall\ j\ \in\ \text{JOB}\ \rightarrow\ ($

   $\min\quad \dfrac{\Sigma_{k \in \Delta \text{idxJobMac}_{i,j}} \#\Delta \text{TimeIdxMac}_{i,k}}{\#\Delta \text{idxJobMac}_{i,j}},\quad$ % least global slack

   $\max\quad \# \Delta \text{TimeJobMac}_{i,j}$ % greatest local slack

$)$

$\text{idxJobMac}_{i,j}\ =\ ?\ (\Rightarrow),$ % query on execution order

$\forall\ i\ \in\ \text{MACHINE}$
$\forall\ j\ \in\ \text{JOB}$
   $\text{t1JobMac}_{i,j}\ =\ ?,$ % query on release

$\min\quad \max_{i \in \text{MACHINE}} \text{t2IdxMac}_{i,\text{nbJob}}.$ % minimize the deadline

Input data of MT10 is as below:

```
10
10
930

0 29 1 78 2  9 3 36 4 49 5 11 6 62 7 56 8 44 9 21
0 43 2 90 4 75 9 11 3 69 1 28 6 46 5 46 7 72 8 30
1 91 0 85 3 39 2 74 8 90 5 10 7 12 6 89 9 45 4 33
1 81 2 95 0 71 4 99 6  9 8 52 7 85 3 98 9 22 5 43
2 14 0  6 1 22 5 61 3 26 4 69 8 21 7 49 9 72 6 53
2 84 1  2 5 52 3 95 8 48 9 72 0 47 6 65 4  6 7 25
1 46 0 37 3 61 2 13 6 32 5 21 9 32 8 89 7 30 4 55
2 31 0 86 1 46 5 74 4 32 6 88 8 19 9 48 7 36 3 79
0 76 1 69 3 76 5 51 2 85 9 11 6 40 7 89 4 26 8 74
1 85 0 13 2 61 6  7 8 64 9 76 5 47 3 52 4 90 7 45
```

The modeling stems from (Zhou 1997). Indexing and sorting, which are the most fundamental concepts in computer science, are used in modeling the scheduling problem. The following conclusions are made for the known and the unknown:

- The durations and the execution order of each job on m machines are known;
- The unknown is the execution order of all the jobs on each machine.

To model the unknown, the following logic variables are introduced:

- Task execution order variable $\text{idxJobMac}_{i,j}$ represents the execution order of job j on machine i. If $\text{idxJobMac}_{i,j}$ is instantiated then the problem becomes solved;

- Time interval variable $TimeJobMac_{i,j}$ represents the time interval of the job j on machine i. If $TimeJobMac_{i,j}$ is instantiated, then all variables will be instantiated;
- Sorted time interval variable $TimeIdxMac_{i,j}$ represents the time interval of the job scheduled j-th on machine i.

Sorted time interval $TimeIdxMac_{i,j}$ can be expressed by $idxJobMac_{i,j}$ and $TimeJobMac_{i,j}$ through the indexing relation as below:

```
∀ i ∈ MACHINE
∀ j ∈ JOB
   TimeJobMac_{i,j} = TimeIdxMac_{i,idxJobMac_{i,j}}'
```

Adding permutation and precedence relations into the indexing relation results in a sorting relation for the set type:

```
∀ i ∈ MACHINE (
  ∀ j < k ∈ JOB
     idxJobMac_{i,j} ≠ idxJobMac_{i,k}'

  ∀ j < k ∈ IDXJOB
     TimeIdxMac_{i,j} ≺ TimeIdxMac_{i,k}'

),
```

To make it easy to understand, the query is simplified: The objective is to instantiate all the task order variables $idxJobMac_{i,j}$. First, the least-slack criterion ($\min \ \Sigma_{k \in IDXJOB} \# \Delta\, TimeIdxMac_{i,k}$) is adopted to select a critical machine i with the least slack for all of its sorted time interval variables.

After the selection of the critical machine i, the choice of a critical job j is done by the following query criteria:

$$\forall\ j\ \in\ JOB\ \rightarrow\ ($$

$$\min\ \frac{\Sigma_{k \in \Delta idxJobMac_{i,j}} \#\Delta TimeIdxMac_{i,k}}{\#\Delta idxJobMac_{i,j}},$$

$$\max\ \ \# \Delta\, TimeJobMac_{i,j}$$

$$)$$

The criteria select such a job j: First, the average slack time of sorted time interval variables whose subscripts ranging over the domain ($\Delta idxJobMac_{i,j}$) of the order variable $idxJobMac_{i,j}$ is the minimum; second, the slack of the time interval variable $TimeJobMac_{i,j}$ is the maximum.

Finally, lower-bound-first binary-domain-splitting is used to enumerate order variables $idxJobMac_{i,j}$.

The objective is to minimize the deadline:

$$\min\ \ \max_{i\ \in\ MACHINE}\ t2IdxMac_{i,nbJob}$$

To facilitate the presentation, some simplification to the model in (Zhou 1997) is made. However, NCL can solve MT10 and all 10×10 instances of (Applegate and Cook 1991). An optimal solution to MT10 (Figure 6.14) is:

Mac 1: [1,29]	[30,72]	[409,493]	[186,256]	[257,262]	[362,408]	[149,185]	[276,361]	[73,148]	[263,275]
Mac 2: [446,523]	[638,665]	[309,399]	[1,81]	[287,308]	[85,86]	[87,132]	[400,445]	[218,286]	[133,217]
Mac 3: [524,532]	[225,314]	[533,606]	[85,179]	[211,224]	[1,84]	[376,388]	[180,210]	[422,506]	[315,375]
Mac 4: [533,568]	[569,637]	[494,532]	[638,735]	[371,396]	[139,233]	[234,294]	[814,892]	[295,370]	[736,787]
Mac 5: [569,617]	[356,430]	[894,926]	[257,355]	[431,499]	[500,505]	[699,753]	[520,551]	[669,694]	[788,877]
Mac 6: [641,651]	[760,805]	[700,709]	[806,848]	[309,369]	[87,138]	[422,442]	[446,519]	[371,421]	[594,640]
Mac 7: [652,713]	[714,759]	[760,848]	[356,364]	[849,901]	[428,492]	[389,420]	[558,645]	[518,557]	[421,427]
Mac 8: [722,777]	[814,885]	[710,721]	[417,501]	[531,579]	[506,530]	[669,698]	[778,813]	[580,668]	[886,930]
Mac 9: [793,836]	[886,915]	[610,699]	[365,416]	[500,520]	[234,281]	[521,609]	[700,718]	[719,792]	[428,491]
Mac 10: [894,914]	[431,441]	[849,893]	[767,788]	[594,665]	[282,353]	[443,474]	[719,766]	[507,517]	[518,593]

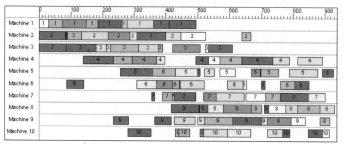

Figure 6.14 An Optimal Solution to MT10

In order to make the model understood easily, an illustration of the relation between task order variable $idxJobMac_{1,\_}$, time interval variable $TimeJobMac_{1,\_}$ and sorted time interval variable $TimeIdxMac_{1,\_}$ for machine 1 is given as below:

$TimeJobMac_{1,\_}$: [1,29] [30,72] [409,493] [186,256] [257,262] [362,408] [149,185] [276,361] [73,148] [263,275]

$TimeIdxMac_{1,\_}$: [1,29] [30,72] [73,148] [149,185] [186,256] [257,262] [263,275] [276,361] [362,408] [409,493]

$idxJobMac_{1,\_}$: 1   2   10   5   6   9   4   8   3   7

For example,

$TimeIdxMac_{1,3} = TimeIdxMac_{1,idxJobMac_{1,3}} = TimeIdxMac_{1,10} = [409,493]$

6.4.6 Minimizing the Cost of a Heat Exchanger

The Heat Exchanger problem (Floudas and Pardalos 1990) is a non-linear constrained optimization problem over real numbers. It requires minimizing the cost function of a heat exchanger. Most of the constraints are linear, but the presence of some non-linear ones plus the very non-linear objective function makes the problem difficult.

This is a good example for testing NCL's solver over floating-point numbers. The NCL description is as follows:

```
Ti1    ∈ [150.0, 240.0],    % linear constraints
To1    ∈ [250.0, 490.0],
Ti2    ∈ [150.0, 190.0],
To2    ∈ [210.0, 340.0],
FE1    ∈ [2.941, 10.0],
```

```
FE2                ∈ [3.158, 10.0],
Fi1                ≥ 0.0,
Fi2                ≥ 0.0,
FB12               ≥ 0.0,
FB21               ≥ 0.0,
Fo1                ≥ 0.0,
Fo2                ≥ 0.0,
T11                = 500.0 - To1,
T12                = 250.0 - Ti1,
T21                = 350.0 - To2,
T22                = 200.0 - Ti2,
Fi1 + Fi2    = 10.0,
Fo2 + FB12   = FE2,
Fo1 + FB21   = FE1,
Fi1 + FB12   = FE1,
Fi2 + FB21   = FE2,

FE2 × (To2 - Ti2) = 600.0,          % non-linear constraints
FE1 × (To1 - Ti1) = 1000.0,
150.0 × Fi1 + To2 × FB12 - Ti1 × FE1 = 0.0,
150.0 × Fi2 + To1 × FB21 - Ti2 × FE2 = 0.0,
```

$$\text{min} \quad 1300 \times \exp(0.6 \times \log(20000 \times 6 / (4 \times \sqrt{T11 \times T12} + (T11+T12)))) +$$
$$1300 \times \exp(0.6 \times \log(12000 \times 6 / (4 \times \sqrt{T21 \times T22} + (T21+T22)))),$$

```
∀ `i` ∈ {`To1`,`To2`,`Ti1`,`Ti2`,`Fi1`,`Fi2`,`Fo1`,`Fo2`}→(
    max   #i,
)
i = ?.
```

The search strategy for this problem is based on the query criterion of greatest slack: to instantiate a float variable i taken from To1, To2, Ti1, Ti2, Fi1, Fi2, Fo1, Fo2, whose domain range (#i) is the greatest. Pay attention to the #i function which has different meanings (respectively float interval width, string length and cardinality) over float variables, string variables and set variables.

NCL solves the problem completely (with proof of optimality). The optimal solution <56825.76171875..56825.76953125> is contained in the following intervals:

```
To1 = <309.9998779296875..309.9999084472656>
To2 = <210.0000000000000..210.0000152587891>
Ti1 = <209.9998779296875..209.9998931884766>
Ti2 = <150.0000000000000..150.0000152587891>
Fi1 = <0.0000047683716..0.0000047683720>
Fi2 = <9.9999942779541..9.9999952316284>
Fo1 = <9.9999933242798..9.9999942779541>
Fo2 = <0.0000057220459..0.0000057220464>
```

Assuming To1, To2, Ti1, Ti2 to be integers, the problem becomes much easier. NCL solves it instantly:

```
To1 = 310, To2 = 210, Ti1 = 210, Ti2 = 150.
```

The optimal solution is proved to be within:

```
<56825.79296875..56825.859375>.
```

6.4.7 Pick-up and Delivery

In the Pick-up and Delivery problem with time windows (PDPTW) (Li and Lim 2001), vehicles deliver goods from origins to destinations subject to capacity and time constraints. Different from (Solomon 1987), cumulative load and capacity constraints, time window constraints, precedence constraints together with coupling constraints must be handled simultaneously.

The whole NCL program is:

```
nbTruck         = 0,                    % number of trucks
capacityTruck   = 0,                    % truck capacity
nbOrder         = 0,                    % number of orders
TRUCK           = [1, nbTruck],
ORDER           = [1, nbOrder],

∀ i ∈ TRUCK(
  sourceTruckᵢ  = -i,                   % origin of truck i
  sinkTruckᵢ    = -(i + nbTruck)        % destination of truck i
),

depot = -1,                             % one depot
SOURCE = {∀ i ∈ TRUCK sourceTruckᵢ},    % origins

SINK   = {∀ i ∈ TRUCK sinkTruckᵢ},      % destinations

SOURCEORDER         = ORDER ∪ SOURCE,
ORDERSINK           = ORDER ∪ SINK,
SOURCEORDERSINK     = ORDER ∪ SOURCE ∪ SINK,

∀ i ∈ SOURCEORDERSINK(          % explicit declaration
  xOrderᵢ             :: 0,      % abscissa
  yOrderᵢ             :: 0,      % ordinate
  demandOrderᵢ        :: 0,      % demand
  w1Orderᵢ            :: 0,      % lower bound of time window
  w2Orderᵢ            :: 0,      % upper bound of time window
  serviceTimeOrderᵢ  :: 0,      % service time
  idxPickupOrderᵢ     :: 0,      % index to pick-up order
  idxDelivrOrderᵢ     :: 0,      % index to delivery order
  TimeWinOrderᵢ = [w1Orderᵢ,w2Orderᵢ],  % time window
```

```
    loadOrder_i ∈ [0,capacityTruck], % truck load at order i
    truckOrder_i ∈ TRUCK                % truck for an order
),

∀ i ∈ {depot} ∪ ORDER(                  % input for depot & orders
    xOrder_i           = 0,
    yOrder_i           = 0,
    demandOrder_i      = 0,
    w1Order_i          = 0,
    w2Order_i          = 0,
    serviceTimeOrder_i = 0,
    idxPickupOrder_i   = 0,
    idxDelivrOrder_i   = 0
),

∀ i ∈ SOURCE ∪ SINK(     % same origins & destinations
    xOrder_i            = xOrder_depot,
    yOrder_i            = yOrder_depot,
    demandOrder_i       = demandOrder_depot,
    TimeWinOrder_i      = TimeWinOrder_depot,
    serviceTimeOrder_i  = serviceTimeOrder_depot,
    idxPickupOrder_i    = 0,
    idxDelivrOrder_i    = 0
),

PICKUPORDER ={∀ i ∈ ORDER (demandOrder_i > 0 ? i : 0)} \ 0,

∀ i,j ∈ SOURCEORDERSINK(
    % distance matrix
    dOrderOrder_{i,j} = ⌊√((xOrder_i -xOrder_j)² +(yOrder_i -yOrder_j)²) +0.5 ⌋,

    % time matrix
    tOrderOrder_{i,j} = dOrderOrder_{i,j} + serviceTimeOrder_i
),

∀ i ∈ TRUCK(
    OrderTruck_i ⊂ ORDER,            % set of orders of truck i
```

$$\text{OrderSourceTruck}_i \qquad = \{\text{sourceTruck}_i\} \cup \text{OrderTruck}_i,$$

$$\text{OrderSinkTruck}_i \qquad = \{\text{sinkTruck}_i\} \cup \text{OrderTruck}_i,$$

$$\text{OrderSourceSinkTruck}_i = \text{OrderSourceTruck}_i \cup \{\text{sinkTruck}_i\},$$

$$\text{truckOrder}_{\text{sourceTruck}_i} \; = i,$$

$$\text{truckOrder}_{\text{sinkTruck}_i} \; = i,$$

$$\text{loadOrder}_{\text{sourceTruck}_i} \; = 0, \qquad \% \text{ initial loading is } 0$$

$$\text{loadOrder}_{\text{sinkTruck}_i} = 0 \qquad\qquad \% \text{ terminal loading is } 0$$

),

$$\text{ORDER} = \cup_{i \in \text{TRUCK}} \text{OrderTruck}_i, \qquad \% \text{ set partitioning over orders}$$

$$\forall \; i < j \in \text{TRUCK}$$
$$\text{OrderTruck}_i \cap \text{OrderTruck}_j = \varnothing,$$

$$\forall \; i \in \text{SOURCEORDER}($$
$$\text{TimeOrder}_i = [\text{t1Order}_i, \text{t2Order}_i], \% \text{ work time from i to next}$$

$$\text{TimeOrder}_i \subset \text{TimeWinOrder}_{\text{depot}},$$

$$\text{nextOrder}_i \in \text{ORDERSINK}, \qquad\qquad \% \text{ successor of order i}$$

$$\text{TimeOrder}_i \prec \text{TimeOrder}_{\text{nextOrder}_i}, \; \% \text{ set sorting for routing}$$

$$\#\text{TimeOrder}_i = \text{tOrderOrder}_{i,\text{nextOrder}_i}, \% \text{ order-next distance}$$

$$i \in \text{OrderSourceTruck}_{\text{truckOrder}_i},$$

$$\text{t1Order}_i \in \text{TimeWinOrder}_i, \qquad\qquad \% \text{ time window constraint}$$

$$\text{loadOrder}_{\text{nextOrder}_i} \qquad\qquad \% \text{ incremental load constraint}$$
$$\qquad = \text{loadOrder}_i + \text{demandOrder}_{\text{nextOrder}_i}$$

),

$$\forall \; i \neq j \in \text{SOURCEORDER}$$
$$\text{nextOrder}_i \neq \text{nextOrder}_j,$$

$$\forall \; i \in \text{PICKUPORDER}($$
$$\text{TimeOrder}_i \prec \text{TimeOrder}_{\text{idxDelivrOrder}_i}, \% \text{ precedence constraint}$$
$$\text{truckOrder}_i = \text{truckOrder}_{\text{idxDelivrOrder}_i}, \% \text{ coupling constraint}$$

$$\text{dOrderOrder}_{i,\text{idxDelivrOrder}_i} = 0 \Rightarrow \text{nextOrder}_i = \text{idxDelivrOrder}_i$$

),

∀ i ∈ TRUCK (
    $\text{t1Order}_{\text{sourceTruck}_i} = 0$,   % trucks depart always at time 0

    ∀ j ∈ $\text{OrderSourceTruck}_i$

      $\text{nextOrder}_j ∈ \text{OrderSinkTruck}_i$,

    $\text{activeTruck}_i ≡ \text{OrderTruck}_i ≠ ∅$,   % active iff nonempty

    $\text{TimeTruck}_i = \bigcup_{j∈\text{OrderSourceTruck}_i} \text{TimeOrder}_j$,

    $\text{TimeTruck}_i ⊂ \text{TimeWinOrder}_{\text{depot}}$
),

∀ i < j ∈ TRUCK(% symmetry breaking
    $\text{activeTruck}_j → \text{activeTruck}_i$,
    sup $\text{OrderSourceTruck}_i$ > sup $\text{OrderSourceTruck}_j$
),

∀ j ∈ PICKUPORDER(
    ∀ i ∈ TRUCK(
      $\text{dSumOrderTruck}_{i,j} =$
          $\sum_{k∈\text{OrderTruck}_i} \max(\text{dOrderOrder}_{k,j}, \text{dOrderOrder}_{k,\text{idxDelivrOrder}_j}$
),

      $\text{dOrderTruck}_{i,j} = \lfloor \text{dSumOrderTruck}_{i,j} / \#\text{OrderTruck}_i + 0.5 \rfloor$,
    ),   % order-to-truck distance

    $\text{DistTruckOrder}_j = \{∀ i ∈ Δ\,\text{truckOrder}_j \quad \underline{\text{dOrderTruck}_{i,j}}\}$,
    $\text{diffDistTruckOrder}_j = \text{DistTruckOrder}_j[2] - \text{DistTruckOrder}_j[1]$,
      % difference between the least two order-truck distances
),

∀ i ∈ SOURCEORDER(
    $\text{DistNextOrder}_i = \{∀ j∈Δ\text{nextOrder}_i \quad \text{dOrderOrder}_{i,j}\}$,
    $\text{diffDistNextOrder}_i = \text{DistNextOrder}_i[2] - \text{DistNextOrder}_i[1]$,
      % difference between the least two order-next distances
),

∀ j ∈ PICKUPORDER → (

```
     min    #∆truckOrder_j,     % fewest trucks

     max    diffDistTruckOrder_j,% least regret: easiest choice

)
∀ i ∈ ∆truckOrder_j → (
     min    dOrderTruck_{i,j} ,     % greedy search

     min    #∆OrderTruck_i      % least slack

)
j ∈ OrderTruck_i ?,


∀ j ∈ SOURCEORDER → (

     min    #∆nextOrder_j,      % fewest successors

     max    diffDistNextOrder_j,% least regret: easiest choice

)
∀ k ∈ ∆nextOrder_j → (

     min    tOrderOrder_{j,k}       % greedy search

)
nextOrder_j = k ?,


∀ j ∈ SOURCEORDER

     t1Order_j = ?,
```

$$\min \ \Sigma_{i \in SOURCEORDER} \#TimeOrder_i - \Sigma_{i \in SOURCEORDER} serviceTimeOrder_i .$$

As commented in the NCL program, there are general parameters such as nbTruck, capacityTruck and nbOrder. Each order i has its coordinates $xOrder_i$, demand $demandOrder_i$, time window [$w1Order_i$, $w2Order_i$], service time $serviceTimeOrder_i$, associated pick-up order $idxPickupOrder_i$ and associated delivery order $idxDelivrOrder_i$. If $demandOrder_i$ is non-negative, it means a pick-up order to which is associated a delivery order $idxDelivrOrder_i$; otherwise, it means a delivery order to which is associated a pick-up order $idxDelivrOrder_i$.

Euclidean distances, rounded to integers, are used in this problem. The distance $dOrderOrder_{i,j}$ between orders i and j is calculated as below:

$$dOrderOrder_{i,j} = \lfloor \sqrt{(xOrder_i - xOrder_j)^2 + (yOrder_i - yOrder_j)^2} + 0.5 \rfloor$$

Different from (Domenjoud et al. 1999) which uses integer sorting with 3 tuples of variables to model vehicle routing and which generates feasible schedules by relaxation and local optimization (see Section 8.1), the model in this book adopts set sorting with 2 tuples of variables and the routing algorithm here is exact.

To each truck i is associated an origin `sourceTruck`$_i$, a destination `sinkTruck`$_i$ and an order set `OrderTruck`$_i$. The `OrderTruck`$_i$, `sourceTruck`$_i$ and `sinkTruck`$_i$ generate a tour for truck i. Truck i is active iff `OrderTruck`$_i$ ≠ ∅. For each order i, the model introduces successor variable `nextOrder`$_i$ and time interval variable `TimeOrder`$_i$ (work and driving time from order i to its successor), with `t1Order`$_i$ and `t2Order`$_i$ being start and completion times. The data model is illustrated in Figure 6.15.

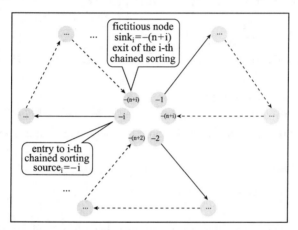

Figure 6.15 Routing By Set Sorting with 2 Tuples of Variables

The modeling of main constraints is explained below:

- "Set sorting with 2 tuples of variables" is used to express that time interval of order i precedes that of its successor, and different orders have different successors:

  $\forall$ i ∈ SOURCEORDER

  `TimeOrder`$_i$ ≺ `TimeOrder`$_{nextOrder_i}$

  $\forall$ $i \neq j$ ∈ SOURCEORDER

  `nextOrder`$_i$ ≠ `nextOrder`$_j$,

- For each order i, the length of the time interval `TimeOrder`$_i$ equals to the time distance (service + driving) from order i to its successor:

  $\forall$ i ∈ SOURCEORDER

  #`TimeOrder`$_i$ = `tOrderOrder`$_{i, nextOrder_i}$,

- For each order i, the balance of the loading of its truck can never be broken. This can be constrained by the relation of Sum of Integers as below.

  $\forall$ k ∈ TRUCK

  $\Sigma_{i \in OrderTruck_k}$`demandOrder`$_i$ = 0,

- Due to the fact that demandOrder$_i$ is not always a positive value for an order i, it is tricky to post the Increment constraint along the routed orders. This is done by introducing the loading variable loadOrder$_i$ which represents the loading amount of the truck, whatever it is, at order i. The advantage of such a modeling is three fold: First, the capacity constraint can be expressed tightly; second, initial and terminal loading of any truck can be expressed concisely; third, of course the Increment relation is a strong constraint.

  $\forall$ i $\in$ SOURCEORDERSINK
  loadOrder$_i$ $\in$ [0, capacityTruck],

  $\forall$ i $\in$ TRUCK(
  loadOrder$_{\text{sourceTruck}_i}$ = 0,   % initial loading is 0
  loadOrder$_{\text{sinkTruck}_i}$ = 0   % terminal loading is 0
  ),
  $\forall$ i $\in$ SOURCEORDER
  loadOrder$_{\text{nextOrder}_i}$ = loadOrder$_i$+demandOrder$_{\text{nextOrder}_i}$'

- Pick-up precedes delivery and should be coupled in a same truck:

  $\forall$ i $\in$ PICKUPORDER(

  TimeOrder$_i$ $\prec$ TimeOrder$_{\text{idxDelivrOrder}_i}$'

  truckOrder$_i$ = truckOrder$_{\text{idxDelivrOrder}_i}$
  ),

- To break symmetry, the model requires that a truck with a lower index is used in preference and it contains greater supremum of the set of orders and origin:

  $\forall$ i < j $\in$ TRUCK(
  activeTruck$_j$ $\rightarrow$ activeTruck$_i$,

  sup OrderSourceTruck$_i$ > sup OrderSourceTruck$_j$,

  ),

Logically it is sufficient to instantiate the successor variable nextOrder$_i$ for each order i. This is efficient when there are only a few trucks. For the general purpose, search can be programmed in 2 steps: first, at the set partitioning level it instantiates the order variable OrderTruck$_i$ for each truck i; next, at the routing level, it instantiates the successor variable nextOrder$_j$ for every order j; the instantiation of the release time variable t1Order$_j$ for all order j is simply a final verification for a solution.

In addition to the least-slack criterion, the NCL model also uses regret-based search rules for solving the problem. To set up the regret criterion for set partitioning, dOrderTruck$_{i,j}$ is introduced to represent "fuzzy" distance from order j to truck i. The formula

$\Sigma_{k \in \text{OrderTruck}_i} \max(\text{dOrderOrder}_{k,j}, \text{dOrderOrder}_{k,\text{idxDelivrOrder}_j})$

sums up the distance for order j to truck i. For pick-up order i, diffDistNextOrder$_i$ is introduced to represent the difference between the second least and the least order-truck distances. If the difference is the biggest, hopefully regret on order-truck choice is the least. To query on OrderTruck$_i$, the search rules are:

- First, select a critical order j in the lexicographic order of (fewest truck candidates, least regret on order-truck choice);
- Next, for order j, with the greedy-search criterion (min dOrderTruck$_{i,j}$) select a truck i such that the distance from truck i to order j is minimal;
- The query "j ∈ OrderTruck$_i$?" triggers the branching: first, try to assign order j to truck i; next, try the inverse logic.

After all orders are assigned to trucks, they should be routed. For each order j, variable diffDistNextOrder$_j$ is introduced to represent the difference between the second least and the least order-successor distances. Search on nextOrder$_j$ follows the rules as below:

- First, select a critical order j in the lexicographic order of (fewest candidate successors, least regret on successor choice);
- Next, for order j, greedily select a successor k with the smallest distance (min tOrderOrder$_{j,k}$);
- The query "nextOrder$_j$ = k?" triggers the branding: first, try to constrain order j's successor to be k; next, try the inverse logic.

The global objective is to minimize the driving time:

$$\min \quad \Sigma_{i \in SOURCEORDER}\#TimeOrder_i - \Sigma_{i \in SOURCEORDER} serviceTimeOrder_i$$

Note that the distances are rounded to integers; the objective is an integer function.

NCL can solve at least 4 problem instances (LC101, LC201, LR101, LRC101) of (Li and Lim 2001) with optimality proofs. Optimal bounds proved are respectively 829 for LC101, 590 for LC201, 1638 for LR101 and 1702 for LRC101. The optimal solutions proved by NCL are(Figure 6.16):

```
LC101
T1: (98, 96, 95, 94, 92, 93, 97, 106, 100, 99)
T2: (32, 33, 31, 35, 37, 38, 39, 36, 105, 34)
T3: (81, 78, 104, 76, 71, 70, 73, 77, 79, 80)
T4: (20, 24, 25, 27, 29, 30, 28, 26, 23, 103, 22, 21)
T5: (67, 65, 63, 62, 74, 72, 61, 64, 102, 68, 66, 69)
T6: (43, 42, 41, 40, 44, 46, 45, 48, 51, 101, 50, 52, 49, 47)
T7: (90, 87, 86, 83, 82, 84, 85, 88, 89, 91)
T8: (5, 3, 7, 8, 10, 11, 9, 6, 4, 2, 1, 75)
T9: (57, 55, 54, 53, 56, 58, 60, 59)
T10: (13, 17, 18, 19, 15, 16, 14, 12)


LC201
T1: (93, 5, 75, 2, 1, 99, 100, 97, 92, 94, 95, 98, 7, 3, 4, 89, 91, 88,
     84, 86, 83, 82, 102, 85, 76, 71, 70, 73, 80, 79, 81, 78, 77, 96,
     87, 90)
T2: (20, 22, 24, 27, 30, 29, 6, 32, 33, 31, 35, 37, 38, 39, 36, 34, 28,
     26, 101, 23, 18, 19, 16, 14, 12, 15, 17, 13, 25, 9, 11, 10, 8, 21)
T3: (67, 63, 62, 74, 72, 61, 64, 66, 69, 68, 65, 49, 55, 54, 53, 56,
     58, 60, 59, 57, 40, 44, 46, 45, 51, 50, 52, 47, 43, 42, 41, 48)
```

```
LR101
T1: (28, 12, 40, 53, 106, 26)
T2: (14, 44, 105, 38, 43, 13)
T3: (39, 23, 104, 67, 55, 25)
T4: (65, 71, 81, 50, 68, 103)
T5: (72, 75, 22, 74, 102, 58)
T6: (30, 51, 101, 9, 66, 1)
T7: (95, 98, 16, 86, 91, 100)
T8: (59, 99, 94, 96)
T9: (92, 42, 15, 87, 57, 97)
T10: (5, 83, 61, 85, 37, 93)
T11: (62, 11, 90, 20, 32, 70)
T12: (45, 82, 18, 84, 60, 89)
T13: (31, 88, 7, 10)
T14: (27, 69, 76, 79, 3, 54, 24, 80)
T15: (33, 29, 78, 34, 35, 77)
T16: (2, 21, 73, 41, 56, 4)
T17: (63, 64, 49, 48)
T18: (52, 6)
T19: (36, 47, 19, 8, 46, 17)

LRC101
T1: (14, 47, 12, 73, 106, 79, 46, 55)
T2: (5, 45, 2, 7, 6, 8, 3, 1, 105, 4)
T3: (63, 76, 104, 51, 22, 49, 20, 24)
T4: (64, 103, 90, 84, 56, 66)
T5: (27, 31, 85, 102, 89, 91)
T6: (83, 23, 21, 19, 18, 48, 25, 101)
T7: (69, 98, 88, 53, 78, 60, 100, 70)
T8: (65, 52, 99, 57, 86, 74)
T9: (59, 75, 87, 97, 58, 77)
T10: (39, 42, 44, 61, 81, 96, 54, 68)
T11: (92, 95, 62, 67, 71, 94, 50, 80)
T12: (33, 28, 29, 30, 26, 34, 32, 93)
T13: (82, 11, 15, 16, 9, 10, 13, 17)
T14: (72, 36, 38, 41, 40, 43, 37, 35)
```

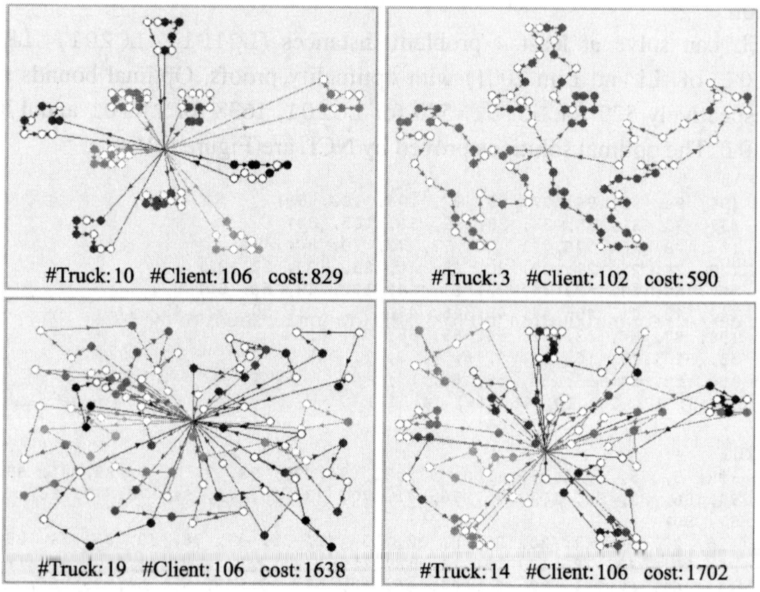

#Truck: 10   #Client: 106   cost: 829

#Truck: 3   #Client: 102   cost: 590

#Truck: 19   #Client: 106   cost: 1638

#Truck: 14   #Client: 106   cost: 1702

Figure 6.16 Solutions to 4 Pick-up and Delivery Problem Instances

6.4.8 Exercises

Job-Shop Scheduling
- How to model and solve the Job-Shop Scheduling problem by a sorting model with 2 tuples of variables?
- How to model and solve the Job-Shop Scheduling problem with a packing model?

Vehicle Routing
- How to simplify the data model and the constraint model if a vehicle routing problem is only related to pick-up or delivery?
- How to modify the data model and the constraint model if a vehicle routing problem involves both depots location and routes planning?
- For a pick-up problem or a delivery problem, the accessibility of a route may be not 100% but a certain rate (for example its reliability is 67%). How to modify the data model and the constraint model to take the route accessibility into consideration and to minimize the transport cost?

References

Aggoun, A., Beldiceanu, N.: Extending CHIP in order to solve complex scheduling and placement problems. Mathl. Comput. Modelling, 17(7), 57–73 (1993)

Andrews, W.S.: Magic Squares and Cubes. New York: Dover (1960)

Applegate, D., Cook, W.: A computational study of the job shop scheduling problem. Operations Research Society of America, 3(2): 149–156 (1991)

Apt, K.R., Wallace, M.: Constraint Logic Programming using Eclipse. Cambridge University Press (2007)

Bleuzen-Guernalec, N., Colmerauer, A.: Optimal narrowing of a block of sortings in optimal time. Constraints 5(1/2): 85–118 (2000)

Booch, G.: Object-Oriented Analysis and Design with Applications. Addison-Wesley (2007)

Bouwkamp, C.J., Duijvestijn, A.J.W.: Catalogue of simple perfect squared squares of orders 21 through 25. Eindhoven University of Technology, Technical Report 92 WSK 03, the Netherlands (1992)

Carlier, J., Pinson, E.: An algorithm for solving the job shop problem. Management Science, 35(2): 164–176 (1989)

Colmerauer, A.: PROLOG II reference manual and theoretical model. Technical report, Groupe Intelligence Articielle, Université Aix-Marseille II (1982)

Colmerauer, A.: An introduction to Prolog III. Communications of the ACM, 33(7): 69–90 (1990)

Colmerauer, A.: Prolog IV Specifications. Reference Manual WP7/R25, Esprit project 5246, TRD Prince (1995)

Conrad, A., Hindricks, T., Morsy, H., Wegener, I.: Solution of the knight's Hamiltonian path problem on chessboards. Discrete Applied Mathematics, 50: 125–134 (1994)

Dincbas, M., Van Hentenryck, P., Simonis, H., Aggoun, A., Graf, T., Berthier, F.: The constraint logic language CHIP. Proc. of the 3rd Annual ACM Symposium on Theory of Computing, 151–158 (1988)

Domenjoud, E., Kirchner, C., Zhou, J.: Generating feasible schedules for a pick-up and delivery problem. Electronic Notes in Discrete Mathematics 1: 36–47 (1999)

Dudeney, H.: In Strand Magazine. Vol. 68, pp. 97 and 214 (1924)

Faure, R.: Le déchargement et le chargement d'un navire. Exercises et problème résolus de recherche opérationnelle, Masson, T3: 279–282 (1991)

Floudas, C.A., Pardalos, P.M.: A Collection of Test Problems for Constrained Global Optimization Algorithms. New York: Springer (1990)

Gambini, I.: A method for cutting squares into distinct squares. Discrete Applied Mathematics, 98(1-2): 65–80 (1999)

Garey, M.R., Johnson, D.S.: Computers and Intractability: A Guide to the Theory of NP-Completeness. W.H. Freeman (1979)

Hall, P.: On representatives of subsets. J. London Math. Soc., 10(37): 26–30 (1935)

Harvey, W., Winterer, T.: Solving the MOLR and social golfers problems. CP'05: 286–300 (2005)

Hoffman, K.L., Padberg, M.: Solving airline crew scheduling problems by branch-and-cut. Management Science, 39(6): 657–682 (1993)

Jaffar, J., Lassez, J.L.: Constraint Logic Programming. Proc. of the 14th ACM POPL Conference, Munich, 111–119 (1987)

Lenstra, J.K., Rinnooy Kan, A.H.G.: Computational complexity of discrete optimization problems. Annals of Discrete Mathematics, 4: 121–140 (1979)

Li, H., Lim, A.: A metaheuristic for the pickup and delivery problem with time windows. Proc. of IEEE International Conference on Tools with Artificial Intelligence, 13: 160–167 (2001)

Muth, J.F., Thompson, G.L.: Industrial Scheduling. Englewood Cliffs, NJ: Prentice-Hall (1963)

Puget, J.-F.: Programmation logique sous contraintes en C++. LMO 1994: 193–202 (1994)

Régin, J.C.: A filtering algorithm for constraints of difference in CSPs. Proc. of AAAI, 1: 362–367 (1994)

Régin, J.C.: Generalized arc consistency for global cardinality constraint. AAAI/IAAI, 1: 209–215 (1996)

Smith, B., Brailsford, S., Hubbard, P.M., Williams, H.B.: The progressive party problem: Integer linear programming and constraint programming compared. Constraints, 1-2: 119–138 (1996)

Smith, D.: So you thought Sudoku came from the Land of the Rising Sun ....The Observer, Sunday, 15 May, 2005 (2005)

Smolka, G.: The Oz programming model. Computer Science Today, 324–343 (1995)

Solomon, M.M.: The vehicle routing and scheduling problems with time window constraints. Operations Research, 35: 254–265 (1987)

Stewart, I.: Calculs d'enfer. Vision Mathématique, 86–88 (1994)

Zhou, J.: A permutation-based approach for solving the Job-shop problem. Constraints, 2(2): 185–213 (1997)

Zhou, J.: Routing by mixed set programming. Proc. of the 8th International Symposium on Operations Research and Its Applications, 157–166 (2009)

7 Industrial Applications

This chapter mainly presents the modeling and solving of three selected industrial problems: Production Scheduling, Personnel Planning and Multi-Modal Transportation Planning. Related to optimization of manufacturing, human and logistic resources, these problems widely exist in industry.

Section 7.1 compares the differences between some academic problems and industrial applications.

Section 7.2 presents the modeling of a Production Scheduling problem based on a packing model. Readers will get a better understanding of the model through the illustration of its solutions by Gantt chart.

Section 7.3 presents the Personnel Planning problem which is formulated with a cumulation model. The solutions to the problem are displayed with Histogram and Gantt chart.

Section 7.4 presents the modeling of a Multi-Modal Transportation Planning problem which deals with the distribution of customer orders over a network with different modes of transport. The problem is described by a routing model and its solutions are visualized by Map.

7.1 Complexity of Industrial Problems

The problems presented in Chapter 6 are from the academic world. Most of them are very hard to solve. However, industrial problems are often much more complex than academic problems:

- Constraints are complex and modeling becomes very difficult. Academic problems usually touch only a few constraints (e.g., the Job-Shop Scheduling problem in Chapter 6 deals with only three kinds of constraints), but industrial problems may have several tens of kinds of constraints or more;
- Problem size is very large. The MT10 instance consists of only 10 jobs to be processed on 10 machines. The number of its tasks is only 100. However, an industrial Production Scheduling problem may amount to 100,000 tasks or more;
- Quick reaction to exceptions and variability (e.g., intuitive interaction and real-time re-optimization) may be strongly required;
- Implementation and practice are difficult: development can be very costly; deployment can take a long time; effect may not be evident immediately.

7.2 Production Scheduling

7.2.1 Problem Definition

This section presents the modeling of a Production Scheduling problem for complex manufacturing; see the literature (Muth and Thompson 1963; Herrmann

2006). Suppose that in a workshop where a large quantity of products are manufactured, equipments are grouped in accordance with their functionalities and tasks of each job are executed along a technological process. The scheduler has to prepare a detailed working plan for each employee, taking earliest start time, deadline and resource capacity constraints into consideration.

In such a context, the Production Scheduling problem consists in allocating resources to tasks in order to efficiently manufacture end products over a time horizon, subject to a variety of complex constraints over resources, jobs and tasks.

Constraints over resources include:

- Work Calendar: Maintenance of equipments, work regulations, week-ends or holidays may all have impacts on the work calendar of a resource. For example, if machine 1 does not work on week-ends, then between 05/02/2009 and 09/02/2009 its work calendar is a date set {'05/02/2009', '06/02/2009', '09/02/2009'};
- Daily Time Slots: Each resource has its availability on each day. For example, if machine 1 does not work during 12:00-14:00 and 18:00-08:00, then its daily time slots are modeled by the set {'08:00'.. '11:59', '14:00'.. '17:59'};
- Resource Capacity: At any time, each resource can only process a limited number of tasks.

Constraints over jobs include:

- Earliest start time: It is the earliest time for a job to be started;
- Latest completion time: It is the latest time for a job to be accomplished;
- Execution order: Jobs need to be executed in a planned execution order, e.g., job A will be executed third among all;
- Precedence: If job A needs to be scheduled before job B, then the beginning of job B must be scheduled after the end of job A;
- Successor: If job B is the successor of job A, then job B will be "immediately" executed after job A without any other in between;
- Coupling: Some jobs are required to be processed on a same resource;
- Inconsistency: Two jobs are said to be inconsistent if they must be processed on different resources;
- Priority: A job with a higher priority should be processed earlier in preference.

Constraints over tasks include:

- Process: Each job consists of tasks along a technological process, synchronized in processing time;
- Resource Requirement: For example, task a requires resource 1 or resource 2;
- Duration: Each task requires a processing time on a certain resource;
- Time Gap: On some resources, a time gap between different jobs may be required;
- Time Window: For example, the start time of task a must be between 10:00 and 12:00.

The scheduling problem may have optimization objectives as below:

- Minimizing the delay of the jobs;
- Minimizing the makespan;
- Maximizing the utilization ratio of resources.

A Production Scheduling problem can be highly complex. It is necessary to use a high-level integrated system for modeling, solving, diagnosing and analyzing, etc. The implementation requires clear concepts and concise models so that a change in the business logic or in customer's requirement necessitates only a little high-level modification of the model rather than a huge quantity of low-level re-coding.

The modeling of a scheduling problem will be illustrated to let readers understand the methodology of programming in NCL.

7.2.2 Data Model

The production scheduling database includes three basic tables: RESOURCE, JOB and TASK. See Table 7.1 to Table 7.3 for the definition:

In a real-world application, user should also consider the tables of products (PRODUCT), technological processes (PROCESS) and orders (ORDER). Their relations are as below:

- PRODUCT gives information such as product identifier (id), product name (name), product type (type), etc.;
- PROCESS defines for each process node its information such as node identifier id, node name name, product identifier idProduct, required resources Resource, etc.;
- ORDER gives information such as order identifier id, order name name, product identifier idProduct and product quantity quantity etc.

Each order may need to be decomposed into some batches (jobs) due to limited resource capacity. Usually, the scheduling system generates the tables of jobs (JOB) and tasks (TASK) from the table of ORDER and PROCESS.

At an abstract level, the basic problem with the RESOURCE, JOB and TASK tables is studied.

Table 7.1   RESOURCE

FIELD	NCL TYPE	DESCRIPTION
id	string	Resource identifier (key)
type	string	Resource type
qtyUnitTime	integer	unit-time production capacity
Schedule	date-time set ("mm/dd/yyyy hh:mm:ss")	Schedule of the resource on service

Table 7.2   JOB

FIELD	NCL TYPE	DESCRIPTION
id	string	Job identifier (key)
priority	integer	Job priority (from lower to higher)
t1	date-time ("mm/dd/yyyy hh:mm:ss")	Earliest start time
t2	date-time ("mm/dd/yyyy hh:mm:ss")	Latest completion time

Table 7.3   TASK

FIELD	NCL TYPE	DESCRIPTION
id	string	Task identifier (key)
name	string	Task name
idJob	string	Job identifier (JOB.id)
idSucc	string	Identifier of succeeding task
typeSync	integer	Synchronization type: 0: release time-due time gap 1: release time-release time gap 2: due time-due time gap
minGap	time("hh:mm:ss")	Lower bound of the time gap to successor
maxGap	time("hh:mm:ss")	Upper bound of the time gap to successor
IdResource	string	Set of identities of candidate resources
quantity	integer	Quantity of the task
TimeWin	date-time set ("mm/dd/yyyy hh:mm:ss")	Time window for release time

Input Program for RESOURCE (ReadResource.n)

To simplify the RESOURCE table, only the fields of id (resource identifier), type (resource type), qtyUnitTime (unit-time production capacity) and Schedule (availability) are considered. Here Schedule is a date-time set of format "mm/dd/yyyy hh:mm:ss". The data input program is:

```
'O' ← database,
'O' ⇒ (SQL:
   "SELECT id,type,qtyUnitTime,Schedule FROM RESOURCE"
),

nbResource = O,
RESOURCE = [1,nbResource],
∀ i ∈ RESOURCE (
   idResource_i              :: "",
   typeResource_i            :: "",
   qtyUnitTimeResource_i     :: 0,

   idResource_i              = O,
   typeResource_i            = O,
   qtyUnitTimeResource_i     = O,
   ScheduleResource_i        = O·"mm/dd/yyyy hh:mm:oo",
),
```

```
IDRESOURCE = {∀ i ∈ RESOURCE idResourceᵢ},

∀ i ∈ IDRESOURCE (
   resourceIdᵢ ∈ RESOURCE,
   idResource_resourceIdᵢ = i,
),
database ← 'O',
```

Input Program for JOB (ReadJob.n)

To simplify the JOB table, only the fields of id (job identifier), priority (job priority), t1 (earliest start time) and t2 (latest completion time) are considered. Here t1 and t2 are date-time constants of format "mm/dd/yyyy hh:mm:ss". The data input program is:

```
'O' ← database,
'O' ⇒ (SQL:"SELECT id, priority, t1, t2 FROM JOB"),

nbJob = O,
JOB = [1, nbJob],
∀ i ∈ JOB (
   idJobᵢ            ::"",
   priorityJobᵢ     ::0,


   idJobᵢ           = O,
   priorityJobᵢ     = O,
   t1Jobᵢ           = O: "mm/dd/yyyy hh:mm:ss",
   t2Jobᵢ           = O: "mm/dd/yyyy hh:mm:ss",
),
database ← 'O',
```

Input Program for TASK (ReadTask.n)

To simplify the TASK table, only the fields of id (task identifier), idJob (job identifier), idSucc (successor identifier), typeSync (type of synchronization with its successor), minGap (lower bound of time gap to its successor), maxGap (upper bound of time gap to its successor), IdResource (set of candidate resource identifiers), quantity (processing quantity of the task) and TimeWin (time window for start time) are considered. Here minGap and maxGap are time constants of format "hh:mm:ss"; TimeWin is a date-time set of format "mm/dd/yyyy hh:mm:ss". If a task does not have a successor, then its successor identifier idSucc is an empty string.

There exist three types of synchronization between a task and its successor:

- 0 (rear-head): a time gap exists between the completion time of a task and

the start time of its successor;
- 1 (head-head): a time gap exists between the start time of a task and the start time of its successor;
- 2 (rear-rear): a time gap exists between the completion time of a task and the completion time of its successor.

The table of TASK is generated from RESOURCE and JOB. The data input program is:

```
'O' ← database,
'O' ⇒ (SQL: "SELECT
        id,idJob,idSucc,typeSync,minGap,
        maxGap,IdResource,quantity,TimeWin FROM TASK"),

nbTask      = O,
TASK = [1, nbTask],
∀ i ∈ TASK(
    idTask_i            :: "",
    idJobTask_i         :: "",
    idSuccTask          :: "",
    typeSyncTask_i      :: 0,
    IdResourceTask_i    :: {""},
    quantityTask_i      :: 0,

    idTask_i            = O,
    idJobTask_i         = O,
    idSuccTask_i        = O,
    typeSyncTask_i      = O,
    minGapTask_i        = O:"hh:mm:ss",
    maxGapTask_i        = O:"hh:mm:ss",
    IdResourceTask_i    = O,
    quantityTask_i      = O,
    TimeWinTask_i       = O : "mm/dd/yyyy hh:mm:ss",

    jobTask_i           ∈ JOB,
    idJob_{jobTask_i}   = idJobTask_i,
),

IDTASK = {∀ i ∈ TASK idTask_i},
```

```
∀ i ∈ IDTASK (
    taskId_i            ∈ TASK,
    idTask_{taskId_i}   = i,
),

∀ i ∈ TASK (
    ResourceTask_i = {∀ j ∈ IdResourceTask_i resourceId_j},

    idSuccTask_i ≠ "" ⇒ (
        succTask_i = taskId_{idSuccTask_i}
        ;
        succTask_i = 0
    ),
),

∀ i ∈ JOB (
    TaskJob_i = {∀ j ∈ TASK (jobTask_j = i? j:0)}\0,

    nbTaskJob_i = #TaskJob_i,
),


minTaskJob = min_{i∈JOB} nbTaskJob_i,
maxTaskJob = max_{i∈JOB} nbTaskJob_i,


database ← 'O',
```

The above program generates for each task i its set of candidate resources $ResourceTask_i$ (subset of RESOURCE) and its successor $succTask_i$ (element of TASK). The program also generates for each job i its set of tasks $TaskJob_i$.

Principal Constants and Critical Variables

Creating a compact data model is important for solving an NP-hard problem. The method is to analyze what are known (constants) and what are unknown (variables).

The most challenging constraint of a Production Scheduling problem is: At any time, there can be at most one task to be scheduled on an exclusive resource. The problem consists in allocating an execution time interval and a resource to each task. So the critical variables for the data model are resource (integer variable) and time interval (set variable).

The following constants are principal:

- For any resource i, $\text{ScheduleResource}_i$ represents the union of its work slots;
- For any task i, durationTask_i represents its effective processing time. The following variables are critical:
- Integer variable resourceTask_i represents the resource allocated to task i;
- Set variable TimeTask_i represents the time interval allocated to task i;
- Set variable WorkTimeTask_i represents the union of working time intervals allocated to task i.

Other logical variables will be introduced along the presentation of the model.

7.2.3 Simplified Optimization Model

This book simplifies the Production Scheduling problem by supposing that there are only three basic data classes: RESOURCE, JOB and TASK. This facilitates the presentation of the essential aspects of production scheduling. The database is identified by database. Its ODBC data source is named jobshop, with empty user name and password.

All resources are supposed to be exclusive in this book.

```
database = ["jobshop" : "" : ""],    % the jobshop database

['Work Directory' "Model\\ReadResource.n"],
['Work Directory' "Model\\ReadJob.n"],
['Work Directory' "Model\\ReadTask.n"],

∀ i ∈ TASK(
    resourceTask_i ∈ ResourceTask_i,

                        % resource requirement constraint
    ScheduleTask_i = ScheduleResource_resourceTask_i,

    TimeTask_i = [t1Task_i, t2Task_i],

                        % time interval of task i
    WorkTimeTask_i = TimeTask_i ∩ ScheduleTask_i,

                        % work calendar constraint

    #WorkTimeTask_i =

        ⌈quantityTask_i / qtyUnitTimeResource_resourceTask_i⌉,

                        % task duration constraint

    t1Task_i ∈ TimeWinTask_i

                        % time window constraint

),
```

$\forall\ i \neq j \in$ TASK

  $\text{TimeTask}_i \cap \text{TimeTask}_j = \varnothing \lor \text{resourceTask}_i \neq \text{resourceTask}_j,$

$\qquad\qquad\qquad$ % cumulative scheduling constraint

$\forall\ i \in$ RESOURCE (

  $\text{TaskResource}_i \subset$ TASK,$\qquad$ % set of tasks on resource i

  $\forall\ j \in$ TASK

    $j \in \text{TaskResource}_i \equiv \text{resourceTask}_j = i,$

),

TASK $= \bigcup_{i \in \text{RESOURCE}} \text{TaskResource}_i,$

$\qquad\qquad\qquad$ % set partitioning over tasks

$\forall\ i \neq j \in$ RESOURCE

  $\text{TaskResource}_i \cap \text{TaskResource}_j = \varnothing,$

$\forall\ i \in$ TASK ($\qquad\qquad\qquad$ % synchronization constraints

  $\text{gapSuccRearHeadTask}_i = \text{t1Task}_{\text{succTask}_i} - \text{t2Task}_i - 1,$

  $\text{gapSuccHeadHeadTask}_i = \text{t1Task}_{\text{succTask}_i} - \text{t1Task}_i - 1,$

  $\text{gapSuccRearRearTask}_i = \text{t2Task}_{\text{succTask}_i} - \text{t2Task}_i - 1,$

  ? typeSyncTask_i (

    0: $\text{gapSuccRearHeadTask}_i \in [\text{minGapTask}_i, \text{maxGapTask}_i];$

    1: $\text{gapSuccHeadHeadTask}_i \in [\text{minGapTask}_i, \text{maxGapTask}_i];$

    2: $\text{gapSuccRearRearTask}_i \in [\text{minGapTask}_i, \text{maxGapTask}_i];$

  ),

),

$\forall\ i \in$ RESOURCE (

  $\text{slackResourceResource}_i = \dfrac{\sum_{k \in \text{TaskResource}_i} \#\Delta\text{resourceTask}_k}{\#\text{TaskResource}_i},$

  $\text{slackTimeResource}_i = \dfrac{\sum_{k \in \text{TaskResource}_i} \#\Delta\text{TimeTask}_k}{\#\text{TaskResource}_i}$

),

```
∀ i ∈ TASK → (
  min    #ΔresourceTask_i,        % least slack

  min    #ΔScheduleTask_i,        % least slack

  min    t1Task_i ,               % sequential search
)
∀ j ∈ ΔresourceTask_i → (
  min    #ΔTaskResource_j,        % least slack

  min    slackResourceResource_j , % least resource slack average

  min    slackTimeResource_j ,    % least time slack average
)
resourceTask_i = j ?,


∀ i ∈ TASK → (
  min    t2Task_i ,               % sequential search

  min    t1Task_i ,               % sequential search

  min    #ΔgapSuccHeadHeadTask_i, % least slack

  min    #ΔgapSuccRearHeadTask_i, % least slack

  min    #ΔgapSuccRearRearTask_i, % least slack
)
TimeTask_i ≠∅ ⇒
  t1Task_i = ?,


∀ i ∈ JOB (
  TimeJob_i = ∪_{j∈TaskJob_i} TimeTask_j,


  ∀ j ∈ TaskJob_i
    t1Task_j ≥ t1Job_i,


  delayJob_i = (
      sup TimeJob_i-t2Job_i > 0 ? sup TimeJob_i - t2Job_i : 0
  ),
```

),

min $\Sigma_{i \in JOB}$delayJob$_i$.   % minimize the total delay of jobs

The resource requirement constraint for task i is expressed as follows:

resourceTask$_i$ ∈ ResourceTask$_i$,

Since the set of available time slots for resource k is ScheduleResource$_k$, for any task i the set of its possible processing time slots ScheduleTask$_i$ is ScheduleResource$_{resourceTask_i}$.

Since TimeTask$_i$ is task i's time interval, the effective processing time can be defined as below:

WorkTimeTask$_i$ = TimeTask$_i$ ∩ ScheduleTask$_i$,

The above constraint is the work calendar constraint, see Figure 7.1.

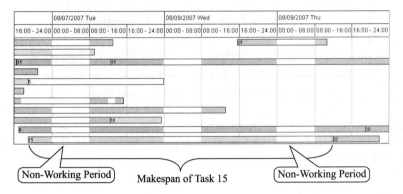

Figure 7.1 The Working Calendar of Resources

Task i's effective processing time is the division of quantity by qtyUnitTime:

#WorkTimeTask$_i$ =

$\lceil$quantityTask$_i$ / qtyUnitTimeResource$_{resourceTask_i}\rceil$,

The start time of task i must fall in its time window TimeWinTask$_i$:

t1Task$_i$ ∈ TimeWinTask$_i$,

The critical constraint of production scheduling is the packing constraint. As shown in Figure 7.2, it requires that two tasks cannot be processed by a same resource at any time:

∀ i ≠ j ∈ TASK

TimeTask$_i$ ∩ TimeTask$_j$ = ∅ ∨ resourceTask$_i$ ≠ resourceTask$_j$,

The model introduces a set variable $\texttt{TaskResource}_i$ for resource $\texttt{i}$, through which a partitioning constraint over tasks can be expressed:

$$\texttt{TASK} = \cup_{\texttt{i} \in \texttt{RESOURCE}} \ \texttt{TaskResource}_i,$$

$$\forall \ \texttt{i} \neq \texttt{j} \in \texttt{RESOURCE}$$

$$\texttt{TaskResource}_i \cap \texttt{TaskResource}_j = \varnothing,$$

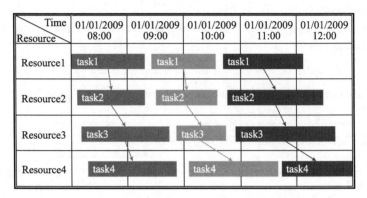

Time Resource	01/01/2009 08:00	01/01/2009 09:00	01/01/2009 10:00	01/01/2009 11:00	01/01/2009 12:00
Resource1	task1	task1	task1		
Resource2	task2	task2	task2		
Resource3	task3	task3	task3		
Resource4	task4	task4	task4		

Figure 7.2 Packing over Resources and Time

For the synchronization on the tasks of a job, three types of time distances are defined between any task $\texttt{i}$ and its successor $\texttt{succTask}_i$. As shown in Figure 7.3, they can be described as below:

$$\texttt{gapSuccRearHeadTask}_i = \texttt{t1Task}_{\texttt{succTask}_i} - \texttt{t2Task}_i -1,$$

$$\texttt{gapSuccHeadHeadTask}_i = \texttt{t1Task}_{\texttt{succTask}_i} - \texttt{t1Task}_i -1,$$

$$\texttt{gapSuccRearRearTask}_i = \texttt{t2Task}_{\texttt{succTask}_i} - \texttt{t2Task}_i -1,$$

Now it is simple to state the synchronization constraints using logical switch:

```
? typeSyncTask_i (
  0: gapSuccRearHeadTask_i ∈ [minGapTask_i,maxGapTask_i];
  1: gapSuccHeadHeadTask_i ∈ [minGapTask_i,maxGapTask_i];
  2: gapSuccRearRearTask_i ∈ [minGapTask_i,maxGapTask_i];
),
```

For the search, the model queries on critical variables in two steps: 1) to instantiate each resource variable $\texttt{resourceTask}_i$ for $\texttt{task}_i$; 2) to instantiate each start time $\texttt{t1Task}_i$ for $\texttt{task}_i$. To be prepared for expressing query criteria, a resource slack variable $\texttt{slackResourceResource}_i$ (representing the average of candidate resources for any task over it) and a time slack variable `slackTimeResource`$_i$ (representing the average of slack in time for any task over it) are defined for resource i:

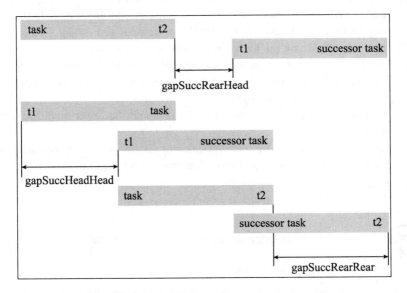

Figure 7.3 Gaps between a Task and Its Successor

$$
\texttt{slackResourceResource}_i = \frac{\sum_{k \in \texttt{TaskResource}_i} \texttt{\#}\Delta\texttt{resourceTask}_k}{\texttt{\#TaskResource}_i} ,
$$

$$
\texttt{slackTimeResource}_i = \frac{\sum_{k \in \texttt{TaskResource}_i} \texttt{\#}\Delta\texttt{TimeTask}_k}{\texttt{\#TaskResource}_i}
$$

To query on `resourceTask`$_i$, the following search strategy is used:

- First, select a critical task i in the lexicographic order of (fewest candidate resources, least slack in processing time, earliest possible start time). The criterion (`min` `#`Δ`resourceTask`$_i$) determines a task i which has the fewest candidate resources; the criterion (`min` `#`Δ`ScheduleTask`$_i$) determines a task i which has the least slack in available time; the criterion (`min` `t1Task`$_i$) determines a task i which has the earliest possible start time;

- Next, for task i select a critical resource j in the lexicographic order of (fewest candidate tasks, least resource slack average, least time slack average). The criterion (`min` `#`Δ`TaskResource`$_j$) determines a resource j with the fewest candidate tasks; the sequential-search criterion (`min` `slackResourceResource`$_j$) determines a resource j with the least resource slack average; the criterion ($\min$ $\underline{slackTimeResource_j}$) determines a resource j with the least time slack average;

- The query "$resourceTask_i = j$?" triggers the branching; first, try to assign resource j to task i; next, try the inverse logic.

To query on $t1Task_i$, the following search strategy is used:

- Select a critical task i in the lexicographic order of (earliest completion time, earliest start time, least slack in rear-head gap, least slack in head-head gap, least slack in rear-rear gap);
- Instantiate the start time variable $t1Task_i$ with the lower-bound-first enumeration mode.

The objective is to minimize the total delay of all the jobs. First, for each job i, any of its tasks should be executed no earlier than its earliest start time:

$\forall j \in TaskJob_i$

$t1Task_j \geq t1Job_i,$

Next, for job i the model introduces the date-time set variable:

$TimeJob_i = \cup_{j \in TaskJob_i} TimeTask_j.$

Since $t2Job_i$ is the job i's latest completion time, the delay of job i is defined as:

$diffTimeJob_i = \sup TimeJob_i - t2Job_i,$

$delayJob_i = (diffTimeJob_i > 0 ? diffTimeJob_i : 0),$

The objective is to minimize the total delay of all jobs:

$\Sigma_{i \in JOB} delayJob_i$

7.2.4 Visualizing Time: Gantt Chart

A Gantt chart is a time chart that illustrates a project schedule (Gantt 1974). In POEM, Gantt chart is a visualization tool for managing time. A solution to a Production Scheduling problem is illustrated using Gantt chart in Figure 7.4.

As shown in the Gantt chart, the vertical axis represents resources and tasks are displayed horizontally in accordance with their processing time. Grey parts in the chart signify non-work time over which the execution of a task is interrupted.

7.2.5 Questions

- How to adjust the data model if each task requires more than one type of resource?
- How to adjust the data model if a resource is not exclusive?

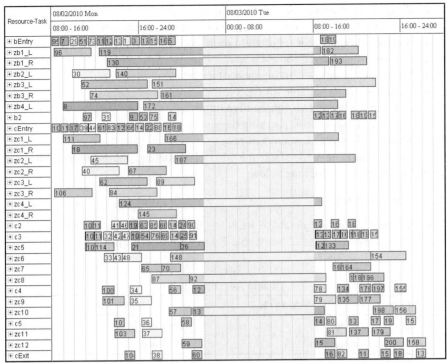

Figure 7.4 Gantt Chart Display of a Solution to a Production Scheduling Problem

7.3 Personnel Planning

7.3.1 Problem Definition

A Personnel Planning problem consists in allocating employees to work shifts (or duties) so as to satisfy the requirements on human resources of different profiles at every time slot. The objective is to assign tasks to the best employees with the best services at the most appropriate times. In this problem, the distribution of the personnel requirement during a future period is predicted based on historical data.

Such a problem often exists in personnel management of a super-market or a call center, etc. For example, call centers exist widely in a variety of businesses such as telecommunication, finance, government, electricity and postal services. As their operation expands, traditional manual planning can no longer guarantee efficient management. An intelligent Personnel Planning system becomes necessary.

If employees are organized into teams, the Personnel Planning system should generate for each team a working schedule over the whole period. Basic concepts for such a system include:

- Slot: time unit, e.g., 15 minutes or 30 minutes;
- Shift: time slot interval of a daily work by an employee, e.g., [1, 16];

- Team: a set of employees of a certain profile.

A Personnel Planning problem usually involves basic constraints as below:

- Number of employees required in each slot and in each profile;
- Number of employees on each day;
- Number of monthly working days of each team;
- Candidate shifts suitable for each team;
- Rest time between two consecutive duties;
- Number of consecutive working days;
- Number of consecutive days of rest.

To help readers to understand the idea of modeling, the Personnel Planning model is presented in NCL as below.

7.3.2 Data Model

The Personnel Planning database includes five basic tables: PROFILE, SLOT, SHIFT, TEAM and DEMAND. See Table 7.4 to Table 7.8 for the definition:

Table 7.4   PROFILE

FIELD	NCL TYPE	DESCRIPTION
id	string	Profile identifier (key)
name	string	Profile name

Table 7.5   SLOT

FIELD	NCL TYPE	DESCRIPTION
id	string	Slot identifier (key)
Time	time set ("hh:mm")	Time interval for the slot

Table 7.6   SHIFT

FIELD	NCL TYPE	DESCRIPTION
id	string	Shift identifier (key)
IdSlot	string set	Set of slot identifiers

Table 7.7   TEAM

FIELD	NCL TYPE	DESCRIPTION
id	string	Team identifier (key)
name	string	Team name
nbStaff	integer	Number of employees
IdProfile	string set	Set of profile identities
IdShift	string set	Set of shift identities

Table 7.8   DEMAND

FIELD	NCL TYPE	DESCRIPTION
idSlot	string	Slot identifier (SLOT.id)
idProfile	string	Profile identifier (PROFILE.id)
date	date ("mm/dd/yyyy")	Date of the demand
minStaff	integer	Minimum number of employees required
maxStaff	integer	Maximum number of employees required

Configuration Program for Parameters (Config.n)

```
database        = ["callcenter" : "" : ""],

minStaffDay     = 40,
maxStaffDay     = 45,

minDayMonth     = 19,
maxDayMonth     = 22,

minDaySequence  = 1,
maxDaySequence  = 6,

minDayRest      = 2,
maxDayRest      = 3,

minSlotRest     = 12,
maxSlotRest     = +∞,
```

The database is identified by `database`. Its ODBC data source is named `callcenter`, with empty user name and password. The parameters `minStaffDay` and `maxStaffDay` represent respectively the minimum and maximum numbers of employees required for each day. `minDayMonth` and `maxDayMonth` represent respectively minimum and maximum numbers of monthly working days of each team. `minDaySequence` and `maxDaySequence` represent respectively the minimum and maximum numbers of consecutive working days for each employee. `minDayRest` and `maxDayRest` represent respectively the minimum and maximum numbers of consecutive days of rest for each employee. Slot is the time unit used in the model. For those teams who are scheduled to work continually for two days, the minimum and the maximum rest time between the duties are respectively `minSlotRest` and `maxSlotRest`.

Input Program for PROFILE (ReadProfile.n)

To simplify the `PROFILE` table, only the fields of `id` (profile identifier) and `name` (profile name) are considered.

```
'O' ← database,
'O' ⇒ (SQL:"SELECT id,name FROM PROFILE   ORDER BY id"),

nbProfile = O,
PROFILE = [1, nbProfile],
∀i ∈ PROFILE(
   idProfile_i        :: "",

   nameProfile_i     :: "",


   idProfile_i       = O,

   nameProfile_i     = O,

),


IDPROFILE = {∀i ∈ PROFILE   idProfile_i},

∀ i ∈ IDPROFILE(
   profileIdProfile_i ∈ PROFILE,

   idProfile_{profileIdProfile_i} = i,
),
database ← 'O',
```

Input Program for SLOT (ReadSlot.n)

To simplify the SLOT table, only the fields of id (slot identifier) and Time (time interval of the slot) are considered. Here Time is a time set constant of format "hh:mm".

```
'O' ← database,
'O' ⇒ (SQL: "SELECT id, Time FROM SLOT ORDER BY id"),

nbSlot = O,
SLOT = [1, nbSlot],
∀ i ∈ SLOT(
   idSlot_i   :: "",

   idSlot_i   = O,

   TimeSlot_i = O : "hh:mm"

),


IDSLOT = {∀i ∈ SLOT   idSlot_i},

∀ i ∈ IDSLOT(
   slotIdSlot_i ∈ SLOT,

   idSlot_{slotIdSlot_i} = i,
```

```
) ,

database ← 'O',
```

For the data class SLOT, $TimeSlot_i$ represents the time interval (format "hh:mm") for slot i.

Input Program for SHIFT (ReadShift.n)

To simplify the SHIFT table, only the fields of id (shift identifier) and Time (work time interval) are considered. Here Time is a time set constant of format "hh:mm".

```
'O' ← database,
'O' ⇒ (SQL:"SELECT id, IdSlot FROM SHIFT ORDER BY id"),

nbShift = O,
SHIFT = [1, nbShift],
∀ i ∈ SHIFT (
   idShift_i          :: "",
   idShift_i        = O,
   IdSlotShift_i    = O,
   SlotShift_i      = {∀ j ∈ IdSlotShift_i  slotIdSlot_j}
) ,

IDSHIFT = {∀ i ∈ SHIFT idShift_i},

∀ i ∈ IDSHIFT (
   shiftIdShift_i ∈ SHIFT,
   idShift_shiftIdShift_i = i
) ,

nonShift = 0,

database ← 'O',
```

For the data class SHIFT, $SlotShift_i$ represents the time slot interval of shift i. The model defines a special parameter nonShift which represents a fictitious non-working shift.

Input Program for TEAM (ReadTeam.n)

To simplify the TEAM table, only the fields of id (team identifier), nbStaff (number of employees), IdProfile (set of profile identities) and IdShift (set of identities of candidate shifts).

```
'O' ← database,
'O' ⇒ (SQL : "SELECT id, IdProfile,IdShift, nbStaff FROM TEAM
        ORDER BY id"),

nbTeam = 0,
TEAM = [1,nbTeam],
∀t ∈ TEAM(
  idTeam_t              :: 0,
  IdProfileTeam_t       :: {""},
  IdShiftTeam_t         :: ∅,
  nbStaffTeam_t         :: 0,
  idTeam_t              = 0,
  IdProfileTeam_t       = 0,
  IdShiftTeam_t         = 0,
  nbStaffTeam_t         = 0,


  ProfileTeam_t = {∀i∈IdProfileTeam_t profileIdProfile_i},
  ShiftTeam_t = {∀i ∈ IdShiftTeam_t shiftIdShift_i}


  ∀p ∈ PROFILE
      nbStaffTeamProfile_{p,t}=(p∈ProfileTeam_t? nbStaffTeam_t: 0),
),

database ← 'O',
```

For the data class TEAM, for team t, ProfileTeam_t represents its set of profiles; nbStaffTeam_t represents the number of its employees, nbStaffTeamProfile_{p,t} represents its number of employees with profile p; ShiftTeam_t represents its set of candidate shifts.

Input Program for DEMAND (ReadDemand.n)

To simplify the DEMAND table, only the fields of idSlot (slot identifier), idProfile (profile identifier), date, minStaff (minimum number of employees required), maxStaff (maximum number of employees required).

```
'O' ← database,
'O' ⇒ (SQL:"SELECT idSlot,idProfile,date,minStaff,maxStaff
    FROM DEMAND ORDER BY date,idSlot,idProfile"),

nbDemand = 0,
DEMAND = [1, nbDemand],
```

```
∀p ∈ PROFILE
∀d ∈ DATE
∀i ∈ SLOT (
   minStaffSlotDateProfile_p,d,i :: 0,
   maxStaffSlotDateProfile_p,d,i :: 0,
),

∀ i ∈ DEMAND (
   idProfileDemand_i :: "",
   idSlotDemand_i     :: 0,
   minStaffDemand_i  :: 0,
   maxStaffDemand_i  :: 0,

   idSlotDemand_i     = O,
   idProfileDemand_i = O,
   dateDemand_i       = O:"mm/dd/yyyy",
   minStaffDemand_i  = O,
   maxStaffDemand_i  = O,

   slotDemand_i          ∈ SLOT,
   idSlotDemand_i        = idSlot_slotDemand_i,


   profileDemand_i     ∈ PROFILE,
   idProfileDemand_i = idProfile_profileDemand_i,

   minStaffSlotDateProfile_profileDemand_i,dateDemand_i,slotDemand_i
              = minStaffDemand_i,
   maxStaffSlotDateProfile_profileDemand_i,dateDemand_i,slotDemand_i
              = maxStaffDemand_i
),
DATE = {∀ i∈ DEMAND  dateDemand_i},
DATE = [date1, date2],


database ← 'O',
```

For any demand i, from constants $profileDemand_i$, $slotDemand_i$, $dateDemand_i$, $minStaffDemand_i$ and $maxStaffDemand_i$, parameters $minStaffSlotDateProfile_{p,d,i}$ (minimum number of required employees) and $maxStaffSlotDateProfile_{p,d,i}$ (maximum number of required employees) can be computed for any profile in any date and at any slot:

```
∀i ∈ DEMAND (
```

$$\text{minStaffSlotDateProfile}_{\text{profileDemand}_i, \text{dateDemand}_i, \text{slotDemand}_i}$$
$$= \text{minStaffDemand}_i,$$
$$\text{maxStaffSlotDateProfile}_{\text{profileDemand}_i, \text{dateDemand}_i, \text{slotDemand}_i}$$
$$= \text{maxStaffDemand}_i$$

),

Finally, the date class DATE can be derived from DEMAND:

$$\text{DATE} = \{\forall\ i \in \text{DEMAND}\ \text{dateDemand}_i\},$$

To keep the model simple, DATE is supposed to be the set of one month's dates from date1 to date2.

Principal Constants and Critical Variables

The Personnel Planning problem amounts to determine the human resource allocation for any profile and at any time slot. The table SHIFT regulates the work schedule of a team. So on any date d, for any team t, the model needs to introduce the following logical variables:

- Boolean variable $\text{activeTeamDate}_{d,t}$ telling if team t works on date d;
- Integer variable $\text{shiftTeamDate}_{d,t}$ telling the work shift for team t on date d;
- Set variable $\text{SlotTeamDate}_{d,t}$ telling the time interval (in slots) for team t on date d;
- Special constant nonShift representing a non-work shift.

The model also defines the following logical variables:

- ActiveTeamDate_d represents the set of teams working on date d;
- ActiveDateTeam_t represents the set of dates on which team t works.

It is more complex to model a team's work sequence. For any team t, the model introduces the following variables:

- nbSequenceTeam_t represents the number of sequences;
- For any sequence i, $\text{DateSequenceTeam}_{t,i}$ represents its date interval with $\text{d1SequenceTeam}_{t,i}$ and $\text{d2SequenceTeam}_{t,i}$ being release and due dates.

Other variables will be introduced in the following model.

7.3.3 Simplified Optimization Model

This book simplifies the Personnel Planning problem by supposing that there are only five basic data classes: PROFILE, SLOT, SHIFT, TEAM and DEMAND. The NCL program models directly on the basic aspect.

```
['Work Directory' "Model\Config.n"],
['Work Directory' "Model\ReadProfile.n"],
['Work Directory' "Model\ReadSlot.n"],
['Work Directory' "Model\ReadShift.n"],
```

```
['Work Directory' "Model\ReadTeam.n"],
['Work Directory' "Model\ReadDemand.n"],
```

$\forall\, d \in DATE\,($

$\quad ActiveTeamDate_d \subset TEAM,$

$\quad \Sigma_{t \in ActiveTeamDate_d} nbStaffTeam_t \in [minStaffDay, maxStaffDay]$

$),$

$\forall\, t \in TEAM\,($

$\quad ActiveDateTeam_t \subset DATE,$

$\quad \#ActiveDateTeam_t \in [minDayMonth,\ maxDayMonth],$

$\quad \forall\, d \in DATE\,($

$\qquad shiftTeamDate_{d,t} \in ShiftTeam_t \cup \{nonShift\},$

$\qquad SlotTeamDate_{d,t} = [s1TeamDate_{d,t}, s2TeamDate_{d,t}],$

$\qquad SlotTeamDate_{d,t} \subset SLOT,$

$\qquad SlotTeamDate_{d,t} = SlotShift_{shiftTeamDate_{d,t}},$

$\qquad activeTeamDate_{d,t} \equiv SlotTeamDate_{d,t} \neq \varnothing,$

$\qquad activeTeamDate_{d,t} \equiv shiftTeamDate_{d,t} \neq nonShift,$

$\qquad activeTeamDate_{d,t} \equiv d \in ActiveDateTeam_t,$

$\qquad activeTeamDate_{d,t} \equiv t \in ActiveTeamDate_d,$

$\quad)$

$),$

$DATE = \cup_{t \in TEAM} ActiveDateTeam_t,$

$\forall\, p \in PROFILE$
$\forall\, d \in DATE$
$\forall\, i \in SLOT\,($
$\quad nbStaffSlotDateProfile_{p,d,i} =$

$\qquad \Sigma_{t \in TeamProfile_p} (i \in SlotTeamDate_{d,t}) \times nbStaffTeamProfile_{p,t},$

$\quad nbStaffSlotDateProfile_{p,d,i} \in$

$\qquad [minStaffSlotDateProfile_{p,d,i}, maxStaffSlotDateProfile_{p,d,i}]$

$),$

$\forall\, t \in$ TEAM
$\forall\, d \in$ [date1, date2-1]
   $(\text{s1TeamDate}_{d+1,t} - \text{s2TeamDate}_{d,t} - 1 + \#\text{SLOT}) \in [\text{minSlotRest}, \text{maxSlotRest}]$,

$\forall\, t \in$ TEAM(
   $\text{nbSequenceTeam}_t \in [0, \#\text{DATE}]$,

   $\forall\, i \in [1, \#\text{DATE}]$(
      $\text{DateSequenceTeam}_{t,i} \subset \text{ActiveDateTeam}_t$,
      $\text{DateSequenceTeam}_{t,i} = [\text{d1SequenceTeam}_{t,i}, \text{d2SequenceTeam}_{t,i}]$,
   ),

   $\forall\, i < j \in [1, \#\text{DATE}]$(
      $\text{DateSequenceTeam}_{t,i} \prec \text{DateSequenceTeam}_{t,j}$,
      $\text{DateSequenceTeam}_{t,j} \neq \varnothing \rightarrow \text{DateSequenceTeam}_{t,i} \neq \varnothing$,
   ),

   $\forall\, i \in [1, \text{nbSequenceTeam}_t]$
      $\#\text{DateSequenceTeam}_{t,i} \in [\text{minDaySequence}, \text{maxDaySequence}]$,

   $\text{ActiveDateTeam}_t = \bigcup_{i \in [1, \text{nbSequenceTeam}_t]} \text{DateSequenceTeam}_{t,i}$,

   $\forall\, i \in [1, \#\text{DATE} - 1]$
      $(\text{d1SequenceTeam}_{t,i+1} - \text{d2SequenceTeam}_{t,i} - 1)$
         $\in [\text{minDayRest}, \text{maxDayRest}]$,
),

$\forall\, d \in$ DATE
$\forall\, i \in$ SLOT
$\forall\, p \in$ PROFILE(
   $\text{lowstaffSlotDateProfile}_{p,d,i} =$
      $\sum_{t \in \text{TeamProfile}_p} (i \in \underline{\text{SlotTeamDate}_{d,t}}) \times \text{nbStaffTeamProfile}_{p,t}$,

   $\text{diffSlotDateProfile}_{p,d,i} =$
      $\text{minStaffSlotDateProfile}_{p,d,i} - \text{lowstaffSlotDateProfile}_{p,d,i}$,
),

$\forall\, d \in$ DATE
$\forall\, s \in$ SHIFT
$\quad$ lackShiftDate$_{d,s}=$

$\quad \sum_{p \in \text{PROFILE}, i \in \text{SlotShift}_s} ($

$\qquad$ (diffSlotDateProfile$_{p,d,i} \geq 0$) $\times$ diffSlotDateProfile$_{p,d,i}$

$\quad$),

$\forall\, d \in$ DATE $\rightarrow$ (
$\quad$ min $\quad$ d,
)
$\forall\, t \in$ TEAM $\rightarrow$ (
$\quad$ min $\quad$ #ΔshiftTeamDate$_{d,t}$,

$\quad$ min $\quad$ #$\underline{\text{ActiveDateTeam}_t}$,
)
$\forall\, s \in \Delta$shiftTeamDate$_{d,t} \rightarrow ($
$\quad$ max $\quad$ lackShiftDate$_{d,s}$
)
shiftTeamDate$_{d,t} = s?$,

$\forall\, d \in$ DATE
$\quad$ excessStaffDate$_d =$

$\quad \sum_{p \in \text{PROFILE}, i \in \text{SLOT}} ($

$\qquad$ nbStaffSlotDateProfile$_{p,d,i}$ - minStaffSlotDateProfile$_{p,d,i}$

$\quad$),

$\quad$ min $\quad \sum_{d \in \text{DATE}}$ excessStaffDate$_d$.

As modeled naturally in the above constraint program, the constraint over "number of employees on each day" is stated as:
$\forall\, d \in$ DATE
$\sum_{t \in \text{ActiveTeamDate}_d}$ nbStaffTeam$_t \in$ [minStaffDay, maxStaffDay],

The constraint over "number of monthly working days of each team" is stated as:
$\forall\, t \in$ TEAM
$\quad$ #ActiveDateTeam$_t \in$ [minDayMonth, maxDayMonth],

Team t on date d can only select a shift from a set of limited candidate shifts:
ShiftTeamDate$_{d,t} \in$ ShiftTeam$_t \cup$ {nonShift},

The domain of shiftTeamDate$_{d,t}$ contains the fictitious shift nonShift. If shiftTeamDate$_{d,t}$ takes value nonShift, it means that team t does not work on date d. So the time slot variable can be computed by the following logic:

$$\texttt{SlotTeamDate}_{d,t} = [\texttt{s1TeamDate}_{d,t}, \texttt{s2TeamDate}_{d,t}],$$

$$\texttt{SlotTeamDate}_{d,t} \subset \texttt{SLOT},$$

$$\texttt{SlotTeamDate}_{d,t} = \texttt{SlotShift}_{\texttt{shiftTeamDate}_{d,t}},$$

For team t on date d, the logical relations between Boolean variable $\texttt{activeTeamDate}_{d,t}$, shift variable $\texttt{shiftTeamDate}_{d,t}$, time slot interval $\texttt{SlotTeamDate}_{d,t}$, set of active teams $\texttt{ActiveTeamDate}_d$ and set of active dates $\texttt{ActiveDateTeam}_t$ are listed below:

$$\texttt{activeTeamDate}_{d,t} \equiv \texttt{SlotTeamDate}_{d,t} \neq \varnothing,$$

$$\texttt{activeTeamDate}_{d,t} \equiv \texttt{shiftTeamDate}_{d,t} \neq \texttt{nonShift},$$

$$\texttt{activeTeamDate}_{d,t} \equiv d \in \texttt{ActiveDateTeam}_t,$$

$$\texttt{activeTeamDate}_{d,t} \equiv t \in \texttt{ActiveTeamDate}_d,$$

NCL uses the weighted cumulation model to express the human resource requirement constraint:

$\forall p \in \texttt{PROFILE}$
$\forall d \in \texttt{DATE}$
$\forall i \in \texttt{SLOT}\,($
    $\texttt{d2SequenceTeam}_{p,d,i} =$

    $\sum_{t \in \texttt{TeamProfile}_p} (i \in \texttt{SlotTeamDate}_{d,t}) \times \texttt{nbStaffTeamProfile}_{p,t},$

    $\texttt{d2SequenceTeam}_{p,d,i} \in$

    $[\texttt{minStaffSlotDateProfile}_{p,d,i}, \texttt{maxStaffSlotDateProfile}_{p,d,i}]$

$)$,

The cumulation model is illustrated in Figure 7.5.

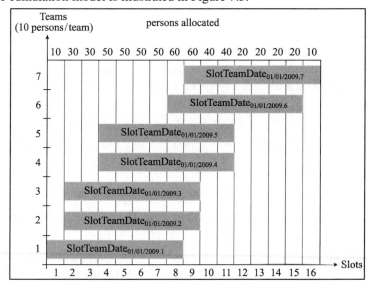

Figure 7.5 The Planning of 7 Teams on 01/01/2009

To make the modeling compact, the cumulation constraint requires
$\mathtt{SlotTeamDate_{d,t}}$ to be an interval.

For any team $\mathtt{t}$, the constraint over the time gap between two consecutive
duties is:

$\forall \mathtt{t} \in \mathtt{TEAM}$

$\forall \mathtt{d} \in \mathtt{[date1, \ date2-1]}$

$\quad(\mathtt{s1TeamDate_{d+1,t}} - \mathtt{s2TeamDate_{d,t}} - 1 + \mathtt{\#SLOT})$

$\qquad \in \mathtt{[minSlotRest, maxSlotRest]},$

It is quite complex to model the work sequences of a team. Based on the
number of sequences $\mathtt{nbSequenceTeam_t}$ and the date interval
$\mathtt{DateSequenceTeam_{t,i}}$ of team $\mathtt{t}$, the interval sequence model (special set
partitioning) is used to express the constraints over work sequences and rest. First,
the work sequences of a team are modeled below:

$\forall \mathtt{t} \in \mathtt{TEAM}\,($

$\quad \mathtt{nbSequenceTeam_t} \in \mathtt{[0, \#DATE]},$

$\quad \forall \mathtt{i} \in \mathtt{[1, \#DATE]}$

$\qquad \mathtt{DateSequenceTeam_{t,i}} =$

$\qquad \mathtt{[d1SequenceTeam_{t,i}, d2SequenceTeam_{t,i}]},$

$\quad \forall \mathtt{i < j} \in \mathtt{[1, \#DATE]}\,($

$\qquad \mathtt{DateSequenceTeam_{t,i}} \prec \mathtt{DateSequenceTeam_{t,j}},$

$\qquad \mathtt{DateSequenceTeam_{t,j}} \neq \varnothing \rightarrow \mathtt{DateSequenceTeam_{t,i}} \neq \varnothing,$

$\quad)\,,$

$\quad \mathtt{ActiveDateTeam_t} =$

$\qquad \bigcup_{\mathtt{i} \in \mathtt{[1, nbSequenceTeam_t]}} \mathtt{DateSequenceTeam_{t,i}},$

$)\,,$

See Figure 7.6 for the model of work sequences.

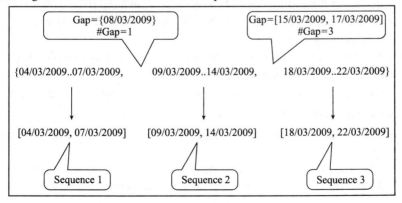

Figure 7.6 Work Sequences and Time Gaps

The constraint over work sequences of team t can be expressed as below:
$$\forall\, i \in [1,\ \text{nbSequenceTeam}_t]$$
$$\#\text{DateSequenceTeam}_{t,i} \in [\text{minDaySequence}, \text{maxDaySequence}],$$

The constraint over "number of consecutive days of rest" can be expressed below:
$$\forall\, i \in [1,\ \#\text{DATE} - 1]$$
$$(\text{d1SequenceTeam}_{t,i+1} - \text{d2SequenceTeam}_{t,i} - 1)$$
$$\in [\text{minDayRest}, \text{maxDayRest}],$$

For search strategy, the model instantiates the shift variable $\text{shiftTeamDate}_{d,t}$ for any team t on any date d. First, for any profile p, any date d and any slot i, some variables are defined as below:

- Number of employees already planned:
$$\text{lowstaffSlotDateProfile}_{p,d,i} =$$
$$\Sigma_{t \in \text{TeamProfile}_p}\, (i \in \underline{\text{SlotTeamDate}_{d,t}})\times \text{nbStaffTeamProfile}_{p,t},$$

- Difference between the minimum employee requirement and the number of employees already planned:
$$\text{diffSlotDateProfile}_{p,d,i} =$$
$$\text{minStaffSlotDateProfile}_{p,d,i} - \text{lowstaffSlotDateProfile}_{p,d,i},$$

Furthermore, for any shift s on any date d, the difference in personnel requirement can be obtained:
$$\text{lackShiftDate}_{d,s} =$$
$$\Sigma_{p \in \text{PROFILE}, i \in \text{SlotShift}_s}\, ($$
$$(\text{diffSlotDateProfile}_{p,d,i} \geq 0)\ \times\ \text{diffSlotDateProfile}_{p,d,i}$$
$$),$$

To query on $\text{shiftTeamDate}_{d,t}$ for any team t on any date d, the search rules are:

- First, select the earliest date d by sequential search ($\min\quad d$), where d corresponds to the subscript d of the non-instantiated shift variable $\text{shiftTeamDate}_{d,t}$;
- Next, for date d select a critical team t in the lexicographic order of (fewest candidate shifts, minimum number of working days). The least-slack criterion ($\min\quad \#\Delta\text{shiftTeamDate}_{d,t}$) selects a team t with the fewest candidate shifts. The greedy criterion ($\min\quad \#\,\text{ActiveDateTeam}_t$) selects a team t which contains the minimum number of already planned working days;
- At last, for date d and team t, the criterion ($\max\quad \text{lackShiftDate}_{d,s}$) selects a shift s with the least lack in human resource requirement;

- The query "shiftTeamDate$_{d,t}$= s?" triggers the branching: first, try to assign shift s to team t on date d; next, try the inverse logic.

The objective is to minimize the excess on the human resource requirement. First, for each date d the model calculates its excess:

excessStaffDate$_d$ =

$\Sigma_{p \in PROFILE, i \in SLOT}$ (

nbStaffSlotDateProfile$_{p,d,i}$ - minStaffSlotDateProfile$_{p,d,i}$

),

The objective function is:

min $\Sigma_{d \in DATE}$ excessStaffDate$_d$.

7.3.4 Visualizing Statistics: Histogram

In POEM, Histogram is a visualization tool for managing statistics. A solution to a Personnel Planning problem is illustrated using Histogram in Figure 7.7.

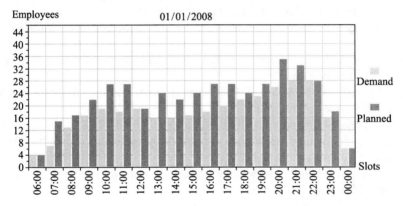

Figure 7.7 Histogram Display of a Solution to a Personnel Planning Problem

As shown in the histogram, the "Demand" bars signify the required human resources over the time horizon (in slots); the "Planned" bars represent a solution which satisfies the demand.

7.3.5 Questions

If there exists a break during a shift and such a break cannot be treated as a working time, how should the data model be adjusted to fit the constraint program?

7.4 Multi-Modal Transportation Planning

7.4.1 Problem Definition

Multi-Modal Transport consists in organizing more than one mode of transport (air, rail, road and water, etc.) to arrange for the flows of goods over a transportation network. Multi-Modal Transport Optimization consists in planning the delivery of goods by different modes of transport through optimal itineraries so as to minimize the cost, to maximize the effectiveness and to maximize the security (Zhou et al. 2007).

In detail, a multi-modal transport optimization problem requires delivering goods for a number of orders from their origins to their destinations, each through a path with a number of legs. Over the transportation network, each leg has its daily schedule, with a certain mode of transport, a duration, a capacity and a unit cost, etc. A solution to the problem should determine the legs and schedules for all orders subject to constraints such as transport mode, time and capacity. The objective is to minimize the total logistic cost.

The following basic concepts are important:

- Site: a node on a transport network;
- Leg: a directed link between two sites, with attributes such as mode of transport and capacity;
- Daily Schedule: daily timetable (set of duties) for a leg;
- Shift: a scheduled trip of a leg, e.g., 8:00-10:00.

Multi-modal transportation planning usually involves basic constraints as below:

- Arrival Time: an order must be delivered between its earliest arrival time and its latest arrival time;
- Requirement on Modes of Transport: an order can only be transported by certain modes of transport;
- Candidate Shifts: possible shifts over a leg;
- Transport Capacity; each mode of transport has a limited capability (in quantity, in volume or in weight);
- Routing: each order is delivered along an itinerary, chained in sites and sorted in time.

7.4.2 Data Model

The multi-modal transportation planning database includes three basic tables: SITE, LEG and ORDER. See Table 7.9 to Table 7.11 for the definition.

Input Program for SITE (ReadSite.n)

To simplify the SITE table, only the fields of id (site identifier) and name (site name) are considered.

```
'O' ← database,
'O' ⇒ (SQL:"SELECT id,name  FROM SITE"),

nbSite     = O,
SITE = [1, nbSite],
∀ i ∈ SITE(
    idSite_i   :: "",
    nameSite_i :: "",
```

$$idSite_i \quad = O,$$
$$nameSite_i = O,$$
$$),$$
$$IDSITE = \{\forall\, i \in SITE\ idSite_i\},$$
$$\forall\, i \in IDSITE\,($$
$$siteId_i \in SITE,$$
$$idSite_{siteId_i} = i,$$
$$),$$
$$database \leftarrow \text{'O'},$$

Table 7.9   SITE

FIELD	NCL TYPE	DESCRIPTION
id	string	Site identifier (key)
name	string	Site name

Table 7.10   LEG

FIELD	NCL TYPE	DESCRIPTION
id	string	Leg identifier (key)
idSite1	string	Origin site identifier
idSite2	string	Destination site identifier
mode	string	Mode of transport (air, rail, road, water, etc.)
time	time ("hh:mm")	Time of transport (in minutes)
Schedule	date-time set ("mm/dd/yyyy hh:mm")	Set of shifts (duties) in date-time
capacity	integer	Transport capacity
costunit	float	Unit cost

Table 7.11   ORDER

FIELD	NCL TYPE	DESCRIPTION
id	string	Order identifier (key)
t1	date-time("mm/dd/yyyy hh:mm")	Earliest arrival time
t2	date-time ("mm/dd/yyyy hh:mm")	Latest arrival time
Mode	string set	Set of allowed modes of transport
quantity	integer	Quantity
idSite1	string	Origin site identifier
idSite2	string	Destination site identifier

After the data class SITE is established, site identities in SITE are mapped into a new data class IDSITE of identities of sites.

Input Program for LEG (ReadLeg.n)

To simplify the LEG table, only the fields of id (site identifier), idSite1 (origin site identifier), idSite2 (destination site identifier), mode (mode of transport), time (time of transport), Schedule (set of transport duties), capacity (transport capacity) and costunit (unit cost) are considered. Here time is of format "hh:mm" and Schedule adopts the format "mm/dd/yyyy hh:mm".

```
'O' ← database,
'O' ⇒ (SQL:"SELECT id,idSite1,idSite2,mode,time,
        Schedule,capacity,costunit FROM LEG ORDER BY id"),

nbLeg = O,
LEG = [1,nbLeg],
∀ r ∈ LEG (
    idLeg_r          :: "",
    idSite1Leg_r     :: "",
    idSite2Leg_r     :: "",
    modeLeg_r        :: "",
    costunitLeg_r    :: 0.0,
    ScheduleLeg_r    :: ∅,
    ShiftLeg_r       :: ∅,

    idLeg_r          = O,
    idSite1Leg_r     = O,
    idSite2Leg_r     = O,
    modeLeg_r        = O,
    timeLeg_r        = O : "hh:mm",
    ScheduleLeg_r    = O : "mm/dd/yyyy hh:mm",
    capacityLeg_r    = O,
    costunitLeg_r    = O,

    site1Leg_r       ∈ SITE,
    site2Leg_r       ∈ SITE,
    idSite1Leg_r     = idSite_site1Leg_r,
    idSite2Leg_r     = idSite_site2Leg_r
```

```
),

SCHEDULE = ∪_{r∈LEG}ScheduleLeg_r,

SHIFT = [1, #SCHEDULE],
∀ s ∈ SHIFT
   t1Shift_s = SCHEDULE[s],

∀ i ∈ SCHEDULE(
   shiftSchedule_i ∈ SHIFT,

   t1Shift_{shiftSchedule_i} = i

),

∀ r ∈ LEG(
   ShiftLeg_r = {∀ i∈ScheduleLeg_r shiftSchedule_i},

   ∀ s ∈ ShiftLeg_r(

      TimeShiftLeg_{r,s} :: {'2000-01-01 00:00'},

      TimeShiftLeg_{r,s} = [t1Shift_s, _],

      #TimeShiftLeg_{r,s} = timeLeg_r

   )

),

∀ i ∈ SITE(
   LegFrSite_i = {∀ r ∈ LEG(site1Leg_r = i ? r:0)}\0,

   LegToSite_i = {∀ r ∈ LEG(site2Leg_r = i ? r:0)}\0

),
database ← 'O',
```

From the data class LEG, the transport timetable SCHEDULE and the data class SHIFT are derived. SCHEDULE is a set of discrete date-times. SHIFT is a compact set of shifts each of which represents abstractly a duty of a leg.

For any leg r, the model introduces its shift set ShiftLeg$_r$. For any shift s on any leg r, the model introduces its time interval TimeShiftLeg$_{r,s}$.

Legs and sites form a transport network. For any site i, LegFrSite$_i$ represents the set of legs exiting from site i and LegToSite$_i$ represents the set of legs coming to site i.

Input Program for ORDER (ReadOrder.n)

To simplify the ORDER table, only the fields of id (order identifier), t1 (earliest delivery time), t2 (latest delivery time), Mode (set of allowed modes of transport), quantity, idSite1 (origin site identifier) and idSite2 (destination site identifier) are considered. Here `t1` and `t2` are of format "mm/dd/yyyy hh:mm".

```
'O' ← database,
'O' ⇒ (SQL:"SELECT id,t1,t2,Mode,quantity,idSite1,idSite2
        FROM ORDER ORDER BY id"),

nbOrder = O,
ORDER = [1, nbOrder],
∀ o ∈ ORDER(
    idOrder_o            :: "",

    ModeOrder_o          :: ∅,

    site1Order_o         ∈ SITE,

    site2Order_o         ∈ SITE,

    idSite1Order_o       ∈ IDSITE,

    idSite2Order_o       ∈ IDSITE,


    idOrder_o            = O,

    minDeadlineOrder_o = O : "mm/dd/yyyy hh:mm",

    maxDeadlineOrder_o = O : "mm/dd/yyyy hh:mm",

    ModeOrder_o          = O,

    quantityOrder_o      = O,

    idSite1Order_o       = O,

    idSite2Order_o       = O,


    idSite1Order_o       = idSite_{site1Order_o},

    idSite2Order_o       = idSite_{site2Order_o},
),

∀ i ∈ SITE(
    OrderOriginSite_i = {∀ o∈ORDER(site1Order_o = i ? o : 0)} \ O,

    OrderDestinSite_i = {∀ o∈ORDER(site2Order_o = i ? o : 0)} \ O,
),

database ← 'O',
```

From the data class ORDER, two constants are derived: $OrderOriginSite_i$ is the set of orders whose origins are all the same (site i) and

`OrderDestinSite`$_i$ is the set of orders whose destinations are all the same (site `i`).

Principal Constants and Critical Variables

The multi-modal transport optimization requires instantiating the legs and schedules for all orders. So the model introduces the following logical variables:

- `LegOrder`$_o$ represents the set of legs for order o;
- `OrderLeg`$_r$ (its counterpart is `LegOrder`$_o$) represents the set of orders for leg r;
- `shiftLegOrder`$_{o,r}$ represents the scheduled shift on leg r for order o;
- `TimeLegOrder`$_{o,r}$ represents the time interval on leg r for order o (start time is `t1LegOrder`$_{o,r}$ and completion time is `t2LegOrder`$_{o,r}$).

Consequently, the solving of a multi-modal transport optimization problem amounts to instantiating `LegOrder`$_o$ for any order o and `shiftLegOrder`$_{o,r}$ for any leg r in `LegOrder`$_o$.

Other logical variables will be explained in the following model.

7.4.3 Simplified Optimization Model

This book simplifies the transport planning problem by supposing that there are only three basic data classes: `SITE`, `LEG` and `ORDER`. The NCL program models the problem directly on the basic aspect. The database name is `MultiModalTransport`, with empty user name and password. The basic model is:

```
database = ["MultiModalTransport" : "" : ""],

['Work Directory' "Model\ReadSite.n"],
['Work Directory' "Model\ReadLeg.n"],
['Work Directory' "Model\ReadOrder.n"],

∀ o ∈ ORDER(
    LegOrder  ⊂ LEG,
           o

    ∀r ∈ LEG(
        shiftLegOrder     ∈ ShiftLeg ,
                     o,r            r

        TimeLegOrder     = [t1LegOrder    ,t2LegOrder    ],
                    o,r              o,r             o,r

        TimeLegOrder     = TimeShiftLeg
                    o,r               r,shiftLegOrder
                                                     o,r

        #TimeLegOrder     = timeLeg ,
                     o,r            r

    ),

    ∀ r ≠ k ∈ LegOrder (
                       o
        site1Leg  ≠ site1Leg ,
                r           k
```

$$\text{site2Leg}_r \neq \text{site2Leg}_k,$$

```
        ),
    ),
```

$\forall\, r \in \text{LEG}($

 $\text{OrderLeg}_r \subset \text{ORDER},$

 $\text{ActiveShiftLeg}_r \subset \text{ShiftLeg}_r,$

 $\forall\, o \in \text{ORDER}$

  $r \in \text{LegOrder}_o \equiv o \in \text{OrderLeg}_r,$

 $\forall\, s \in \text{ShiftLeg}_r($

  $\text{OrderShiftLeg}_{r,s} \subset \text{OrderLeg}_r,$

  $\text{activeShiftLeg}_{r,s} \equiv \text{OrderShiftLeg}_{r,s} \neq \varnothing,$

  $\text{activeShiftLeg}_{r,s} \equiv s \in \text{ActiveShiftLeg}_r,$

  $\text{quantityShiftLeg}_{r,s} = \sum_{o \in \text{OrderShiftLeg}_{r,s}} \text{quantityOrder}_o,$

  $\text{quantityShiftLeg}_{r,s} \leq \text{capacityLeg}_r,$

 ),

 $\text{OrderLeg}_r = \bigcup_{s \in \text{ShiftLeg}_r} \text{OrderShiftLeg}_{r,s},$

 $\forall\, s \neq i \in \text{ShiftLeg}_r$

  $\text{OrderShiftLeg}_{r,s} \cap \text{OrderShiftLeg}_{r,i} = \varnothing,$

  $\forall\, o \in \text{OrderLeg}_r($

   $\text{modeLeg}_r \in \text{ModeOrder}_o,$

   $\text{shiftLegOrder}_{o,r} \in \text{ActiveShiftLeg}_r,$

   $o \in \text{OrderShiftLeg}_{r,\text{shiftLegOrder}_{o,r}},$

  ),

 $\text{quantityLeg}_r = \sum_{o \in \text{OrderLeg}_r} \text{quantityOrder}_o,$

 $\text{quantityLeg}_r \leq \#\text{ActiveShiftLeg}_r \times \text{capacityLeg}_r,$

$)$,

$ORDER = \bigcup_{r \in LEG} OrderLeg_r,$

$\forall\, o \in ORDER\,($
  $sinkOrder_o = -o,$

  $firstLegOrder_o \in LegOrder_o \cap LegFrSite_{site1Order_o},$
  $lastLegOrder_o \in LegOrder_o \cap LegToSite_{site2Order_o},$

  $BodyLegOrder_o \subset LegOrder_o,$

  $LegOrder_o = \{firstLegOrder_o\} \cup BodyLegOrder_o,$

  $t1Order_o = t1LegOrder_{o,firstLegOrder_o},$
  $t2Order_o = t2LegOrder_{o,lastLegOrder_o},$

  $t2Order_o \in [minDeadlineOrder_o,\ maxDeadlineOrder_o],$

  $site1Leg_{firstLegOrder_o} = site1Order_o,$
  $site2Leg_{lastLegOrder_o} = site2Order_o,$

  $\forall\, r \in LEG\,($

    $nextLegOrder_{o,r} \in$
    $(BodyLegOrder_o \cap LegFrSite_{site2Leg_r}) \cup \{sinkOrder_o\},$

    $r \notin LegOrder_o \rightarrow nextLegOrder_{o,r} = sinkOrder_o,$
  $)$,

  $nextLegOrder_{o,lastLegOrder_o} = sinkOrder_o,$

  $\forall\, r \neq k \in LegOrder_o$
    $nextLegOrder_{o,r} \neq nextLegOrder_{o,k},$

  $\forall\, r \in LegOrder_o\,($

    $TimeLegOrder_{o,r} \subset [t1Order_o, t2Order_o],$

$$\text{TimeLegOrder}_{o,r} \prec \text{TimeLegOrder}_{o,\text{nextLegOrder}_{o,r}},$$

$$\text{site1Leg}_{\text{nextLegOrder}_{o,r}} = \text{site2Leg}_r,$$

$$),$$

$$),$$

$\forall\, i \in \text{SITE}\,($

$$\text{OrderFrSite}_i = \bigcup_{r \in \text{LegFrSite}_i} \text{OrderLeg}_r,$$

$$\text{OrderToSite}_i = \bigcup_{r \in \text{LegToSite}_i} \text{OrderLeg}_r,$$

$$\text{quantityFrSite}_i = \sum_{o \in \text{OrderFrSite}_i} \text{quantityOrder}_o,$$

$$\text{quantityFrSite}_i \le \sum_{r \in \text{LegFrSite}_i} \#\text{ActiveShiftLeg}_r \times \text{capacityLeg}_r,$$

$$\text{quantityToSite}_i = \sum_{o \in \text{OrderToSite}_i} \text{quantityOrder}_o,$$

$$\text{quantityToSite}_i \le \sum_{r \in \text{LegToSite}_i} \#\text{ActiveShiftLeg}_r \times \text{capacityLeg}_r,$$

$$\text{RefOriginOrderSite}_i =$$

$$\{\forall\, r \in \text{LegToSite}_i \ \grave{}\text{OrderLeg}_r\grave{}\} \cup \{\grave{}\text{OrderOriginSite}_i\grave{}\},$$

$$\text{RefDestinOrderSite}_i =$$

$$\{\forall\, r \in \text{LegFrSite}_i \ \grave{}\text{OrderLeg}_r\grave{}\} \cup \{\grave{}\text{OrderDestinSite}_i\grave{}\},$$

$$\text{OrderSite}_i = \bigcup_{\grave{}o\grave{} \in \text{RefOriginOrderSite}_i} O,$$

$$\forall\, \grave{}O\grave{} \ne \grave{}P\grave{} \in \text{RefOriginOrderSite}_i$$

$$O \cap P = \varnothing,$$

$$\text{OrderSite}_i = \bigcup_{\grave{}o\grave{} \in \text{RefDestinOrderSite}_i} O,$$

$$\forall\, \grave{}O\grave{} \ne \grave{}P\grave{} \in \text{RefDestinOrderSite}_i$$

$$O \cap P = \varnothing,$$

$$),$$

$\forall\, r \in \text{LEG}$
$\forall\, o \in \text{ORDER}\,($

$$\text{mayBeFirstLegForOrder}_{r,o} \equiv \text{site1Leg}_r = \text{site1Order}_o,$$

$$\text{mayBeLastLegForOrder}_{r,o} \equiv \text{site2Leg}_r = \text{site2Order}_o,$$

),

$\forall$ o $\in$ ORDER $\rightarrow$ (

   min $\underline{\text{t2Order}_o}$,

   min $\#\Delta\text{LegOrder}_o$,

)

$\forall$ r $\in \Delta$LegOrder$_o$ $\rightarrow$ (

   max   mayBeFirstLegForOrder$_{r,o}$,

   max   mayBeLastLegForOrder$_{r,o}$,

   min $\#\Delta$shiftLegOrder$_{o,r}$,

)

r $\in$ LegOrder$_o$?,

$\forall$ o $\in$ ORDER $\rightarrow$ (

   min $\underline{\text{t2Order}_o}$,

   min $\#$LegOrder$_o$,

)

$\forall$ r $\in$ LegOrder$_o$ $\rightarrow$ (

   min   t1LegOrder$_{o,r}$,

)

$\forall$ s $\in \Delta$shiftLegOrder$_{o,r}$ $\rightarrow$ (

   min $\#\Delta$OrderShiftLeg$_{r,s}$,

)

shiftLegOrder$_{o,r}$ = s?,

$\forall$ o $\in$ ORDER

   costOrder$_o$ = $\Sigma_{r\in\text{LegOrder}_o}$costunitLeg$_r$ $\times$ quantityOrder$_o$,

cost =$\lceil\Sigma_{\text{o} \in \text{ORDER}}$ costOrder$_o\rceil$,

min   cost.

First, based on shiftLegOrder$_o$ and TimeLegOrder$_{o,r}$, constraints over shifts on any leg r for any order o can be illustrated as below:

- For all shifts on leg r, the domain is ShiftLeg$_r$. So for all order o shift-LegOrder$_{o,r}$ $\in$ ShiftLeg$_r$;

- From the shift timetable $TimeShiftLeg_{r,s}$, the shift time interval corresponding to the shift variable $shiftLegOrder_{o,r}$ can be derived through indexing: $TimeShiftRoute_{r,shiftRouteOrder_{o,r}}$;

- The duration of a shift is given, i.e., $\#TimeLegOrder_{o,r} = timeLeg_r$

Second, for any leg r, the model introduces the variable $OrderShiftLeg_{r,s}$ to represent the set of orders for shift s. Clearly the $OrderShiftLeg_{r,s}$'s form a set partition of $OrderLeg_r$:

$$OrderLeg_r = \cup_{s \in ShiftLeg_r} OrderShiftLeg_{r,s},$$

$$\forall s \neq i \in ShiftLeg_r$$

$$OrderShiftLeg_{r,s} \cap OrderShiftLeg_{r,i} = \varnothing,$$

The constraint over the transport modes is:

$$\forall r \in LEG$$

$$\forall o \in OrderLeg_r$$

$$modeLeg_r \in ModeOrder_o,$$

The model introduces a set variable $ActiveShiftLeg_r$ to represent the set of active shifts on leg r. Thus, with a new Boolean variable $activeShiftLeg_{r,s}$ used to represent if shift s is active on leg r, the following equivalences about $OrderShiftLeg_{r,s}$ and $ActiveShiftLeg_r$ can be concluded:

$$activeShiftLeg_{r,s} \equiv OrderShiftLeg_{r,s} \neq \varnothing,$$

$$activeShiftLeg_{r,s} \equiv s \in ActiveShiftLeg_r,$$

Since the quantity of the transported orders for any shift s of leg r cannot be greater than $capacityLeg_r$ (capacity of the leg), the capacity constraint is:

$$quantityShiftLeg_{r,s} = \Sigma_{o \in OrderShiftLeg_{r,s}} quantityOrder_o,$$

$$quantityShiftLeg_{r,s} \leq capacityLeg_r,$$

More globally for any leg r, the capacity constraint becomes:

$$quantityLeg_r = \Sigma_{o \in OrderLeg_r} quantityOrder_o,$$

$$quantityLeg_r \leq \#ActiveShiftLeg_r \times capacityLeg_r,$$

Legs and sites form a transport network. For any site i, $OrderFrSite_i$ represents the set of orders exiting from site i and $OrderToSite_i$ represents the set of orders coming to site i. The total quantity of all orders from site i cannot be greater than the capacity of all active shifts on all the legs from the site:

$$quantityFrSite_i = \Sigma_{o \in OrderFrSite_i} quantityOrder_o,$$

$$quantityFrSite_i \leq \Sigma_{r \in LegFrSite_i} \#ActiveShiftLeg_r \times capacityLeg_r,$$

Symmetrically, the total quantity of all orders going to site i cannot be greater than the capacity of all active shifts on all the legs to the site:

$$\text{quantityToSite}_i = \Sigma_{o \in \text{OrderToSite}_i} \text{quantityOrder}_o,$$

$$\text{quantityToSite}_i \leq \Sigma_{r \in \text{LegToSite}_i} \#\text{ActiveShiftLeg}_r \times \text{capacityLeg}_r,$$

On the transport network, the total quantity of the orders stays the same. For any site i, the set of orders starting at and coming to site i is equal to the set of orders terminating at and exiting from site i. The relations are:

$$\text{RefOriginOrderSite}_i =$$

$$\{\forall r \in \text{LegToSite}_i \;\; `\text{OrderLeg}_r`\} \cup \{`\text{OrderOriginSite}_i`\},$$

$$\text{RefDestinOrderSite}_i =$$

$$\{\forall r \in \text{LegFrSite}_i \;\; `\text{OrderLeg}_r`\} \cup \{`\text{OrderDestinSite}_i`\},$$

$$\text{OrderSite}_i = \cup_{`o` \in \text{RefOriginOrderSite}_i} o,$$

$$\forall `O` \neq `P` \in \text{RefOriginOrderSite}_i$$

$$O \cap P = \varnothing,$$

$$\text{OrderSite}_i = \cup_{`o` \in \text{RefDestinOrderSite}_i} o,$$

$$\forall `O` \neq `P` \in \text{RefDestinOrderSite}_i$$

$$O \cap P = \varnothing,$$

Customer orders flow on the transport network in a scheduled and routed way. NCL uses "set sorting with 2 tuples of variables" to model the routing constraint. For such a chained sorting, it is important to select the "chained objects" among which the "entry" and "exit" are the most crucial objects. Sometimes, "entry" and "exit" need to be created, that is, they may be fictitious objects in a sorting chain.

For any order o, the model selects its "legs" as the chained objects. The variable LegOrder_o is used to represent the set of chained legs for order o. For the "exit" of the sorted legs, the model creates a fictitious leg sinkOrder_o to terminate the chain. In this example, no "entry" is introduced. But a new integer variable firstLegOrder_o is created to represent the first leg selected by order o. Similarly, the last leg before the exit sinkOrder_o is represented by another integer variable lastLegOrder_o. With firstLegOrder_o and lastLegOrder_o excluded from LegOrder_o, the rest is labeled by a set variable BodyLegOrder_o. See Figure 7.8 for an illustration of the modeling idea.

The relation over the chained objects of order o is:

$$\text{LegOrder}_o = \{\text{firstLegOrder}_o\} \cup \text{BodyLegOrder}_o,$$

If order o covers more than one leg, its first leg is different from its last leg. The relations are:

$$\#\text{LegOrder}_o > 1 \equiv \text{lastLegOrder}_o \in \text{BodyLegOrder}_o,$$

$$\#\text{LegOrder}_o > 1 \equiv \text{lastLegOrder}_o \neq \text{firstLegOrder}_o,$$

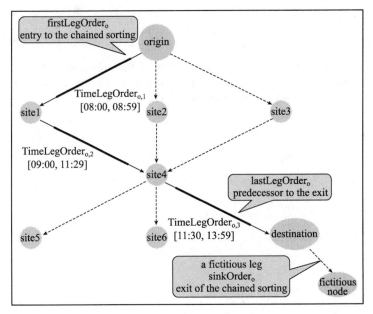

Figure 7.8 Sorting with 2 Tuples of Variables for Multi-Modal Transportation Planning

The model needs to constrain departure time $t1Order_o$ and arrival time $t2Order_o$ over order o:

$$t1Order_o = t1LegOrder_{o,firstLegOrder_o},$$

$$t2Order_o = t2LegOrder_{o,lastLegOrder_o},$$

Arrival time of order o should be constrained by its delivery deadline. The constraint over the order o's end time is:

$$t2Order_o \in [minDeadlineOrder_o, maxDeadlineOrder_o],$$

The first leg for order o should start at its origin site $site1Order_o$:

$$site1Leg_{firstLegOrder_o} = site1Order_o,$$

The last leg for order o should terminate at its destination site $site2Order_o$:

$$site2Leg_{lastLegOrder_o} = site2Order_o,$$

Moreover, the model introduces a succeeding leg variable $nextLegOrder_{o,r}$ for leg r of order o. The relations around the succeeding legs are:

- The domain constraint over successor variables:

  $$nextLegOrder_{o,r} \in$$

  $$(BodyLegOrder_o \cap LegFrSite_{site2Leg_r}) \cup \{sinkOrder_o\},$$

- If a leg r is not in the set of legs ($LegOrder_o$) of order o, then the model lets its successor be the fictitious exit $sinkOrder_o$:

  $$r \notin LegOrder_o \rightarrow nextLegOrder_{o,r} = sinkOrder_o,$$

Apparently, the successor to the last leg for order o is the exit $\texttt{sinkOrder}_o$:

$\texttt{nextLegOrder}_{o,\texttt{lastLegOrder}_o} = \texttt{sinkOrder}_o,$

For all legs of $\texttt{LegOrder}_o$, their successors are distinct:

$\forall\, r \neq k \in \texttt{LegOrder}_o$

$\qquad \texttt{nextLegOrder}_{o,r} \neq \texttt{nextLegOrder}_{o,k},$

The routing for order o involves the chaining of times and sites along its legs. For any leg r of any order o:

- The chained precedence relation over times is:

$\texttt{TimeLegOrder}_{o,r} \prec \texttt{TimeLegOrder}_{o,\texttt{nextLegOrder}_{o,r}},$

- The chained connection relation over sites is:

$\texttt{site1Leg}_{\texttt{nextLegOrder}_{o,r}} = \texttt{site2Leg}_r,$

For the search strategy: first, the model instantiates the set of legs $\texttt{LegOrder}_o$ for all order o; next, it instantiates the shift variable $\texttt{shiftLegOrder}_{o,r}$ for all leg r of order o. The preparation work is to define a Boolean variable $\texttt{mayBeFirstLegForOrder}_{r,o}$ to check the possibility for leg r to be the first leg of order o:

$\texttt{mayBeFirstLegForOrder}_{r,o} \equiv \texttt{site1Leg}_r = \texttt{site1Order}_o,$

Symmetrically, a Boolean variable $\texttt{mayBeLastLegForOrder}_{r,o}$ is defined to check the possibility for leg r to be the last leg of order o:

$\texttt{mayBeLastLegForOrder}_{r,o} \equiv \texttt{site2Leg}_r = \texttt{site2Order}_o,$

To query on $\texttt{LegOrder}_o$ for order o, the search rules are:

- First, to select a critical order in the lexicographic order of (earliest arrival time, fewest candidate legs). The criterion ($\texttt{min}\quad \texttt{t2Order}_o$) selects an order o with the earliest arrival time; the criterion ($\texttt{min}\quad \#\triangle\texttt{LegOrder}_o$) selects an order o with the fewest candidate legs;
- Next, for order o, select a critical leg r in the lexicographic order of (most probable to be the first leg, most probable to be the last leg, fewest candidate shifts). The greedy criterion ($\texttt{max}\quad \texttt{mayBeFirstLegForOrder}_{r,o}$) selects a leg with the greatest possibility to be the first leg for order o; the greedy criterion ($\texttt{max}\quad \texttt{mayBeLastLegForOrder}_{r,o}$) selects a leg with the greatest possibility to be the last leg for order o; the least-slack criterion ($\texttt{min}\quad \#\triangle\texttt{shiftLegOrder}_{o,r}$) selects a leg r with the fewest candidate shifts;
- The query "$r \in \texttt{LegOrder}_o$?" triggers the branching: first, try to assign leg r to order o; next, try the inverse logic.

As soon as all legs for all the orders are known, the model queries on shifts of any leg r for any order o to instantiate the shift variable $\texttt{shiftLegOrder}_{o,r}$:

- First, select a critical order o in the lexicographic order of (earliest arrival time, fewest legs). The criterion ($\texttt{min}\quad \texttt{t2Order}_o$) selects an order o with the earliest arrival time; the criterion ($\min$ $\# \text{LegOrder}_o$) selects an order o with the fewest legs. Note that now LegOrder_o is known. So the criterion is a greedy one;

- Second, for order o, the sequential-search criterion ($\min$ $\text{t1LegOrder}_{o,r}$) selects a critical leg r with the earliest start time;
- Third, for order o and leg r, the criterion ($\min$ $\# \triangle \text{OrderShiftLeg}_{r,s}$) selects a shift s with the fewest candidate orders;
- The query "$\text{shiftLegOrder}_{o,r} = s$?" triggers the branching: first, try to assign shift s to leg r for order o; next, try the inverse logic;

The objective is to minimize the total transport cost. First, the cost function of each order is:

$$\text{costOrder}_o = \Sigma_{r \in \text{LegOrder}_o} \text{costunitLeg}_r \times \text{quantityOrder}_o,$$

The objective function is:

$$[\Sigma_{o \in \text{ORDER}} \text{ costOrder}_o].$$

The model presented above is a general one. In practice user may be faced with simpler cases. For example, the number of transits may be limited to be not greater than 2 and a transit may be limited to take place at a hub which is a small subset of the sites. In this case of limited number of transits, for example 2, the modeling can be simplified further as below:

- Use variables leg1Order_o, leg2Order_o, leg3Order_o instead of LegOrder_o to represent the legs of order o over the transportation network.
- No need to use the routing model and to introduce the successor variable $\text{nextLegOrder}_{o,r}$ for an order o.
- The site chaining relation over the itinerary of an order becomes:

$$\text{site1Order}_o = \text{site1Leg}_{\text{leg1Order}_o},$$
$$\text{site2Leg}_{\text{leg1Order}_o} = \text{site1Leg}_{\text{leg2Order}_o},$$
$$\text{site2Leg}_{\text{leg2Order}_o} = \text{site1Leg}_{\text{leg3Order}_o},$$
$$\text{site2Leg}_{\text{leg3Order}_o} = \text{site2Order}_o,$$

- The precedence relation over the itinerary becomes:

$$\text{TimeLegOrder}_{o,\text{leg1Order}_o} \prec \text{TimeLegOrder}_{o,\text{leg2Order}_o},$$

$$\text{TimeLegOrder}_{o,\text{leg2Order}_o} \prec \text{TimeLegOrder}_{o,\text{leg3Order}_o},$$

- Finally, user needs to study other relations over leg1Order_o, leg2Order_o and leg3Order_o. For example, in which case they are distinct legs? In which case they are in fact a single leg?

7.4.4 Visualizing Geographical Information: Map

In POEM, Map is a visualization tool for managing geographical information. A solution to a multi-modal transport planning problem is illustrated using Map in Figure 7.9.

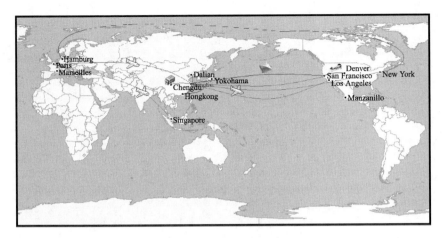

Figure 7.9 Map Display of a Solution to a Multi-Modal Transportation Planning Problem

As shown in the map, different modes of transport by air, rail, road or water are used to accomplish the tasks on a world-wide transportation network.

7.4.5 Questions

The multi-modal transportation planning model presented in this book just handles capacity constraints in terms of quantity. However, in practice people should also take volume and weight into consideration. A question is: how to modify the data model and the program so as to introduce capacity constraints over volume and weight?

References

Gantt, H.L.: Work, Wages and Profits. Easton, Pennsylvania, Hive Publishing Company (1974)

Herrmann, J.W. (editor): Handbook of Production Scheduling, Springer, New York (2006)

Muth, J.F., Thompson, G.L.: Industrial Scheduling. Englewood Cliffs, NJ: Prentice-Hall (1963)

Zhou, J., Zhou, J., Zhou, J., Courtet, Y., Wu, W., Ni, H.: Logistics planning using the POEM language system. ERCIM News 2007(68) (2007)

8 Relaxation and Decomposition

This chapter presents two practical approaches to solving problems using NCL: relaxation and decomposition.

Section 8.1 proposes a local optimization method which relaxes a portion of a candidate solution and locally evolves to a better one in an iterative manner. A complete NCL program for the Traveling Salesman Problem illustrates a basic idea of local optimization by relaxation.

Section 8.2 studies the issues of solving complex problems by decomposition. On one hand, the solving of the Pick-up and Delivery problem is re-visited to present model decomposition methods. On the other hand, the solution to a large-scale Production Scheduling problem illustrates the approach of data decomposition to reduce the complexity of industrial problems.

8.1 Local Optimization by Relaxation

Relaxation is a frequently used technique in mathematical optimization. Usually it is about relaxing a strict constraint by replacing it with a weaker one that can be satisfied more easily, for example, linear relaxation used in mathematical programming. In this book, it concerns re-optimization: The system relaxes a portion of a candidate solution and locally evolves to a better one in an iterative manner. As recommended in Section 6.1.1, using such techniques to improve the quality of a solution is helpful.

8.1.1 Relaxation and Interaction

A solution may need to be maintained from time to time. Computer is inflexible. When conditions change or when human expertise is needed, human interaction over a solution becomes necessary.

During a human-machine interaction, generally the system needs to deal with such a scenario: 1) A portion of an old solution needs to be retained; 2) New constraints introduced by an interaction needs to be added; 3) Other parts of the solution will be relaxed for a local optimization.

An interaction method can be designed as follows: After introducing constraints of 1) and 2), the system relaxes the rest of the solution to expand a local solution space and carries out re-optimization over it. If there is a solution, then the interaction succeeds; otherwise it fails and the system rejects the interaction.

Designing a relaxation strategy is important for an interaction method. It consists in retaining and/or dropping parts of an old solution, that is, deciding which parts of the solution need to be fixed and/or relaxed. The interaction logic depends on user's application logic and it is often based on scenarios. For example, some standard interaction may be: inserting a new order into a production schedule, deleting a planned order canceled by the customer, or modifying the start time of a planned task.

A human-machine interaction, when automated, can become a heuristic method for local optimization in NCL. This will be presented in the following.

8.1.2 Local Optimization

For combinatorial problems, by "exact solver" the author means its algorithms are based on exhaustive enumeration with a search tree. However, in limited time a tree search algorithm cannot always guarantee the quality of its solutions; an exact solver cannot break through the NP-hardness of a problem. So a practical way is to treat the model as an optimization operator and to iterate local optimization with the operator to improve solutions.

As a programming language, NCL offers user an easy method for local optimization to handle complex problems: local optimization by relaxation. The extent of relaxation determines the local space for re-optimization and depends on the scalability of NCL's algorithms. The principle is that relaxation should generate enough "potential" for local optimization and in the same time it should ensure that NCL can contain combinatorial explosion so as to compute a locally optimized solution.

From the author's point of view, iterative optimization based on relaxation is in fact an NCL version of heuristic methods such as local search (Hoos and Stutzler 2005). Usually a human-machine interaction logic can be borrowed to design such a heuristic.

8.1.3 Iterative Optimization for TSP

It is a good example to illustrate relaxation and iterative optimization through the solving of TSP (Traveling Salesman Problem) (Applegate et al. 2006). NCL can efficiently solve small-size TSPs in reasonable time. For a large-size TSP, iterative optimization will be very useful.

NCL's TSP model is organized at two levels: The optimization operator is `TSP.n` and peripherally the master model is an iteration script `ScriptTsp.n`.

The idea of iterative optimization for TSP is: Based on an initial solution, by relaxing a portion of the solution within a relaxation window and by fixing the rest of the solution, NCL re-optimizes in the relaxed solution space to compute a local optimum. This process goes in an iterative manner until no better solution is found.

Iteration Script (ScriptTsp.n)

```
['Work Directory'  "Model\ReadTsp.n"],

maxBacktrack  = 100,
maxTime       = 60,
sizeRelax     = 20,
shiftRelax    = 4,
```

```
nbLoop          = #SOURCENODE ÷ shiftRelax,

prog            = ['Work Directory' "TSP.n"],
config          = ['Work Directory' "ncl.cfg"],

iterationBuf = ["iteration buffer" : _],

'@' ⇒ (
  ∀ loop ∈ [0, nbLoop](
    tsp_loop = [prog, config , 1],

    ? tsp_loop(
        "optimal solution proved" : loop = 0 → '.';

        "no solution exists",
        "stopped without solution" : loop > 0
    )

  )
).
```

After the script includes `['Work Directory' "Model\ReadTsp.n"]` (data-reading program) into the model, some parameters are configured: `maxBacktrack` represents the maximum number of backtracks allowed for computing a solution. If this limit is exceeded, NCL will terminate with no solution; `maxTime` is the maximum time of computation above which NCL will terminate; the iteration buffer `iterationBuf` serves as a register of solutions for the TSP operator; `sizeRelax` and `shiftRelax` define respectively the size and the shifting step of the relaxation window; from `shiftRelax` the model calculates the number of iterations `nbLoop` (`#SOURCENODE ÷ shiftRelax`).

ScriptTsp.n will execute the TSP operator for (nbLoop+1) times: initially `loop = 0` and sub-model `TSP.n` will be called to compute a first solution; next, the script calls the TSP operator for `nbLoop` times to relax a previous solution and computes a locally optimized new solution.

Note that if in the first pass the solver finds an optimal solution and proves its optimality, the system can terminate immediately by forcing '.' to be true; there is no more need for further optimization.

Data Model (ReadTsp.n)

```
source              = 1,
sink                = 0,
SOURCE              = {source},
```

```
SINK                    = {sink},

SOURCENODE              = O,
SOURCENODE              = SOURCE ∪ NODE,
NODE ∩ SOURCE           = ∅,
NODESINK                = NODE ∪ SINK,
SOURCENODESINK          = SOURCE ∪ NODE ∪ SINK,

∀ i,j ∈ SOURCENODESINK
  dNodeNode_{i,j} :: O,

∀ i ∈ SOURCENODESINK(
  xNode_i :: 0.0,

  yNode_i :: 0.0,
),

∀ i ∈ SOURCENODE (
  _           = O,

  xNode_i     = O,

  yNode_i     = O,
),

xNode_{sink} = xNode_{source},
yNode_{sink} = yNode_{source},

∀ i,j ∈ SOURCENODE
  dNodeNode_{i,j} = O,

dNodeNode_{source,sink} = O,
dNodeNode_{sink,source} = O,
dNodeNode_{sink,sink}   = O,

∀ i ∈ SINK
∀ j ∈ SOURCENODESINK(
  dNodeNode_{i,j} = dNodeNode_{source,j},

  dNodeNode_{j,i} = dNodeNode_{j,source},
),

IDX = [1, #SOURCENODE],
```

The data-reading program sets up a data model: source represents the TSP origin (any node can be selected to be source); the model then creates a fictitious TSP node sink to represent the destination; SOURCENODE represents all TSP nodes except for destination; NODESINK represents all nodes except for origin; finally, SOURCENODESINK represents all nodes including origin and destination.

Abscissa xNode$_i$ for node i, ordinate yNode$_i$ for node i and the distance matrix dNodeNode$_{i,j}$ (for node i and j) over SOURCENODESINK are defined and are input from a data pool.

Finally, the set of indices is introduced: IDX = [1, #SOURCENODE].

This data model is set up to formulate set sorting with 2 tuples of variables to state the routing constraint for TSP. See Figure 8.1.

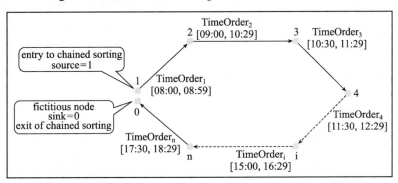

Figure 8.1 Modeling TSP by Set Sorting With 2 Tuples of Variables

Optimization Operator (TSP.n)

```
∀ i ∈ SOURCENODE (
    nextNode_i ∈ NODESINK,

    TimeNode_i = [t1Node_i, t2Node_i],

    TimeNode_i ⊂ [1, distance],


    #TimeNode_i = dNodeNode_i,nextNode_i'

    TimeNode_i ≺ TimeNode_nextNode_i'


    DistNextNode_i = {∀ j ∈ ∆nextNode_i  dNodeNode_i,j},

    diffDistNextNode_i = DistNextNode_i[2] - DistNextNode_i[1],

        % difference between the least two node-successor distances
),


∀ i ≠ j ∈ SOURCENODE
```

```
       nextNode_i ≠ nextNode_j,


  ∀ i ∈ IDX
     nodeIdx_i ∈ SOURCENODE,


  ∀ i ∈ IDX \ 1
     nodeIdx_i = nextNode_nodeIdx_{i-1},

  ∀ i < j ∈ IDX
     nodeIdx_i ≠ nodeIdx_j,

  t1Node_source = 1,


  ∀ i ∈ NODE → (
     min    #ΔnextNode_i,

     max    diffDistNextNode_i,

  )
  ∀ k ∈ ΔnextNode_i → (

     min    dNodeNode_{i,k},

  )
  nextNode_i = k?,


  distance = Σ_{i∈SOURCENODE} #TimeNode_i,


  min    distance,

  ['Work Directory' "Model\RelaxTsp.n"],

  ['Work Directory' "Model\WriteTsp.n"],

  'Backtrack Count' > maxBacktrack ∧
  'Local Time' > maxTime → '.'.
```

Similar to the Pick-up and Delivery model, for each node i the TSP model introduces a successor variable $nextNode_i$ and a time interval variable $TimeNode_i$ (work and driving time from node i to its successor), with $t1Node_i$ being start time and $t2Node_i$ being completion time.

The modeling of main constraints is explained as follows: "set sorting" model is used to express that time interval $TimeNode_i$ for node i precedes that of its successor and different nodes have different successors:

```
  ∀ i ∈ SOURCENODE (
```

```
#TimeNode_i = dNodeNode_{i,nextNode_i}'

TimeNode_i ≺ TimeNode_{nextNode_i}'
),
∀ i ≠ j ∈ SOURCENODE
    nextNode_i ≠ nextNode_j,
```

Apparently, a solution is obtained if every successor variable $nextNode_i$ for node i is instantiated.

In addition to the least-slack criterion, the model also uses regret-based search rules to solve the problem. $DistNextNode_i$ is introduced to represent the set of distances from i to all possible candidate successors. When querying on successor variable $nextNode_i$, the search rules are:

- First, select a critical node i in the lexicographic order (fewest candidate successors, least regret on successor choice). Least regret means greatest easiness on the choice of a successor. The definition of the "easiness of choice" function is: difference between the second least and the least distances: $DistNextNode_i[2]-DistNextNode_i[1]$.
- Next, for node i, greedily select a successor k with the smallest distance: min $dNodeNode_{i,j}$.
- The query "$nextNode_i$ = k?" triggers the branching: first, try to constrain i's successor to be k; next, try the inverse logic.

To make the model $RelaxTsp.n$ executable, an integer variable $nodeIdx_i$ representing the node that is visited i-th in a TSP tour is introduced. The description of such a relation is as follows:

```
∀ i ∈ IDX \ 1
    nodeIdx_i = nextNode_{nodeIdx_{i-1}}'

∀ i < j ∈ IDX
    nodeIdx_i ≠ nodeIdx_j,
```

The objective is to minimize the driving time:

$$distance = \Sigma_{i \in SOURCENODE} \#TimeNode_i,$$

Finally, to be prepared for iterative optimization, the TSP operator embeds the relaxation program $RelaxTsp.n$ and solution output program $WriteTsp.n$ by included files:

```
['Work Directory' "Model\RelaxTsp.n"],
['Work Directory' "Model\WriteTsp.n"],
```

Relaxation Program (RelaxTsp.n)

```
loop > 0 ⇒ (
  'O' ← iterationBuf,

  distance < 0,
```

```
idx1Relax = (loop - 1) × shiftRelax + 1,
idx2Relax = idx1Relax + sizeRelax - 1,
IdxToRelax = [idx1Relax, idx2Relax] ∪ [1, idx2Relax-#IDX],

∀ i ∈ IDX
  fixedNodeIdx_i = O,


∀ i ∈ IDX \ IdxToRelax \ 1
  nextNode_{fixedNodeIdx_{i-1}} = fixedNodeIdx_i,


iterationBuf ← 'O',
).
```

Relaxation logic is coordinated by the logical variables $nodeIdx_i$ and $fixedNodeIdx_i$. In an iterative manner, NCL relaxes a portion of a solution obtained previously with a relaxation window IdxToRelax, fixes the rest of the solution and carries out a local optimization over the relaxed space to compute better solutions. Constants sizeRelax and shiftRelax represent respectively the size and the shifting step of the relaxation window.

Solution Output (WriteTsp.n)

```
iterationBuf ← '@',

@(distance "\n"),

∀ i ∈ IDX
  @(nodeIdx_i "\t"),


'@' ← iterationBuf.
```

Solutions are stored in buffer iterationBuf which contains the driving time distance (the objective) and instantiated nodes in the order of a TSP trip: $nodeIdx_i$ stands for the node visited at i-th step of the trip.

In this book, the method of iterative optimization will be illustrated by solving the Danzig42 instance from TSPLIB.

As shown in Figure 8.2, when the model gives a solution with distance = 879, two parts of the solution are separated, with the one outside the dotted circle being fixed and the other inside the circle being relaxed. NCL re-optimizes over the relaxed part to obtain a locally optimized solution with distance = 739. After a number of iterations, the model gets an optimal solution to the Danzig42 problem instance as shown in Figure 8.3.

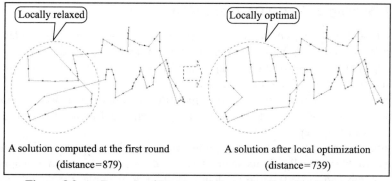

Figure 8.2 An Example of Iterative Optimization Based on Relaxation

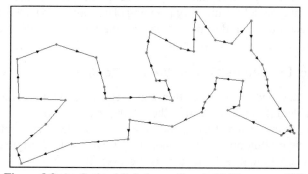

Figure 8.3 An Optimal Solution to Danzig42 (distance = 699)

Exercises for TSP

Readers are encouraged to improve the strategy of relaxation and iterative optimization. From the literature of operations research, quite a lot of pairwise exchange heuristics can be borrowed in the TSP operator (TSP.n) for iterative optimization. A simple idea is to use discrete relaxation windows instead of interval windows.

Another exercise for readers is the use of function instead of sub-model to encapsulate the TSP operator.

8.2 Solving by Decomposition

In Section 6.1.1, problem decomposition is recommended as one of the principles for modeling. In practice, instead of solving a problem in one pass, the solving of a large-size problem in NCL can be decomposed in two ways:

- Decomposing the problem model into sub-models and solving the sub-problems respectively;
- Decomposing the problem data into groups and solving the sub-problems iteratively.

Normally, an NP-hard problem can quickly become intractable for any solver as the problem size increases. So due to limited scalability, solving by decomposition is a practical approach in real-world applications.

8.2.1 Solving by Model Decomposition

If the model of a problem can be decomposed into sub-models, it is an ideal way of decomposing; the solving of the problem can often be greatly simplified. Model decomposition discussed in this chapter is different from MP and CP decomposition methods proposed in (Hooker 2002).

There are two kinds of model decomposition. The first one is to decompose a problem "statically" to well separated sub-problems and then to solve the sub-problems step by step.

Another kind of model decomposition, which is more general, is to decompose a problem "dynamically" in its search tree. To do so, it requires more insight into the problem and more flexible modeling skills. For example, the vehicle routing model can be decomposed dynamically to a set partitioning model for truck loading and a routing model for itinerary planning. The solving of the problem is complete and exact after such decomposition. But the behavior of the NCL engine in the search tree becomes very different.

8.2.2 Model Decomposition for Vehicle Routing

To illustrate the model decomposition approach, the solving of the Pick-up and Delivery problem (Li and Lim 2001; Zhou 2009) is re-visited.

In Chapter 6, the search strategy for the Pick-up and Delivery problem (in general for vehicle routing problems) is modeled at two levels: First, to assign orders to trucks; second, to link each order to its successor if any.

Previous Search Rules

```
∀ j ∈ PICKUPORDER → (

    min    #ΔtruckOrder_j,       % fewest trucks

    max    diffDistTruckOrder_j, % least regret: easiest choice

)

∀ i ∈ ΔtruckOrder_j → (

    min    dOrderTruck_{i,j} ,    % greedy search

    min    #ΔOrderTruck_i        % least slack

)

j ∈ OrderTruck_i?,

∀ j ∈ SOURCEORDER → (

    min    #ΔnextOrder_j,        % fewest successors

    max    diffDistNextOrder_j,  % least regret: easiest choice

)
```

$\forall\ k\ \in\ \Delta\text{nextOrder}_j\ \rightarrow\ ($

 min $\text{tOrderOrder}_{j,k}$ % greedy search

)

$\text{nextOrder}_j\ =\ k\ ?,$

$\forall\ j\ \in\ \text{SOURCEORDER}$

 $\text{t1Order}_j\ =\ ?,$

However, the above search strategy does not take into consideration local properties of the search tree: After set partitioning of orders is finished, the route of every truck can be optimized separately and simultaneously. That is, the problem will become decomposable after all orders are assigned to trucks; local optimal solutions to the sub-problems of routing for all the trucks constitute a global optimal solution. This suggests that the search depth after truck loading can be reduced by the number of trucks.

To exploit efficiently the sub-structure of the search tree, the NCL program needs to be rewritten for its search rules. The approach is to encapsulate the functionality of local optimization and search queries into a function. For doing this, a predicate (Boolean function) $<\text{queryForTruck}>$ is defined. In the predicate, the instantiation of successor variables nextOrder_j and release time variables t1Order_j for all order j in $\text{SourceOrderTruck}_i$ of truck i should be accomplished locally.

Query Predicate

$<\text{queryForTruck}>(\text{truck})$ % define a query predicate

(

 min $\sum_{j \in \text{SourceOrderTruck}_{\text{truck}}}\#\text{TimeOrder}_j,$

            % local optimization objective

 $\forall\ j\ \in\ \text{SourceOrderTruck}_{\text{truck}}\ \rightarrow\ ($

  min $\#\Delta\text{nextOrder}_j,$ % fewest successors

  max $\text{diffDistNextOrder}_j,$% least regret: easiest choice

)

 $\forall\ k\ \in\ \Delta\text{nextOrder}_j\ \rightarrow\ ($

  min $\text{tOrderOrder}_{j,k}$ % greedy search

)

 $\text{nextOrder}_j\ =\ k\ ?$ % local query

),

The function <queryForTruck> has one integer argument truck which represents the index of a truck. In the function, a local objective is stated to tell the NCL engine to carry out a local optimization:

$$\min \quad \Sigma_{j \in SourceOrderTruck_{truck}} \#TimeOrder_j,$$

The search queries and the objective defined in the function are "local". This means each time a query in this function is executed, a complete search within the scope of the function should be done before the query moves out of the function.

After the definition of the function, the only thing left to do is to state the query predicate for each truck:

```
∀ i ∈ TRUCK

   queryForTruck(i),
```

With dynamic model decomposition, the search tree for the routing problem can be much shorter and the efficiency of the model can be greatly improved. Note that parallel computing will be very useful for functions.

In practice, system variables such as 'Local Time', 'Backtrack Count', 'Solution Count', 'O', '@' and '.' can be used to control the local search and the local optimization.

8.2.3 Solving by Data Decomposition

Even after the model decomposition, sub-problems can still be too complex to be solved directly. To further reduce the complexity, user can decompose problem data into groups and to solve the corresponding local problems in steps as below:

- Sorting the original data into groups in terms of some criteria, e.g., for production scheduling, sorting by job deadlines, by earliest release dates or by processing durations, etc..
- Solving the local problem for a group in such a way: 1) Relax partially the local solution to the previous group (if any) and merge the relaxed part into the current group so as to smoothly connect these two consecutive groups. 2) Solve the problem corresponding to the merged group.
- Generating a global solution by sequentially relaxing, merging and solving in an iterative manner.

Data decomposition is indispensable for industrial applications due to limited scalability of a solver. Suppose, for example, the complexity of an NP-hard problem is $O(2^n)$ where n is the size of the problem. As n increases, the problem will quickly become intractable. But if the data is decomposed into m groups of sizes $n1, \ldots, nm$, the complexity for the solver will be $O(m \times \max(2^{n1}, \ldots , 2^{nm}))$. What is important is the heuristic of decomposition and the efficiency of local optimization.

8.2.4 Data Decomposition for Production Scheduling

To illustrate the data decomposition method, some peripheral programs for solving the Production Scheduling problem (see Chapter 7) is given below.

Sorting Data

For the Production Scheduling problem, jobs should be sorted before decomposing the data. The idea is to assign an index $idxJob_i$ to each job i. The job-sorting program is given below.

```
IDX = [1,nbJob],

∀ i ∈ JOB
   idxJob_i ∈ IDX,

∀ i ∈ IDX (
   jobIdx_i ∈ JOB,
   idxJob_jobIdx_i = i,
   TaskIdx_i = TaskJob_jobIdx_i,
),

∀ i ≠ j ∈ JOB
   idxJob_i ≠ idxJob_j,

∀ i ∈ JOB → (
   min    idxJob_i ,    % sequential search: least job index
   min    t2Job_i,     % sequential search: earliest completion time
   min    t1Job_i,     % sequential search: earliest start time
)
idxJob_i = ??.       % double question mark signifies fast query
```

Based on a heuristic of sequential search in the lexicographic order of (least job index, earliest completion time, earliest start time), a direct construction of a sorting for the jobs is feasible. So a fast-query for the sorting is used in the above program. Note that fast query is symbolized by a double question mark (??). The system will immediately terminate (that is, there is no need to backtrack) once a solution is obtained.

Partitioning Data

After sorting the jobs, NCL decomposes them into groups. With all the jobs numbered from 1 to nbJob, the program segments the indices into nbGroup groups while balancing the numbers of tasks in the groups. For this, the interval sequence model (a special case of set partitioning) is used to decompose data. The job-partitioning program is given below.

```
maxTaskGroup = 0,          % max number of tasks for a group
```

```
minGroup = ⌈nbTask / maxTaskGroup⌉,
maxGroup = ⌈nbTask / minTaskJob⌉,

nbGroup ∈ [minGroup, maxGroup],
GROUP = [1, nbGroup],

∀ i ∈ [1, maxGroup] (
    IdxGroupᵢ ⊂ IDX,                    % job indices are grouped

    IdxGroupᵢ = [_, idx2Groupᵢ],

    TaskGroupᵢ = ∪ⱼ∈IdxGroupᵢ TaskIdxⱼ,
),


∀ i ∈ GROUP

    #TaskGroupᵢ ≤ maxTaskGroup,

∀ i ∈ [1, nbGroup-1]

    #TaskGroupᵢ + #TaskIdx_idx2Groupᵢ+1 > maxTaskGroup,
                % these 2 constraints settle the partitioning


∀ i ∈ GROUP
    IdxGroupᵢ ≠ ∅,

IDX = ∪ᵢ∈GROUP IdxGroupᵢ,          % interval sequence model
∀ i < j ∈ GROUP

    IdxGroupᵢ ≺ IdxGroupⱼ.
                % set partitioning with precedence relation
```

Without any search, NCL groups all jobs definitely in the pre-search phase. For example, suppose that there are 10 jobs (nbJob = 10) with 119 tasks (nbTask = 119); maximum number of tasks for a group is 30 (maxTaskGroup = 30); the indices of the jobs and the numbers of tasks are:

- Job Index: 1 2   3   4   5   6   7   8   9   10
- #TaskIdxᵢ: 15 12   12 10 9 17   11 10 8   15

In this case, the job-partitioning model will give the result as below:

- #TaskGroupᵢ: 27   22   26   29   15
- IdxGroupᵢ: [1,2]   [3,4]   [5,6]   [7,9]   {10}

Decomposing and Merging

A Production Scheduling problem may consist of up to 100,000 tasks or even more. Apparently it is not feasible to solve such a large-scale problem in one pass.

To construct a solution to such a problem, solving by decomposing and merging is an appropriate approach.

This section explains the steps for solving a real-world industrial Production Scheduling problem. The problem requires scheduling tasks over one week. After decomposing the jobs into groups, NCL solves the local problems group by group in a sequential manner. Figure 7.4 in Section 7.2 displays a local solution to the first group.

A weekly schedule constructed by relaxing and merging local solutions is illustrated in Figure 8.4. Such an approach seems to be very practical in industrial applications and usually can generate feasible solutions of good quality.

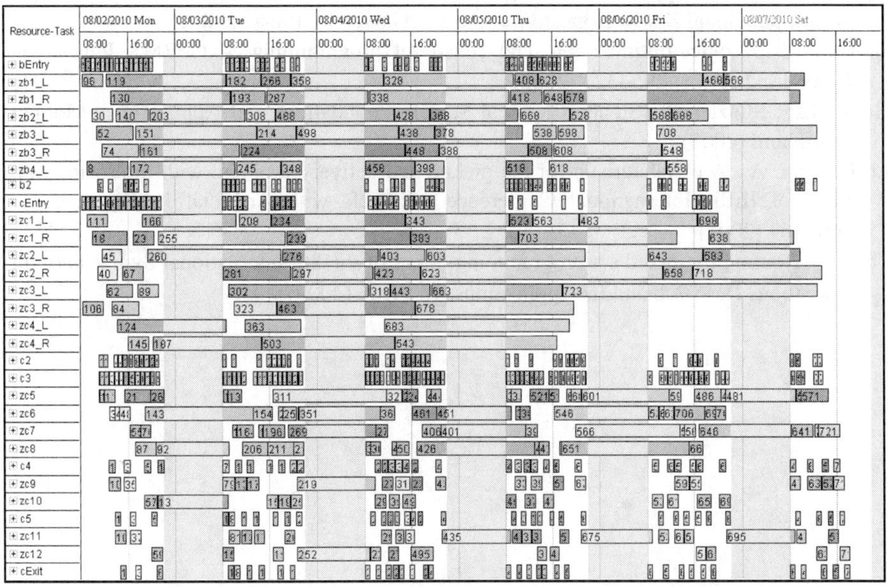

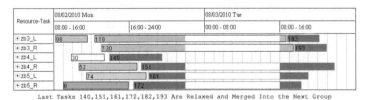

Figure 8.4 A Weekly Schedule after Relaxing and Merging Local Solutions

Figure 8.5 illustrates the idea of solving by decomposing and merging.

Figure 8.5 Solving by Decomposing and Merging

- Sorting jobs and partitioning them while balancing the numbers of tasks for the groups;
- Solving the local problem of the first group, relaxing the last tasks (182, 193, 140, 151, 161, 172) on the resources and fixing all other tasks (96, 119, 130, 30, 52, 74, 8), shifting to the next group, solving its problem, merging the consecutive solutions, going on sequentially and iteratively till the last group.

References

Applegate, D.L., Bixby, R.E., Chvátal, V., Cook, W.J.: The Traveling Salesman Problem: A Computational Study. Princeton: Princeton University Press (2006)

Hooker, J.N.: Logic, optimization, and constraint programming. INFORMS Journal on Computing, 14(4): 295–321 (2002)

Hoos, H.H., Stutzler, T.: Stochastic Local Search: Foundations and Applications, Morgan Kaufmann (2005)

Li, H., Lim, A.: A metaheuristic for the pickup and delivery problem with time windows. Proc. of IEEE International Conference on Tools with Artificial Intelligence, 13: 160–167 (2001)

Zhou, J.: Routing by mixed set programming. Proc. of the 8th International Symposium on Operations Research and Its Applications, 157–166 (2009)

Appendix 1   The Grammar in TeX

This appendix is a more structured presentation of the NCL grammar in TeX. The grammar is ambiguous in terms of derivation and is vague in terms of reduction. But it is "intuitive" and is in accordance with mathematical logic conventions. Technically the ambiguity can be disambiguated by using constraints such as precedence and associativity for mathematical operations and the vagueness can be accommodated by replacing conflict rules with context-sensitive ones. For a more rigorous study on the grammar, readers are referred to Chapter 3.

Overall Structure

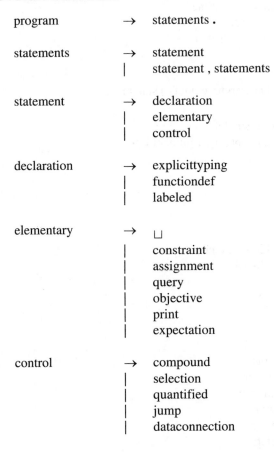

program	→	statements .
statements	→	statement
	|	statement , statements
statement	→	declaration
	|	elementary
	|	control
declaration	→	explicittyping
	|	functiondef
	|	labeled
elementary	→	⊔
	|	constraint
	|	assignment
	|	query
	|	objective
	|	print
	|	expectation
control	→	compound
	|	selection
	|	quantified
	|	jump
	|	dataconnection

Declaration

Explicit Typing

explicittyping	→	bool :: bool
	|	float :: float
	|	int :: int
	|	dtime :: dtime
	|	str :: str
	|	boolref :: boolref
	|	floatref :: floatref
	|	integralref :: integralref
	|	setref :: setref
	|	intset :: intset
	|	dtimeset :: dtimeset
	|	strset :: strset
	|	refset :: refset

Function Definition

functiondef	→	<ID> (argumentdefs) statement

argumentdefs	→	argumentdef
	|	argumentdef , argumentdefs

argumentdef	→	⊔
	|	ID

Label

labeled	→	< ID > statement
	|	(labeled)

Elementary Statement

Constraint

constraint	→	boolctr
	|	numctr
	|	dtimectr
	|	strctr
	|	refctr
	|	setctr

boolctr	→	bool = bool
	|	bool \neq bool

	\neg bool
	bool \wedge bool
	bool \vee bool
	bool \oplus bool
	bool \rightarrow bool
	bool \equiv bool
	bool \not\equiv bool
	boolsubmodel
	sqlquery
	oscommand
	boolgroup
	(boolctr)

boolgroup → boolcst
	boolvar
	boolfunc
	boolextract
	\bigwedge refset
	\bigvee refset
	\bigoplus refset
	\bigwedge subidx bool
	\bigvee subidx bool
	\bigoplus subidx bool

numctr → float \in [float , float]
	float \not\in [float , float]
	int \in intset
	int \not\in intset
	num = num
	num \neq num
	num < num
	num \leq num
	num > num
	num \geq num
	(numctr)

dtimectr → dtime \in dtimeset
	dtime \not\in dtimeset
	dtime = dtime
	dtime \neq dtime
	dtime < dtime
	dtime \leq dtime
	dtime > dtime
	dtime \geq dtime
	(dtimectr)

strctr	$\rightarrow$	str \in strset
	|	str \not\in strset
	|	str = str
	|	str \neq str
	|	(strctr)

refctr	$\rightarrow$	ref \in refset
	|	ref \not\in refset
	|	ref = ref
	|	ref \neq ref
	|	(refctr)

setctr	$\rightarrow$	set = set
	|	set \neq set
	|	set \prec set
	|	set \not\prec set
	|	set \succ set
	|	set \not\succ set
	|	set \subset set
	|	set \not\subset set
	|	set \supset set
	|	set \not\supset set
	|	(setctr)

Assignment

assignment	$\rightarrow$	boolvar := bool
	|	floatvar := float
	|	intvar := int
	|	dtimevar := dtime
	|	strvar := str
	|	boolrefvar := boolref
	|	floatrefvar := floatref
	|	integralrefvar := integralref
	|	setrefvar := setref
	|	intsetvar := intset
	|	dtimesetvar := dtimeset
	|	strsetvar := strset
	|	refsetvar := refset

Optimization Objective

objective	$\rightarrow$	min float
	|	max float
	|	min float ; step
	|	max float : step

	min int
	max int
	min int : step
	max int : step
	min dtime
	max dtime
	min dtime : step
	max dtime : step
	(objective)

step   →   num

           | dtime

Query and Search

query   →   standardquery

           | fastquery

           | (query)

standardquery   →   expression = ? enummode

           | bool \equiv ? enummode

           | bool ?

fastquery   →   expression = ?? enummode

           | bool \equiv ?? enummode

           | bool ??

Enumeration Mode

enummode   →   ⊔

           | (directedmode)

           | (bool ? directedmode : directedmode)

directedmode   →   \rightarrow

           | \Rightarrow

           | \leftarrow

           | \Leftarrow

Query Criterion

criteria   →   criterion

           | criterion , criteria

           | (criteria)

criterion   →   ⊔

           | \min bool

           | \max bool

	\min float
	\max float
	\min int
	\max int
	\min dtime
	\max dtime

Output

print	→	@ expression
	|	@ expression : dataformat
	|	(print)

Data Format

dataformat	→	alignment
	|	floatformat
	|	dtimeformat

floatformat	→	(decimallen , alignment)

alignment	→	int

decimallen	→	int

dtimeformat	→	"dd/mm/yyyy hh"
	|	"mm/dd/yyyy hh"
	|	"yyyy-mm-dd hh"
	|	"dd/mm/yyyy hh:mm"
	|	"mm/dd/yyyy hh:mm"
	|	"yyyy-mm-dd hh:mm"
	|	"dd/mm/yyyy hh:mm:ss"
	|	"mm/dd/yyyy hh:mm:ss"
	|	"yyyy-mm-dd hh:mm:ss"
	|	"dd/mm/yyyy"
	|	"mm/dd/yyyy"
	|	"yyyy-mm-dd"
	|	"yyyymmdd"
	|	"hh"
	|	"hh:mm"
	|	"hh:mm:ss"
	|	""

Expectation

expectation	→	?? bool
	|	(expectation)

Control

Control statements here include those of logical and temporal controls presented in Chapter 3.

Compound Statement

compound	→	grouped
	|	included
	|	soft
	|	(message : statements)

Grouped Statement

grouped	→	(statement , statements)

Included File

included	→	[path]
	|	(included)
path	→	str
	|	concatenation

Soft Statement

soft	→	(bool : statements)

Custom Message

message	→	str
	|	concatenation

Selection

selection	→	switch
	|	ifthenelse

Switch

switch	→	? float (floatswitch)
	|	? integral (intswitch)
	|	? set (setswitch)
	|	(switch)
floatswitch	→	floatbranch
	|	floatbranch ; floatswitch
floatbranch	→	⊔ : statements
	|	floatcase : statements
floatcase	→	float

		float , floatcase
integralswitch	$\rightarrow$	integralbranch
	|	integralbranch ; integralswitch
integralbranch	$\rightarrow$	⊔ : statements
	|	integralcase : statements
integralcase	$\rightarrow$	integral
	|	integral , integralcase
setswitch	$\rightarrow$	setbranch
	|	setbranch ; setswitch
setbranch	$\rightarrow$	⊔ : statements
	|	setcase : statements
setcase	$\rightarrow$	set
	|	set , setcase

If-Then-Else

ifthenelse	$\rightarrow$	bool \Rightarrow boolswitch
	|	(ifthenelse)
boolswitch	$\rightarrow$	statements
	|	(statements ; statements)

Quantification

quantified	$\rightarrow$	existential
	|	universal
	|	(quantified)

Existential Quantification

existential	$\rightarrow$	\exists index statement
	|	\exists indices statement

Universal Quantification

universal	$\rightarrow$	\forall index body
	|	\forall indices body
body	$\rightarrow$	statement
	|	\rightarrow (criteria) statement

Indexing

index	$\rightarrow$	varidx \in set

	varidx \in set : varidx \neq integral
	varidx \in set : varidx \leq integral
	varidx \in set : varidx \geq integral
	varidx \in set : varidx < integral
	varidx \in set : varidx > integral

indices	→	varidxlist \in set

doubleidx	→	index , index
	|	doublevaridx \in set

doublevaridx	→	varidx \leq varidx
	|	varidx < varidx
	|	varidx \geq varidx
	|	varidx > varidx
	|	varidx \neq varidx
	|	varidx , varidx

varidxlist	→	varidx , varidx
	|	varidx , varidxlist

subidx	→	_ { varidx = integral } ^ { integral }
	|	_ { index }
	|	_ { doubleidx }

varidx	→	ID
	|	`ID`

Jump

jump	→	>> ID
	|	(jump)

Data Connection

dataconnection	→	\bigcirc \leftarrow poolhandle
	|	poolhandle \leftarrow \bigcirc
	|	'\bigcirc' \leftarrow poolhandle
	|	poolhandle \leftarrow '\bigcirc'
	|	@ \leftarrow poolhandle
	|	poolhandle \leftarrow @
	|	'@' \leftarrow poolhandle
	|	poolhandle \leftarrow '@'

poolhandle	→	int

Expression

expression	$\rightarrow$	bool
		float
		integral
		set

integral	$\rightarrow$	int
		dtime
		str
		ref

| num | $\rightarrow$ | float |
| | | int |

Boolean

| bool | $\rightarrow$ | constraint |

Float

float	$\rightarrow$	+ float
		− float
		float + num
		int + float
		float − num
		int − float
		float \times num
		int \times float
		float \times bool
		bool \times float
		num / num
		\frac { num } { num }
		floatgroup
		(float)

floatgroup	$\rightarrow$	floatcst
		floatvar
		floatfunc
		floatextract
		| float |
		{ float } ^ { num }
		{ int } ^ { float }
		(bool ? float : num)
		(bool ? int : float)
		\min (float , float)
		\max (float , float)

	\min subidx { float }
	\max subidx { float }
	\sum subidx { float }
	\arccos { num }
	\arcsin { num }
	\arctan { num }
	\cos { num }
	\sin { num }
	\tan { num }
	\exp { num }
	\log { num }
	\sqrt { num }

Integer

int	→	+ int
	|	− int
	|	bool + bool
	|	bool + int
	|	int + bool
	|	int + int
	|	int − int
	|	bool \times bool
	|	bool \times int
	|	int \times bool
	|	int \times int
	|	int \div int
	|	int \mod int
	|	intgroup
	|	(int)

intgroup	→	intcst
	|	intvar
	|	intfunc
	|	intextract
	|	pool
	|	\lfloor num \rfloor
	|	\lceil num \rceil
	|	| int |
	|	{ int } ^ { int }
	|	(bool ? int : int)
	|	\min (int , int)
	|	\max (int , int)
	|	# { str }
	|	# { set }

	\inf { intset }
	\sup { intset }
	\sum { intset }
	\sum subidx { int }
	\sum subidx { bool }
	\min subidx { int }
	\max subidx { int }
	intsetgroup [int]

Date/Time

dtime	$\rightarrow$	dtime + int
		dtime – dtime
		dtime + bool
		dtime \times int
		int \times dtime
		dtime \div dtime
		dtime \mod dtime
		dtimegroup
		(dtime)

dtimegroup	$\rightarrow$	dtimecst
		dtimevar
		dtimefunc
		dtimeextract
		(bool ? dtime : dtime)
		min (dtime , dtime)
		max (dtime , dtime)
		\inf { dtimeset }
		\sup { dtimeset }
		\sum { dtimeset }
		\sum subidx { dtime }
		\min subidx { dtime }
		\max subidx { dtime }
		dtimesetgroup [int]
		dtimegroup [dtimeattribute]

dtimeattribute	$\rightarrow$	"dd/mm/yyyy"
		"mm/dd/yyyy"
		"yyyy-mm-dd"
		"hh"
		"hh:mm"
		"hh:mm:ss"
		"yyyy"
		"mm"
		"dd"

String

str	$\rightarrow$	strgroup
	|	strsubmodel
	|	(str)

Grouped String

strgroup	$\rightarrow$	strcst
	|	strvar
	|	strfunc
	|	(bool ? str : str)
	|	(concatenation)
	|	strgroup [int]
	|	strgroup [int .. int]

Concatenation

concatenation	$\rightarrow$	group group
	|	group concatenation

group	$\rightarrow$	boolgroup
	|	floatgroup
	|	intgroup
	|	dtimegroup
	|	strgroup
	|	boolrefgroup
	|	floatrefgroup
	|	integralrefgroup
	|	setrefgroup
	|	intsetgroup
	|	dtimesetgroup
	|	strsetgroup
	|	refsetgroup

Reference

ref	$\rightarrow$	boolref
	|	floatref
	|	integralref
	|	setref

boolref	$\rightarrow$	boolrefgroup
	|	(boolref)

floatref	$\rightarrow$	floatrefgroup
	|	(floatref)

| integralref | $\rightarrow$ | integralrefgroup |

	|	(integralref)
setref	$\rightarrow$	setrefgroup
	|	(setref)
boolrefgroup	$\rightarrow$	`bool`
	|	boolrefvar
	|	boolreffunc
	|	(bool ? boolref : boolref)
floatrefgroup	$\rightarrow$	`float`
	|	floatrefvar
	|	floatreffunc
	|	(bool ? floatref : floatref)
integralrefgroup	$\rightarrow$	`integral`
	|	integralrefvar
	|	integralreffunc
	|	(bool ? integralref : integralref)
setrefgroup	$\rightarrow$	`set`
	|	setrefvar
	|	setreffunc
	|	(bool ? setref : setref)

Set

set	$\rightarrow$	intset
	|	strset
	|	dtimeset
	|	refset
intset	$\rightarrow$	intset \setminus int
	|	intset \setminus intset
	|	intset \cap intset
	|	intset \cup intset
	|	intset >> int
	|	intset << int
	|	intsetgroup
	|	(intset)
intsetgroup	$\rightarrow$	intsetcst
	|	intsetvar
	|	intsetfunc
	|	intsetextract
	|	[int , int]

	\{ intcollection \}
	(bool ? intset : intset)
	\bigcap subidx intset
	\bigcup subidx intset
	intsetgroup [int .. int]

dtimeset	→	dtimeset \setminus dtime
		dtimeset \setminus dtimeset
		dtimeset \cap dtimeset
		dtimeset \cup dtimeset
		dtimeset >> int
		dtimeset << int
		dtimesetgroup
		(dtimeset)

dtimesetgroup	→	dtimesetcst
		dtimesetvar
		dtimesetfunc
		dtimesetextract
		[dtime , dtime]
		\{ dtimecollection \}
		(bool ? dtimeset : dtimeset)
		\bigcap subidx dtimeset
		\bigcup subidx dtimeset
		dtimesetgroup [dtimeattribute]
		dtimesetgroup [int .. int]

strset	→	strset \setminus str
		strset \setminus strset
		strset \cap strset
		strset \cup strset
		strsetgroup
		(strset)

strsetgroup	→	strsetcst
		strsetvar
		strsetfunc
		strsetextract
		\{ strcollection \}
		(bool ? strset: strset)
		\bigcap subidx strset
		\bigcup subidx strset

| refset | → | refset \setminus ref |
| | | refset \setminus refset |

		refset \cap refset
		refset \cup refset
		refsetgroup
		(refset)

refsetgroup	→	refsetcst
		refsetvar
		refsetfunc
		refsetextract
		\{ refcollection \}
		(bool ? refset : refset)
		\bigcap refset
		\bigcup refset
		\bigcap subidx refset
		\bigcup subidx refset

intcollection	→	intlist
		\forall index int
		\forall doubleidx int

intlist	→	int
		int .. int
		int , intlist
		int .. int , intlist

dtimecollection	→	dtimelist
		\forall index dtime
		\forall doubleidx dtime

dtimelist	→	dtime
		dtime .. dtime
		dtime , dtimelist
		dtime .. dtime , dtimelist

strcollection	→	strlist
		\forall index str
		\forall doubleidx str

| strlist | → | str |
| | | str , strlist |

refcollection	→	reflist
		\forall index ref
		\forall doubleidx ref

| reflist | $\rightarrow$ | ref |
| | \| | ref , reflist |

Constant

| boolcst | $\rightarrow$ | T |
| | \| | F |

| floatcst | $\rightarrow$ | FLOAT |

| intcst | $\rightarrow$ | INT |
| | \| | \infty |

| dtimecst | $\rightarrow$ | DTIME |

| strcst | $\rightarrow$ | STR |

| intsetcst | $\rightarrow$ | \emptyset |

| dtimesetcst | $\rightarrow$ | \emptyset |

| strsetcst | $\rightarrow$ | \emptyset |

| refsetcst | $\rightarrow$ | \emptyset |

Variable

| boolvar | $\rightarrow$ | var |
| | \| | systembool |

| floatvar | $\rightarrow$ | var |
| | \| | systemfloat |

| intvar | $\rightarrow$ | var |
| | \| | systemint |

| dtimevar | $\rightarrow$ | var |
| | \| | systemtime |

| strvar | $\rightarrow$ | var |
| | \| | systemstr |

| boolrefvar | $\rightarrow$ | var |

| floatrefvar | $\rightarrow$ | var |

| integralrefvar | $\rightarrow$ | var |

setrefvar	$\rightarrow$	var

intsetvar	$\rightarrow$	var

dtimesetvar	$\rightarrow$	var

strsetvar	$\rightarrow$	var

refsetvar	$\rightarrow$	var

var	$\rightarrow$	ID
	|	ID _{ subscripts }
	|	input
	|	_

subscripts	$\rightarrow$	integral
	|	integral , subscripts

System Variable

systembool	$\rightarrow$	'\bigcirc'
	|	'@'
	|	'˙'
	|	"

systemfloat	$\rightarrow$	'Global Time'
	|	'Local Time'

systemint	$\rightarrow$	'Model Depth'
	|	'Trace Level'
	|	'Solution Count'
	|	'Backtrack Count'
	|	'Search Depth'

systemtime	$\rightarrow$	'dd/mm/yyyy hh'
	|	'mm/dd/yyyy hh'
	|	'yyyy-mm-dd hh'
	|	'dd/mm/yyyy hh:mm'
	|	'mm/dd/yyyy hh:mm'
	|	'yyyy-mm-dd hh:mm'
	|	'dd/mm/yyyy hh:mm:ss'
	|	'mm/dd/yyyy hh:mm:ss'
	|	'yyyy-mm-dd hh:mm:ss'
	|	'dd/mm/yyyy'
	|	'mm/dd/yyyy'

		'yyyy-mm-dd'
		'yyyymmdd'
		'hh'
		'hh:mm'
		'hh:mm:ss'

| systemstr | $\rightarrow$ | 'Work Directory' |

Input

input	$\rightarrow$	\bigcirc
		\bigcirc : dtimeformat
		\bigcirc : delimiter

| delimiter | $\rightarrow$ | STR |

Extraction

| boolextract | $\rightarrow$ | \overline { bool } |
| | | \underline { bool } |

floatextract	$\rightarrow$	\overline { float }
		\underline { float }
		# { float }

intextract	$\rightarrow$	\overline { int }
		\underline { int }
		# (poolhandle , delimiter)

| dtimeextract | $\rightarrow$ | \overline { dtime } |
| | | \underline { dtime } |

intsetextract	$\rightarrow$	\Delta { bool }
		\Delta { int }
		\overline { intset }
		\underline { intset }
		\Delta { intset }

dtimesetextract	$\rightarrow$	\Delta { dtime }
		\overline { dtimeset }
		\underline { dtimeset }
		\Delta { dtimeset }

strsetextract	$\rightarrow$	\Delta { str }
		\overline { strset }
		\underline { strset }

	|	\Delta \{ strset \}
refsetextract	→	\Delta \{ ref \}
	|	\overline \{ refset \}
	|	\underline \{ refset \}
	|	\Delta \{ refset \}

Function

boolfunc	→	func
floatfunc	→	func
intfunc	→	func
dtimefunc	→	func
strfunc	→	func
boolreffunc	→	func
floatreffunc	→	func
integralreffunc	→	func
setreffunc	→	func
intsetfunc	→	func
dtimesetfunc	→	func
strsetfunc	→	func
refsetfunc	→	func
func	→	ID (arguments)
arguments	→	argument
	|	argument , arguments
argument	→	⊔
	|	expression

Data Pool

| pool | → | buffer |

	|	textfile
	|	database
buffer	$\rightarrow$	[id : strbuf]
textfile	$\rightarrow$	[id]
database	$\rightarrow$	[id : user : password]
id	$\rightarrow$	str
	|	concatenation
strbuf	$\rightarrow$	id
user	$\rightarrow$	id
password	$\rightarrow$	id

Sub-Model

boolsubmodel	$\rightarrow$	submodel
strsubmodel	$\rightarrow$	submodel
submodel	$\rightarrow$	[prog , config , level]
prog	$\rightarrow$	int
config	$\rightarrow$	int
level	$\rightarrow$	int

SQL Query

sqlquery	$\rightarrow$	(SQL : commands)
	|	(SQL : \forall index command)
commands	$\rightarrow$	command
	|	command , commands
command	$\rightarrow$	⊔
	|	str
	|	concatenation

OS Command

oscommand	$\rightarrow$	(OS : commands)
	|	(OS : \forall index command)

Appendix 2 The ComPoem Component

Description

ComPoem is POEM's ActiveX component for Microsoft Windows. Through ComPoem, an optimization model in NCL can be called by an application program in another language. For example,

- with Visual C++ user can develop an application with IDE (Integrated Development Environment); a ComPoem component can be added through the menu "Components and Controls".
- with Visual Basic user can develop an application with IDE; a ComPoem component can be added through the menu "Components".
- with Java user can develop an application calling ComPoem through API.

Properties

WorkDirectory [String]:   Input : Work directory (optional)

ProgramFile [String]:   Input : Path of the program file
InputFile [String]:   Input : Path of the input file (optional)
OutputFile [String]:   Input : Path of the output file (optional)
ConfigFile [String]:   Input : Path of the config file (optional)

ProgramBuffer [String]:   Input : Program buffer
InputBuffer [String]:   Input : Input buffer
OutputBuffer [String]:   Input : Output buffer
ConfigBuffer [String]:   Input : Config buffer

TraceFile [String] :   Input : Path of the trace file (optional)
TraceLevel [Integer]:   Input : Level (0-3) for tracing (optional)

Functions

GetNclStatus:
     Return: Between 0 and 2
     0:      NCL is stopped
     1:      NCL is running
     2:      NCL is suspended

GetSolutionCount:
     Return: Number of solutions; by default it is 0.

GetObjectiveCount:
   Return: Number of optimization objectives (either integer or float);
   by default it is 0.

GetObjectiveName [Integer]:
   Input: Number (starting from 1) of the integer/float objective function
   Return: Objective name (string); by default it is NULL.

GetObjectiveType [Integer]:
   Input: Number (starting from 1) of the integer/float objective function
   Return: Between 0 and 4
   0:        No objective
   1:        Minimize integer objective
   2:        Maximize integer objective
   3:        Minimize float objective
   4:        Maximize float objective

GetIntObjective [Integer]:
   Input: Index (starting from 1) of the integer objective function
   Return: Value of the integer objective function

GetFloatObjective [Integer]:
   Input: Index (starting from 1) of the float objective function
   Return: Value of the float objective function

ExecuteNcl: Execute NCL engine
StopNcl: Stop NCL engine
SuspendNcl: Suspend NCL engine
ResumeNcl: Resume NCL engine

SetTaskView [Integer]:
   Input: 0 or 1
   0:        Hide ComPoem's Task View Window
   1:        Show ComPoem's Task View Window

SetTaskPriorityLevel [Integer]: Set the priority of the task in Windows.
   Input: Between −2 and 2
   2:        Highest
   1:        Above normal
   0:        Normal (default value)
   −1:   Below normal
   −2:   Lowest

Events

TaskMsg (lCode [Integer], **szMsg** [String]):
Return a value about a task's state.
lCode is the message code and it has the following meaning:
  0:   ComPoem is stopped
  1:   ComPoem is running
  2:   ComPoem is suspended
  −1: Warning
  −2: Error
  −3: Exception
szMsg is the message text.

NclMsg (lCode [Integer], **szMsg** [String]): Message Handler
lCode is the message code; see Section 5.7.3 for more information.
szMsg is the message text.

Index